Fast-Track A&E

Beat The Queue, Beat The Clock
(How To Skip Queues in Hospitals)

Louistas Nyuyse

Author Of The Best Seller "Think Like A Virus"

Copyright © 2023 Louistas Nyuyse

All rights reserved. No part of this publication may be reproduced, distributed, or transmitted in any form or by any means, including photocopying, recording, or any other electronic or mechanical methods, without the prior written permission of the publisher, except in the case of brief quotations embodied in critical reviews and certain other noncommercial uses permitted by copyright law. For permission, write to the publisher at:

Greatness University Publishers
London, UK
www.greatnessuniversity.co.uk

ISBN: 978-1-913164-05-8
ISBN-13: 978-1-913164-05-8

DEDICATION

This Book Is Dedicated To

My Lovely Parent: Nyuyse Phillip And Labeh Evelyne

And My Beautiful Daughter: Maisie Nyuyse And Alyssa Nyuyse

For Their Unconditional Love.

Also To Tom Saviour, And The A&E Nurses In Royal Surrey

And Ambulance Staff, Who Saved Me After I Drowned.

Find Out More About Healthcare Innovation

in **Think Like A VIRUS:** *The C.O.R.O.N.A. Effect*

Fast-Track A&E

Dear Reader,

Whether you are a Healthcare Practitioner or a Patient, I invite you to embark on an insightful journey into healthcare, designed to empower you with knowledge and practical strategies from deep experience. "Mastering The Healthcare System," Part 1 of the book, begins with a global view of healthcare systems, leading into proactive health management and effective communication with healthcare professionals. Pain management, understanding emergency care, the connection between mental and physical health, specific health conditions, the growing role of telemedicine, preparing for hospital visits, and fostering mindset and emotional resilience form the core of this section.

Part 2, "Practical Tips for Beating A&E Queues," translates theory into actionable advice. It covers navigating health challenges, etiquette in A&E, understanding diagnoses, managing pain in A&E, and explores alternative pain relief methods. A highlight is Chapter 7, "Hospital From The Sky: An A-Z Journey," which offers a poetic perspective on the healthcare experience.

This book is more than just information; it's a tool for empowerment in your health journey, blending practical advice with reflective insights. It aims to inspire you to take charge of your health and navigate the complexities of healthcare with confidence.

Here's to your journey towards informed health decisions and a deeper understanding of the intricate world of healthcare.

Wishing you, good health and enlightenment. *Louistas Nyuyse*

CONTENTS

PART 1: MASTERING THE HEALTHCARE SYSTEM   **1**

Chapter 1: Understanding Healthcare Systems Globally   1

Chapter 2: Proactive Health Management   45

Chapter 3: Effective Communication with Healthcare Professionals   71

Chapter 4: Pain Management   89

Chapter 5: When to Seek Emergency Care   113

Chapter 6: Mental Health and Its Role in Physical Well-being   127

Chapter 7: Dealing with Specific Conditions   145

Chapter 8: Role of Telemedicine in Modern Healthcare   173

Chapter 9: Preparing for Hospital Visits   211

Chapter 10: Mindset and Emotional Resilience   245

PART 2: PRACTICAL TIPS FOR BEATING A&E QUEUES   269

Chapter 1: When Health Challenges Arise   269

Chapter 2: A&E Etiquettes   281

Chapter 3: Navigating The Diagnosis   291

Chapter 4: Pain Management in A&E and Beyond   303

Chapter 5: Alternative Approaches to Pain Relief   313

Chapter 6: Navigating Family Dynamics   325

Chapter 7: Hospital From The Sky: An A-Z Journey   333

References   341

Glossary   346

About The Author   349

ACKNOWLEDGMENTS

In the bustling world of healthcare, this book has been a journey of discovery, inspiration, and countless cups of coffee. My heartfelt gratitude goes to my family for their unwavering support and patience. Their endurance of my late-night writing marathons and my 'brain food' experiments has been nothing short of heroic.

A special thank you to my inquisitive healthcare studies student, whose challenging questions sparked the idea for this book. Your curiosity has been a guiding light in my research.

To Amanda Dean, my mentor in the dynamic A&E realm – your wisdom has been invaluable. And to my colleagues, the unsung heroes of healthcare, thank you for your stories and insights, which have enriched every page.

Lastly, to the patients I've had the honor to care for – you are the heart of this book. Your resilience and stories have been my inspiration, shaping the chapters within.

This book is a tapestry woven from many lives. To everyone who contributed – thank you for enriching its narrative.

Now, let's turn the page and begin anew – with a fresh cup of coffee, of course. Cheers!!

PART 1

MASTERING THE HEALTHCARE SYSTEM

Chapter 1:

Understanding Healthcare Systems Globally

Introduction to Global Healthcare Systems.

Introduction to Global Healthcare Systems:

In the intricate tapestry of modern society, healthcare systems stand out as fundamental threads, vital to the well-being and functioning of communities across the globe. These systems, diverse in their structures and operations, serve a unifying purpose: to promote, restore, and maintain health. They are not merely an assortment of hospitals, clinics, and medical professionals, but a reflection of a society's values, its socio-economic dynamics, and its commitment to the welfare of its citizens.

From bustling cities in the developed world to remote villages in developing nations, healthcare systems represent a promise – a promise of healing, care, and support. They are complex organisms, pulsating with the collective efforts of countless individuals working towards a common goal: health for all. This aspiration, enshrined in the World Health Organization's principle of "Health for All", encapsulates the ideal that good health should be a reachable goal for every individual, regardless of geography, socio-economic status, or cultural background.

The importance of healthcare systems extends beyond the confines of medical buildings. These systems are pivotal in shaping a nation's productivity, stability, and progress. A healthy populace is the cornerstone of a thriving society – it fuels the workforce, nurtures future generations, and reduces the burden of disease and disability. Conversely, when healthcare systems falter, the repercussions are profound and far-reaching, impacting not just physical health, but mental well-being, economic growth, and the social fabric of communities.

In this globalized world, where diseases know no borders, and health challenges are increasingly complex, understanding the nuances of different healthcare systems becomes paramount. It is not just a matter of academic interest but a practical necessity. By examining how various countries approach healthcare - from the state-funded National Health Service (NHS) in the United Kingdom to the insurance-based models in the United States and the hybrid systems found in Asia and Europe - we gain valuable insights into the strengths and weaknesses of these models. This knowledge is crucial in navigating the challenges of the 21st century, from managing pandemics to addressing the burgeoning burden of chronic diseases.

Therefore, this chapter aims to embark on a journey through the world's healthcare landscapes. It will explore the intricate workings of different healthcare systems, their foundational principles, and the lessons they offer. This exploration is not just a foray into the mechanics of health policy and administration; it is an endeavor to understand how humanity cares for its most vulnerable, how societies prioritize resources, and how nations strive towards the lofty but attainable goal of health for every individual.

Highlighting the Diversity in Healthcare Systems Globally:

The diversity in healthcare systems across the globe is as varied as the cultures and nations they serve. Each system is a unique mosaic, composed of historical, economic, political, and social elements that shape its approach to delivering healthcare.

State-Funded Systems:

In countries like the United Kingdom, healthcare is predominantly state-funded, exemplified by the National Health Service (NHS). The NHS is a beacon of universal healthcare, providing comprehensive services from the cradle to the grave, funded primarily through taxation.

Similarly, in Scandinavia and other parts of Europe, state-funded healthcare models prioritize equitable access, with an emphasis on preventative care and social welfare.

Insurance-Based Models:

Contrasting the state-funded systems are the insurance-based models, most notably in the United States. Here, healthcare is largely provided by private sector businesses and jointly paid for by private health insurance, out-of-pocket payments, and government funding programs like Medicare and Medicaid.

This model often results in a diverse range of services and providers, but also creates disparities in access and quality, contingent upon an individual's insurance coverage.

Hybrid Systems:

Many countries employ hybrid models that combine elements of both state-funded and insurance-based systems. For instance, Germany and Japan utilize a social health insurance system where healthcare is financed through employer and employee contributions to various sickness funds.

In Canada, there is a publicly funded healthcare system providing universal coverage for essential healthcare services, with private insurance covering additional services.

Developing World Models:

In many developing countries, healthcare systems face distinct challenges, often characterized by limited resources, underfunding, and infrastructure constraints. These systems may rely heavily on international aid and non-governmental organizations for support.

Despite these challenges, there are innovative approaches in countries like Rwanda, where community-based health insurance and decentralized healthcare delivery have made significant strides in improving access and quality.

Innovative and Emerging Models:

With advancements in technology and a push towards personalized medicine, new models of healthcare delivery are emerging. Telemedicine and digital health services are revolutionizing access, particularly in remote or underserved areas.

Countries like Singapore are pioneering integrated healthcare models, where data-driven and preventive approaches are leading to efficient and effective healthcare delivery.

The global landscape of healthcare is a kaleidoscope of systems, each reflecting the values, priorities, and capacities of its society. Understanding this diversity is not only fascinating in its own right but also crucial in learning how different nations tackle common health challenges. It highlights that there is no one-size-fits-all approach to healthcare; rather, each system offers valuable lessons and innovative solutions that can inspire improvements and reforms in other countries.

The National Health Service (NHS) in the UK:

Overview of the NHS, its history, and how it operates

The National Health Service (NHS), established in 1948, stands as a towering example of a universal healthcare system, rooted in the principles of equity and accessibility. Its inception was a groundbreaking moment in British social history, embodying the post-war consensus that healthcare should be a right for all, not a privilege for the few.

Historical Context:

The NHS was born out of the idealism of the post-World War II era, under the guidance of Health Minister Aneurin Bevan. It was founded on the principle that good healthcare should be available to all, regardless of wealth.

This was a transformative shift from the pre-war period, where healthcare was largely provided by a mix of charity, municipal, and private providers, often at a cost that was prohibitive for many.

Fast-Track A&E

How the NHS Operates:

Funded primarily through taxation, the NHS provides a wide range of health services including general practitioner (GP) services, hospital care, dental care, and more, free at the point of use for UK residents.

The NHS is structured into four regional systems: NHS England, NHS Scotland, NHS Wales, and Health and Social Care in Northern Ireland, each with some degree of autonomy.

Key Principles:

The founding principles of the NHS are based on providing a comprehensive service available to all, free at the point of need, and based on clinical need, not the ability to pay. These principles have guided the NHS for over seven decades.

Challenges and Evolution:

Over the years, the NHS has faced numerous challenges including rising costs, an aging population, and increasing demand for services.

The system has evolved in response, with reforms aimed at improving efficiency, patient choice, and the integration of services. Examples include the introduction of Primary Care Trusts (PCTs), and more recently, Clinical Commissioning Groups (CCGs) in England.

Technological advancements and a greater focus on preventive care are also shaping the way the NHS operates.

Global Influence:

The NHS has had a profound influence globally, serving as a model for other countries seeking to establish universal healthcare systems. Its commitment to free healthcare at the point of delivery remains a powerful example of a healthcare system based on equity and social justice.

The NHS, with its rich history and enduring principles, continues to be a source of national pride and a beacon of universal healthcare. Its journey from inception to the present day offers valuable insights into the challenges and triumphs of providing healthcare as a public service.

Funding Model, Services Provided, and Patient Experiences in the NHS:

Funding Model:

The NHS is predominantly funded through general taxation and National Insurance contributions. This central funding model ensures that the cost of healthcare services is shared across the entire population, facilitating free access at the point of use.

Additional funding comes from prescription charges, dental fees, and opticians' charges, although there are exemptions for various groups (e.g., children, elderly, low-income individuals).

This funding model reflects the NHS's core principle of collective responsibility for health. It's a system designed to pool risk and resources, ensuring that those in need can access healthcare regardless of their financial situation.

Fast-Track A&E

Services Provided:

General Practitioner (GP) Services: GPs act as the primary point of contact for most medical concerns. They provide consultations, diagnose illnesses, prescribe medications, and refer patients to specialist services when necessary.

Hospital Services: This includes emergency care, surgical procedures, maternity services, and specialist treatments. Hospitals in the NHS are typically large, centralized facilities providing a broad range of services.

Community and Mental Health Services: These encompass a range of services from health visiting and district nursing to mental health care and rehabilitation services.

Dental Care and Optometry: While these services are part of the NHS, they often come with charges, albeit at regulated rates.

Prescription Medications: Prescriptions are subsidized under the NHS, with a standard charge per item, though many groups are exempt from these charges.

Patient Experiences:

Accessibility: One of the most lauded aspects of the NHS is its accessibility. The principle of healthcare free at the point of use means that patients do not face financial barriers to accessing care.

Quality of Care: The NHS is generally well regarded for the quality of care it provides, especially in critical care and emergency services. However, experiences can vary, and some areas, like mental health services, face challenges with long waiting times.

Waiting Times: A significant challenge for the NHS is managing waiting times, both in terms of accessing GP appointments and waiting for specialist treatments or surgeries. This is often attributed to high demand and resource constraints.

Patient Satisfaction: Surveys generally indicate a high level of patient satisfaction with NHS services, particularly praising the dedication and professionalism of NHS staff. However, concerns about waiting times and access to services, particularly in mental health and dentistry, are recurring themes.

Response to COVID-19: The NHS's response to the COVID-19 pandemic highlighted both its strengths and the challenges it faces. The rapid deployment of emergency services and the vaccine rollout showcased its capacity for effective response under pressure, while also highlighting resource constraints and staff burnout.

The NHS's funding model, its comprehensive range of services, and the experiences of its patients paint a picture of a healthcare system deeply rooted in principles of equity and universality. While it faces challenges, particularly in terms of funding and resource allocation, the NHS continues to be a model of how a health system can provide high-quality care accessible to all.

Medicare and Healthcare in the USA:

Structure of Medicare:

Medicare is a federal health insurance program primarily for people aged 65 and older, though it also covers younger individuals with certain disabilities and diseases. Established in 1965 under the Social Security Act, Medicare was designed to provide health insurance to populations who might otherwise have no coverage.

Medicare is divided into four parts:

Part A (Hospital Insurance): Covers inpatient hospital stays, care in a skilled nursing facility, hospice care, and some home health care.

Part B (Medical Insurance): Covers certain doctors' services, outpatient care, medical supplies, and preventive services.

Part C (Medicare Advantage Plans): A private insurance option that covers all Part A and Part B services and typically includes Part D (prescription drug coverage), often with extra benefits.

Part D (Prescription Drug Coverage): Adds prescription drug coverage to the Original Medicare, some Medicare Cost Plans, some Medicare Private-Fee-for-Service Plans, and Medicare Medical Savings Account Plans.

Medicare's Role in the Broader US Healthcare System:

Medicare plays a critical role in the American healthcare landscape by providing a safety net for older adults and people with disabilities, two groups that often face higher health risks and medical costs.

While Medicare provides a foundation of health security, it doesn't cover all medical expenses or the cost of most long-term care. Many beneficiaries purchase supplemental insurance to cover gaps in Medicare coverage.

Medicare also serves as a benchmark for other health plans in terms of payment rates for health services and coverage decisions. It often leads the way in introducing new payment models aimed at improving care quality and controlling costs, such as the shift from fee-for-service to value-based care.

The program significantly influences the US healthcare system's economics, impacting healthcare providers, private insurance companies, and overall national health expenditures.

Medicare's policies and reforms, such as the introduction of the Affordable Care Act (ACA), have broader implications for the healthcare system, influencing policy decisions and healthcare delivery models across the public and private sectors.

Medicare's complexity and its interplay with the private insurance market reflect the multifaceted nature of the US healthcare system. It's a pivotal program that underscores the challenges and debates surrounding healthcare in the United States, including issues of accessibility, affordability, and the balance between public and private roles in health insurance and care delivery.

Private vs Public Healthcare Options in the USA:

The United States healthcare system is characterized by a mix of both private and public elements, creating a complex landscape of healthcare options. Understanding this dichotomy is key to comprehending the broader US healthcare context.

Private Healthcare:

Insurance: Private health insurance, often provided as an employee benefit but also available for individual purchase, is a cornerstone of the US healthcare system. Major providers include companies like UnitedHealth, Anthem, and Aetna.

Providers and Facilities: Private healthcare facilities, including hospitals and clinics, make up a significant portion of the healthcare infrastructure in the U.S. These facilities often boast advanced technologies and shorter wait times but can be more expensive.

Direct Out-of-Pocket Payments: For those without insurance or with limited coverage, healthcare often requires direct payments at the time of service, which can be prohibitively expensive.

Quality and Choice: Private healthcare typically offers a broader choice of providers and facilities and is perceived as offering superior quality, especially for elective procedures and specialized care.

Public Healthcare:

Medicare: As previously discussed, Medicare is a federal program primarily for those 65 and older, providing a range of healthcare services.

Medicaid: A state and federal program that provides health coverage for low-income individuals and families. Medicaid coverage varies by state, as states have significant leeway in determining the extent of coverage.

The Children's Health Insurance Program (CHIP): Provides health coverage to eligible children, through both Medicaid and separate CHIP programs.

Veterans Health Administration (VHA): Provides healthcare services to eligible military veterans at VHA medical centers and outpatient clinics.

Affordable Care Act (ACA) Exchanges: Also known as Obamacare, the ACA created health insurance exchanges where individuals and families can purchase health insurance, often with subsidies for lower-income individuals.

Comparative Aspects:

Accessibility: Public healthcare programs are designed to increase healthcare accessibility, particularly for vulnerable populations. However, eligibility criteria can be a barrier. Private healthcare is more readily accessible to those with employer-provided plans or who can afford private insurance.

Cost: Public healthcare options are generally more affordable for eligible individuals, with costs subsidized by government funding. Private healthcare, while offering more options, can be expensive, especially for those without insurance.

Quality and Efficiency: There's a perception that private healthcare offers higher quality and efficiency, though this can vary widely. Public healthcare providers also deliver high-quality care, but resource constraints can sometimes impact service delivery.

The coexistence of public and private healthcare in the USA creates a diverse but fragmented landscape. This system allows for choice and innovation but also leads to disparities in access and quality. The ongoing debate about healthcare in the U.S. often centers around finding the right balance between private and public elements to create a more equitable and efficient healthcare system.

European Healthcare Models:

Key Examples of Models

European healthcare systems are often cited as examples of efficient and equitable healthcare delivery. Two key models that have influenced these systems are the Beveridge and Bismarck models. Each represents a different approach to organizing and financing healthcare.

1. The Beveridge Model:

Characteristics: Named after William Beveridge, the architect of the British welfare state, this model features healthcare financed and provided by the government through tax payments. Healthcare is delivered to all citizens and is primarily free at the point of use.

Examples:

United Kingdom: The National Health Service (NHS) is a classic example of the Beveridge model. It is funded through taxation, and the government manages the hospitals and employs the healthcare professionals.

Spain and Italy: These countries also have healthcare systems based on the Beveridge model, offering universal coverage with a strong focus on primary and preventive care.

Advantages: High levels of health equity and accessibility, and usually lower per capita costs due to government control over prices.

Challenges: Can be prone to long waiting times for elective procedures and underfunding issues, especially in times of economic downturn.

2. The Bismarck Model:

Characteristics: Named after the Prussian Chancellor Otto von Bismarck, who first introduced the model in Germany in the 19th century, this model is based on insurance plans financed jointly by employers and employees through payroll deduction. These plans cover all citizens and are not-for-profit.

Examples:

Germany: Known for its efficiency and high-quality care, the German healthcare system operates with a multitude of "sickness funds" that provide healthcare to the population.

France and Belgium: These countries have similar systems, with a combination of employer-employee funded plans and government subsidies to ensure universal coverage.

Advantages: Provides a balance of state oversight and market competition, generally resulting in high-quality care and choice for patients.

Challenges: Managing costs can be challenging due to the complex interplay of multiple insurers and providers.

Comparative Analysis:

Access and Equity: Both models excel in providing universal healthcare, but the Beveridge model is often more equitable due to its uniformity and simplicity.

Quality and Choice: The Bismarck model typically offers greater choice and potentially shorter waiting times but can be more complex to navigate.

Cost Control: Beveridge systems have more direct government control over costs, which can lead to more effective overall cost containment. Bismarck systems, with their blend of competition and regulation, also strive to balance costs and quality.

Public Satisfaction: Satisfaction levels can vary within both models, but they generally score higher in public satisfaction compared to more privatized systems, as seen in some other parts of the world.

In summary, both the Beveridge and Bismarck models have shaped European healthcare systems, reflecting a commitment to universal coverage and healthcare as a right. While each has its unique strengths and challenges, they offer valuable lessons in the pursuit of efficient, equitable, and high-quality healthcare.

Differences in Funding, Accessibility, and Quality of Care in European Healthcare Models:

The Beveridge and Bismarck models, while both committed to providing universal healthcare, exhibit notable differences in funding, accessibility, and quality of care.

1. Funding:

Beveridge Model:

Funded primarily through general taxation. This method simplifies funding and administration, as there's no need for a collection of premiums or multiple insurance providers.

The government's control over funding can lead to more effective cost containment but also poses risks of underfunding, especially in economic downturns or due to political decisions.

Bismarck Model:

Funded through payroll deductions and employer contributions, creating a multitude of insurance funds. These funds are usually non-profit and tightly regulated.

This model can provide more stable and diversified funding

sources but may lead to higher administrative costs due to the complexity of managing multiple funds.

2. Accessibility:

Beveridge Model:

Generally, offers high levels of accessibility with minimal barriers for the population, as healthcare is provided free at the point of use for all residents.

However, challenges such as long waiting times for certain procedures and specialist care can impact accessibility and patient satisfaction.

Bismarck Model:

Also provides high accessibility, with mandatory coverage for all citizens. The competition among funds can lead to innovation and efficiency in services.

The complexity of insurance plans and potential for variations in coverage can sometimes make navigation and accessibility more challenging for patients.

3. Quality of Care:

Beveridge Model:

The quality of care is generally high, with a strong focus on primary and preventive care. The model's simplicity can facilitate integrated care pathways and efficient use of resources.

Quality can be impacted by budget constraints and resource

limitations, leading to variations in service availability and facility conditions.

Bismarck Model:

Typically associated with high-quality healthcare, benefiting from competition and choice. Patients often have better access to specialists and shorter wait times for elective procedures.

The reliance on multiple providers and insurers can lead to discrepancies in the standard of care, depending on the insurance plan and providers.

Comparative Summary:

The Beveridge model, with its state-funded and provided approach, tends to excel in equitable access and cost control but can face challenges in wait times and resource allocation.

The Bismarck model, characterized by its insurance-based approach, often offers greater choice and potentially higher-quality care but can be more complex and less equitable in terms of coverage variations.

Both models share a common goal of universal healthcare coverage, but their different approaches to funding and organization result in distinct experiences for patients in terms of accessibility and quality of care.

Hence, the Beveridge and Bismarck models each have their unique advantages and challenges. The choice of model often reflects a country's social, economic, and political values and priorities. Understanding these differences is crucial for policymakers and healthcare professionals as they strive to balance equity, quality, and efficiency in healthcare delivery.

Healthcare in Asia: Japan, Singapore, and India

Asian healthcare systems display a remarkable diversity, reflecting the varied economic, cultural, and political landscapes of the region. Examining the healthcare systems of Japan, Singapore, and India offers insights into different approaches to health policy and management.

1. Japan: Universal Coverage with a Focus on Preventive Care

System Overview: Japan's healthcare system is known for its universal coverage, achieved through a compulsory health insurance model. All residents are required to enroll in either an employer-based plan or the national health insurance program.

Funding: The system is funded through premiums, co-payments, and taxes. The government tightly controls costs, especially for services and medications.

Accessibility and Quality: Japan has high accessibility to healthcare services, with a strong emphasis on preventive care and regular health check-ups. The quality of healthcare is generally excellent, contributing to Japan's high life expectancy.

Challenges: Japan faces challenges related to its aging population, including rising healthcare costs and the need for more long-term care services.

2. Singapore: A Hybrid Model Emphasizing Personal Responsibility

System Overview: Singapore's healthcare system is a unique hybrid model, combining government-run and market-based elements. It's built on the principles of individual responsibility and affordable healthcare for all.

Funding: The system is funded through a combination of compulsory health savings accounts (Medisave), government-subsidized insurance for major illnesses (Medishield Life), and out-of-pocket payments.

Accessibility and Quality: The system ensures high accessibility with a focus on efficiency and cost-effectiveness. Healthcare facilities in Singapore are known for their high quality and use of advanced technologies.

Challenges: The system's reliance on personal savings and individual responsibility can pose challenges for lower-income groups and elderly citizens.

3. India: A Developing System with Wide Disparities

System Overview: India's healthcare system is a mix of public and private sectors. The public sector aims to provide universal healthcare but is underfunded and overstretched, leading to a significant role for private healthcare providers.

Funding: Public healthcare is funded by the government, while private healthcare is mostly paid for out-of-pocket or through private insurance.

Accessibility and Quality: There is a wide disparity in

healthcare accessibility and quality in India, with significant differences between urban and rural areas, and between public and private healthcare services.

Challenges: Major challenges include underfunding in the public sector, lack of infrastructure, inadequate healthcare in rural areas, and the rising cost of private healthcare.

Comparative Analysis:

Universal vs. Mixed Models: Japan and Singapore have achieved near-universal healthcare coverage, albeit through different models, while India is still grappling with achieving this goal.

Quality and Efficiency: Japan and Singapore are known for high-quality healthcare, with Singapore particularly noted for its efficiency and innovation. In contrast, India's healthcare quality varies widely, with excellence in some private facilities but struggles in the public sector.

Equity and Accessibility: Japan's system is characterized by its equity and accessibility, while Singapore's model, though efficient, relies heavily on individual responsibility. India faces significant challenges in healthcare equity and accessibility.

These three examples underscore the diversity in healthcare approaches in Asia, shaped by each country's unique socio-economic context. Japan and Singapore offer models of efficiency and innovation, while India's system reflects the challenges faced by many developing countries in providing equitable and quality healthcare.

Healthcare in Australia, New Zealand, and Indonesia

Exploring the healthcare systems of Australia, New Zealand, and Indonesia offers a glimpse into different approaches and challenges in providing healthcare in the Asia-Pacific region.

1. Australia: A Blend of Public and Private Healthcare

System Overview: Australia's healthcare system is known for its hybrid model, which includes a universal public health insurance program called Medicare and a private health sector.

Funding: Medicare, funded by tax revenues, provides free or subsidized healthcare services to Australian citizens and permanent residents. Private healthcare is funded through private health insurance premiums and out-of-pocket payments.

Accessibility and Quality: The Australian healthcare system is generally well-regarded for its accessibility and quality of care. Medicare ensures that basic healthcare is accessible to all, while private insurance offers more choices and shorter waiting times for certain procedures.

Challenges: Despite its strengths, the system faces challenges like long waiting times for certain public healthcare services and rising healthcare costs.

2. New Zealand: Publicly Funded, Focused on Equity

System Overview: New Zealand's healthcare system is

predominantly publicly funded, offering free or heavily subsidized healthcare services to residents. It operates under the principle of providing equitable healthcare access for all.

Funding: The system is funded through general taxation. It provides a broad range of services, including hospital treatment, primary care, pharmaceuticals, and mental health services.

Accessibility and Quality: The quality of healthcare in New Zealand is high, with a strong focus on public health and preventive care. However, there are concerns about accessibility and waiting times, particularly for non-urgent procedures.

Challenges: Key challenges include managing the growing demand for healthcare services due to an aging population and ensuring equitable access for all, including the indigenous Maori population.

3. Indonesia: An Emerging Universal Healthcare System

System Overview: Indonesia has been working towards a universal healthcare system through the implementation of its National Health Insurance program (Jaminan Kesehatan Nasional or JKN).

Funding: JKN aims to cover all Indonesian citizens and is funded through a combination of government contributions, employer and employee contributions, and individual premiums.

Accessibility and Quality: While the goal is to provide universal coverage, there are still challenges in terms of accessibility, especially in rural and remote areas. The quality of healthcare varies significantly between urban and rural regions.

Challenges: Indonesia faces numerous challenges in its pursuit of universal healthcare, including funding shortfalls, uneven distribution of healthcare resources, and the need to improve the quality of healthcare services.

Comparative Analysis:

Public vs. Private Roles: Australia's system balances public and private sectors, while New Zealand focuses more on public provision. Indonesia is in the process of expanding public healthcare coverage.

Quality and Accessibility: Both Australia and New Zealand offer high-quality healthcare, though both grapple with issues of accessibility and efficiency. Indonesia is working to improve both the quality and accessibility of its healthcare services.

Challenges: Common challenges across these systems include managing healthcare costs, ensuring equitable access, and adapting to demographic changes like aging populations.

These examples from the Asia-Pacific region illustrate varied approaches to healthcare, influenced by each country's economic, social, and political contexts. Australia and New Zealand have established systems that balance quality and accessibility, while Indonesia is in the midst of significant healthcare reforms to achieve universal coverage.

Differences in Funding, Accessibility, and Quality of Care in Australia, New Zealand, and Indonesia

1. Funding:

Australia: The Australian healthcare system is funded through a mix of government taxation (for the public system) and private payments (for the private system). Medicare, the public insurance program, is financed through a specific income tax levy, alongside general government revenues.

New Zealand: New Zealand's healthcare system is primarily funded by the government through general taxation. This public funding covers a wide range of health services, with some co-payments required for certain services, particularly in primary care.

Indonesia: Indonesia's National Health Insurance program (JKN) is funded through a combination of government funding, contributions from employed citizens and their employers, and individual premiums from self-employed or non-working citizens.

2. Accessibility:

Australia: While Medicare provides broad accessibility to essential healthcare services, there are still gaps that are filled by private insurance. Private insurance offers quicker access to elective surgeries and certain specialists.

New Zealand: New Zealand's system provides widespread access to healthcare. However, accessibility issues arise in terms of long waiting times for elective procedures and certain specialist services. Rural areas may also face challenges in accessing healthcare.

Indonesia: Accessibility in Indonesia is a work in progress with the JKN. Urban areas generally have better access to healthcare services compared to rural and remote regions. The JKN aims to improve accessibility, but infrastructure and resource distribution remain significant challenges.

3. Quality of Care:

Australia: The quality of healthcare in Australia is generally high, with both the public and private sectors providing advanced medical care. However, there can be variations in quality and availability of services, particularly between urban and rural areas.

New Zealand: The quality of care in New Zealand is also high, with a strong focus on public health and primary care. However, as with Australia, disparities exist, particularly affecting the indigenous Maori population and in more remote regions.

Indonesia: The quality of healthcare services in Indonesia varies widely, with high-quality care available in major cities and private facilities but limited in rural and remote areas. The government is focusing on improving quality across the board as part of its healthcare reforms.

Comparative Summary:

Funding Models: Australia and New Zealand have robust public funding mechanisms, supplemented by private spending, ensuring broad coverage. Indonesia is still developing its public funding model to achieve universal coverage.

Accessibility: Australia and New Zealand provide high accessibility, though with some challenges in wait times and rural healthcare. Indonesia is working to increase accessibility, particularly for its rural population.

Quality of Care: All three countries strive for high-quality healthcare, with Australia and New Zealand achieving this more consistently. Indonesia faces more significant challenges in ensuring quality healthcare for its entire population.

These three healthcare systems in the Asia-Pacific region reflect different stages and strategies in providing healthcare to their populations. Australia and New Zealand have established systems with a strong public foundation, complemented by private options, while Indonesia is navigating the complex process of expanding and improving its healthcare system to meet the needs of its diverse and dispersed population.

Comparative Analysis of Healthcare Systems in Australia, New Zealand, and Indonesia

When comparing the healthcare systems of Australia, New Zealand, and Indonesia, it's essential to consider how each country approaches coverage, quality, and efficiency, reflecting their unique socio-economic contexts.

Fast-Track A&E

1. Coverage:

Australia: Offers comprehensive coverage through its public Medicare system, supplemented by private health insurance. Most residents have access to a wide range of essential health services. The dual system allows for greater choice, although it can create disparities based on private insurance.

New Zealand: Provides universal coverage with a strong public healthcare system. There's a smaller role for private insurance compared to Australia. Coverage is extensive, although there are concerns about equity for the Maori and Pacific populations.

Indonesia: Is in the process of expanding coverage through the JKN system. While significant strides have been made towards universal coverage, there are still gaps, especially in remote and rural areas.

2. Quality of Care:

Australia: Known for high-quality healthcare, both in the public and private sectors. It offers advanced medical technology and highly trained healthcare professionals. Quality can vary regionally, with rural areas sometimes facing disadvantages.

New Zealand: Also provides high-quality care with an efficient public health system. However, like Australia, New Zealand faces challenges in ensuring the same level of quality across all regions and communities.

Indonesia: Quality varies significantly across the country. Urban areas, especially in Java and Bali, have high-quality facilities, but there is a notable disparity in rural and less developed regions.

3. Efficiency:

Australia: Generally efficient, especially in primary care and emergency services. However, the system faces challenges like rising healthcare costs and the need for more integration between public and private sectors.

New Zealand: Efficient in terms of cost management and public health outcomes but faces issues with long waiting times for certain elective procedures and specialist services.

Indonesia: Efficiency is hindered by the vast geographical spread of the country and the disparity in healthcare resources. The JKN has made some improvements in efficiency, but there is still a long way to go in terms of infrastructure and resource allocation.

Overall Comparative Analysis:

Australia and New Zealand: Both have well-established healthcare systems with universal coverage, high-quality care, and relatively efficient operations. They face common challenges like managing rising costs and ensuring equitable access across all regions and communities.

Indonesia: While making significant progress, Indonesia's healthcare system is still developing. It faces challenges in achieving universal coverage, ensuring consistent quality across the archipelago, and improving overall efficiency in healthcare delivery.

Australia and New Zealand exemplify mature healthcare systems with robust public funding and a commitment to universal coverage, though they face ongoing challenges in equity and cost management. Indonesia represents an emerging system with ambitious goals for universal coverage and improving quality, navigating the complexities of a diverse and dispersed population.

Comparative Analysis of Healthcare Systems: Global Perspective

In comparing the healthcare systems of the UK (Beveridge model), Germany (Bismarck model), the USA, Japan, Singapore, India, Australia, New Zealand, and Indonesia, we assess them on three key parameters: coverage, quality, and efficiency.

1. Coverage:

Universal Coverage Models (UK, Japan, Singapore, Australia, New Zealand): These countries have systems designed to provide healthcare access to all citizens, either through state-funded models (UK, New Zealand) or through compulsory insurance schemes (Japan, Singapore, Australia). They generally achieve high coverage but may face challenges in service disparities or long wait times.

Mixed Coverage Models (Germany, USA, India, Indonesia): Germany, with its Bismarck model, provides universal coverage through employer-based and private insurance, ensuring broad access. The USA has a more fragmented system with Medicare, Medicaid, private insurance, and uninsured populations, leading to significant disparities in coverage. India and Indonesia are working towards universal coverage, but still face substantial gaps, particularly in rural and underserved areas.

2. Quality of Care:

High-Quality Care (UK, Germany, Japan, Singapore, Australia, New Zealand): These countries are generally recognized for high-quality healthcare services, with well-developed public health systems and advanced medical technologies. However, regional disparities and resource limitations can affect the uniformity of quality.

Variable Quality (USA, India, Indonesia): In the USA, the quality of care can be excellent, especially in well-funded private healthcare settings, but varies widely. India and Indonesia also display significant variations in quality, with urban centers often having better-quality services compared to rural areas.

3. Efficiency:

Efficient Systems (UK, Germany, Japan, Singapore, New Zealand): These countries, with their more centralized or streamlined healthcare systems, generally exhibit higher efficiency in terms of cost management and healthcare delivery. However, they can face issues like overburdened services and long wait times for elective procedures.

Mixed Efficiency (Australia, USA, India, Indonesia): Australia balances efficiency between public and private sectors but faces challenges in integrating these systems. The USA's healthcare system is often criticized for high costs and inefficiencies despite high expenditure. India and Indonesia, with their developing healthcare infrastructure, are working to improve efficiency but are hindered by resource constraints and uneven distribution of healthcare facilities.

Overall Comparative Summary:

Universal Coverage Countries: These systems tend to provide broad access to healthcare with high-quality services but may face challenges in wait times and service disparities.

Mixed Coverage Countries: These systems offer varying degrees of coverage, often with high-quality care available, but face challenges in ensuring equitable access for all populations and efficiently managing resources.

Developing Systems (India, Indonesia): These are characterized by efforts to expand coverage and improve quality, but face significant challenges in infrastructure, funding, and disparities between urban and rural healthcare services.

While universal coverage systems like those in the UK, Japan, and Singapore tend to excel in providing equitable access and high-quality care, they are not without challenges in efficiency and service consistency. The mixed models, such as in the USA and Germany, offer varying levels of coverage and quality, often influenced by the interplay of public and private sectors. Developing systems like India and Indonesia face unique challenges in expanding coverage, enhancing quality, and achieving efficiency amidst economic and demographic changes.

Learning from Different Healthcare Systems: Global Insights

The diverse healthcare systems across the world, each with its unique strengths and challenges, offer valuable lessons that countries can learn from each other. Here are some key insights:

1. From Universal Coverage Systems (UK, Japan, Singapore, Australia, New Zealand):

Preventive Care and Public Health: These countries often emphasize preventive care and robust public health programs, leading to better health outcomes and cost savings. Others can adopt similar strategies to improve overall population health and reduce the burden on healthcare systems.

Cost Control Measures: The control of medical costs in countries like the UK and Japan, through government negotiation and regulation, can be a model for countries struggling with escalating healthcare costs.

2. From Mixed Coverage Systems (Germany, USA):

Innovation and Choice: The USA, despite its challenges, is a leader in medical innovation and offers a wide choice of healthcare providers. This can be a model for countries looking to foster innovation and improve service quality.

Balanced Insurance Models: Germany's Bismarck model demonstrates how a well-regulated insurance-based system can achieve universal coverage with high-quality care.

Countries reforming their insurance systems can learn from Germany's approach.

3. From Developing Systems (India, Indonesia):

Resource Optimization: Developing countries like India and Indonesia are often forced to innovate and optimize limited resources. Their approaches to community-based healthcare and mobile health initiatives can offer lessons in delivering healthcare in resource-constrained settings.

Public-Private Partnerships: The role of private sector involvement in expanding healthcare access and quality in these countries can provide insights into effective public-private collaboration.

Common Lessons:

Health Equity: The importance of health equity as demonstrated by universal coverage systems is a critical lesson for all. Ensuring that all segments of the population have access to healthcare is fundamental to a well-functioning system.

Technology and Digital Health: Countries like Singapore and Australia are advancing in digital health. Their use of technology for better health data management and telemedicine can be a guide for others.

Aging Populations: Many developed countries are dealing with aging populations. Learning how they manage this demographic shift, including long-term care and geriatric healthcare, is vital for countries that will soon face similar challenges.

Public Participation and Awareness: Effective healthcare systems often involve public participation and health awareness campaigns. Educating the public about health issues and involving them in health decisions can lead to better health outcomes.

While each healthcare system has its unique context, there are universal lessons in balancing cost, quality, and access, managing public and private roles in healthcare, and innovating to meet the changing health needs of the population. Learning from each other's experiences, successes, and challenges can guide countries in enhancing their healthcare systems to meet the needs of their citizens.

Challenges and Future Trends in Global Healthcare

Healthcare systems worldwide face a set of common challenges, which are shaping future trends in healthcare. These challenges include aging populations, rising healthcare costs, and issues of health equity.

1. Aging Populations:

Challenge: Many countries are experiencing an increase in the proportion of elderly citizens due to higher life expectancy and lower birth rates. This demographic shift puts additional pressure on healthcare systems, with increased demand for long-term care, geriatric care, and management of chronic conditions.

Future Trends: We are likely to see an expansion in services targeting the elderly, including home-based care and telemedicine, as well as a greater focus on preventive care to ensure healthier aging. There's also an emerging trend in developing technologies like AI and robotics to assist in elderly care.

2. Rising Healthcare Costs:

Challenge: Healthcare costs are escalating globally, driven by factors such as technological advancements, expensive treatments, and administrative inefficiencies. This rise challenges the sustainability of healthcare systems and limits access to care, particularly in countries without universal coverage.

Future Trends: To address this, there's a growing emphasis on value-based care, where reimbursement is tied to patient outcomes rather than services provided. Additionally, there's a push towards cost transparency and the adoption of AI and big data analytics to identify cost-saving opportunities and reduce wastage.

3. Health Equity:

Challenge: Disparities in healthcare access and quality exist within and between countries. Factors such as socioeconomic status, race, gender, and geography can significantly influence an individual's health outcomes.

Future Trends: Addressing health equity is becoming a central focus, with efforts to improve access in underserved areas, enhance cultural competence among healthcare providers, and implement policies that promote equity. Digital health technologies, like mobile health applications, are also seen as tools to bridge gaps in access.

4. Integrating Technology in Healthcare:

Trend: The increasing integration of technology in healthcare is a key trend. This includes the expansion of telehealth, use of electronic health records, wearable health devices, and AI-driven diagnostics and treatment plans.

Impact: These technologies can potentially improve efficiency, access, and personalized care. However, they also present challenges in data security, privacy, and ensuring equitable access to the technologies.

5. Public Health and Preventive Care:

Trend: There's a renewed focus on public health and preventive care, as evidenced by the global response to the COVID-19 pandemic. This includes not only combating infectious diseases but also addressing lifestyle-related health issues.

Impact: Preventive care can reduce the long-term burden on healthcare systems and improve population health outcomes. This shift requires investment in public health infrastructure and community-based health initiatives.

6. Mental Health:

Emerging Focus: Mental health is increasingly recognized as a critical component of overall health, leading to a broader integration of mental health services in primary care settings and a push towards de-stigmatization.

Future Approach: Expect to see more holistic approaches to healthcare that include mental well-being, along with the use of digital tools to provide mental health support.

While the challenges facing global healthcare are significant, the future is likely to be integrated, focused on both equity and efficiency and technology driven.

Emerging Trends in Healthcare: Digital Health and Personalized Medicine

The landscape of global healthcare is rapidly evolving, with significant advancements in digital health and personalized medicine. These trends are reshaping how healthcare is delivered, making it more efficient, effective, and patient-centered.

1. Digital Health:

Telemedicine and Telehealth: The use of telemedicine has skyrocketed, particularly accentuated by the COVID-19 pandemic. It allows patients to receive medical advice, diagnosis, and treatment remotely, significantly increasing accessibility, especially in rural or underserved areas.

Mobile Health Applications: Smartphone apps for health monitoring and management are becoming increasingly popular. These apps range from fitness and nutrition tracking to managing chronic conditions like diabetes.

Wearable Technology: Wearable devices like fitness trackers, smartwatches, and even smart clothing collect health data in real-time, providing valuable insights into a person's health and lifestyle.

Electronic Health Records (EHRs): EHRs improve the efficiency and coordination of care by securely storing and sharing patient information across different healthcare providers.

Artificial Intelligence and Machine Learning: AI is being used for predictive analytics (identifying patients at risk), helping with diagnostic processes, and personalizing treatment plans.

2. Personalized Medicine:

Genomics and Genetic Testing: Advances in genomics are enabling more personalized medical treatments. Genetic testing can now identify predispositions to certain diseases, allowing for early intervention and personalized treatment plans.

Pharmacogenomics: This field combines pharmacology and genomics to understand how an individual's genetic makeup affects their response to drugs. This knowledge can help in selecting the most effective and least harmful medications for patients.

Targeted Therapies: Especially in cancer treatment, targeted therapies use drugs that specifically target the molecular changes that are driving the disease. These treatments can be more effective and less harmful than traditional treatments.

Regenerative Medicine: This area includes stem cell therapy and tissue engineering, which hold the potential to regenerate damaged tissues and organs, offering solutions for previously untreatable conditions.

3. Challenges and Considerations:

Data Security and Privacy: With the increasing use of digital tools, protecting patient data and maintaining privacy is paramount.

Health Equity: There is a risk that these advanced technologies could widen the health equity gap, as they may be less accessible to low-income or rural populations.

Regulation and Ethics: The rapid development of these technologies poses challenges in regulation and raises ethical questions, particularly around genetic data and AI decision-making in healthcare.

Digital health and personalized medicine are at the forefront of transforming healthcare. They offer the promise of more accessible, efficient, and tailored healthcare services. However, as these technologies advance, it's crucial to address challenges related to equity, ethics, and data security to ensure they benefit all segments of society.

Understanding Healthcare Systems in a Globalized World

Summary of Key Findings:

Diverse Models and Approaches: The exploration of global healthcare systems reveals a rich tapestry of models, from the state-funded systems like the UK's NHS to the insurance-based approaches in the USA and hybrid models in countries like Australia. Each system reflects its socio-economic context and cultural values.

Universal Coverage vs. Accessibility and Quality: Countries with universal healthcare coverage, such as those in Europe and Asia (e.g., Japan, Singapore), generally excel in providing equitable access. However, challenges like long wait times and regional disparities in service quality persist. In contrast, systems with mixed coverage models, like the USA, offer high-quality services but face significant issues in equitable access and affordability.

Emerging Trends: The rise of digital health and personalized medicine is reshaping healthcare delivery. Telemedicine, AI, wearable technology, and advances in genomics are paving the way for more efficient, personalized, and accessible healthcare. However, these advancements bring challenges in data privacy, health equity, and regulatory oversight.

Common Global Challenges: Aging populations, rising healthcare costs, and health equity remain universal challenges. These issues require innovative solutions, policy reforms, and international collaboration to ensure sustainable and equitable healthcare systems.

The Importance of Learning from Each Other: The diversity in healthcare systems offers opportunities for cross-learning. For instance, the cost control measures in the UK can provide valuable lessons for countries grappling with rising healthcare expenses, while the innovation and choice in the US healthcare system can inspire improvements in service quality globally.

Emphasizing the Global Context:

In our interconnected world, understanding different healthcare systems is more than an academic exercise; it is a necessity for global health and development. As health challenges become increasingly transnational with issues like pandemics, climate change-related health impacts, and the international migration of health professionals, a deep understanding of various healthcare systems becomes crucial.

Learning from the successes and challenges of different healthcare models can guide countries in enhancing their healthcare systems to better meet the needs of their populations. This understanding also facilitates international cooperation in health initiatives, policy making, and tackling global health emergencies.

Chapter 2

Proactive Health Management

Lifestyle Modifications for Disease Prevention:

The Role of Diet:

The cornerstone of disease prevention often lies not in medical intervention, but in daily lifestyle choices, with diet playing a pivotal role. A balanced diet, rich in essential nutrients, acts as a powerful tool in warding off various chronic diseases.

Preventing Diabetes:

A diet high in fiber, whole grains, and lean proteins, while low in processed sugars and unhealthy fats, can help regulate blood sugar levels. This balance is crucial in preventing type 2 diabetes.

Incorporating foods with a low glycemic index, such as whole oats, lentils, and most fruits, helps in maintaining stable blood glucose levels.

Combatting Heart Disease:

Heart disease prevention benefits from a diet low in saturated and trans fats, which are commonly found in fried foods, some baked goods, and processed snacks.

Foods rich in omega-3 fatty acids, like salmon, walnuts, and flaxseeds, can contribute to heart health by reducing blood pressure and decreasing the risk of arrhythmias.

Cancer Prevention:

Diets abundant in fruits and vegetables, which are high in antioxidants, vitamins, and minerals, can reduce the risk of certain types of cancer. These foods combat oxidative stress and inflammation, known contributors to cancer development.

Regular consumption of cruciferous vegetables like broccoli, cauliflower, and Brussels sprouts has been linked to a lower risk of colon and other cancers.

General Guidelines:

Adopt a diet that is diverse and colorful, ensuring a wide range of nutrients. Each color in fruits and vegetables represents different vitamins, minerals, and antioxidants.

Emphasize whole foods over processed ones, aiming for natural sources of nutrients.

Portion control is also crucial; even healthy foods can contribute to weight gain and related health issues if consumed in excessive amounts.

Cultural and Regional Diets:

Acknowledge and incorporate cultural and regional dietary preferences. For example, the Mediterranean diet, rich in plant-based foods, olive oil, and fish, is renowned for its health benefits, particularly in cardiovascular health.

No single diet fits all; dietary choices should consider cultural preferences, availability of food, and individual health needs.

Embracing a balanced diet is a fundamental step in proactive health management. By focusing on nutrient-rich foods and avoiding those that contribute to health issues, individuals can significantly reduce the risk of chronic diseases. This dietary approach, combined with other lifestyle modifications, forms a solid foundation for long-term health and disease prevention.

The Mediterranean Diet, DASH Diet, and Other Nutritional Plans

1. The Mediterranean Diet:

Overview: The Mediterranean diet is inspired by the eating habits of countries bordering the Mediterranean Sea. It is renowned for its cardiovascular benefits and has been associated with longevity.

Key Components: This diet emphasizes:

- High consumption of fruits, vegetables, whole grains, legumes, and nuts.
- Healthy fats such as olive oil instead of butter.
- Flavouring foods with herbs and spices instead.
- Limited intake of red meat, and a focus on fish and poultry.
- Moderate consumption of red wine, though this is optional and should be in moderation.

Health Benefits: Research has linked the Mediterranean diet to a reduced risk of heart disease, stroke, type 2 diabetes, and certain types of cancer.

2. The DASH Diet:

Overview: DASH stands for Dietary Approaches to Stop Hypertension. It was originally developed to lower blood pressure without medication but is now recognized for its overall health benefits.

Key Components: The DASH diet focuses on:

- High intake of vegetables, fruits, and whole grains.
- Inclusion of dairy products that are low in fat.
- Lean meats, fish, poultry, nuts, and beans.
- Limitation on foods high in saturated fat, such as fatty meats, full-fat dairy products, and tropical oils like coconut and palm oil.

Reduction in sodium intake.

Health Benefits: It's proven effective in lowering blood pressure and LDL (bad) cholesterol in the blood. It also aids in weight loss and offers diabetes prevention benefits.

3. Other Nutritional Plans:

Plant-Based Diets: Emphasizing foods derived from plants, including vegetables, grains, nuts, seeds, legumes, and fruits, while minimizing or excluding animal products. Known for reducing the risk of heart disease, hypertension, diabetes, and certain cancers.

Paleo Diet: Focuses on consuming foods that were likely available to early humans, such as lean meats, fish, fruits, vegetables, nuts, and seeds. It excludes processed foods, grains, dairy, and legumes. The Paleo diet is sometimes chosen for weight loss or lifestyle reasons but lacks certain nutritional elements like dietary fiber from whole grains.

Ketogenic (Keto) Diet: A high-fat, low-carbohydrate diet that shifts the body's metabolism away from carbs and towards fat and ketones. Originally developed for managing epilepsy, it has gained popularity for weight loss. It emphasizes healthy fats, moderate protein, and very low carbohydrates.

Each of these diets offers a unique approach to eating and has its own set of health benefits. The Mediterranean and DASH diets are particularly notable for their cardiovascular benefits and their emphasis on balance and moderation, making them widely recommended by nutritionists and healthcare professionals. While dietary needs can vary based on individual health conditions, lifestyle, and personal preferences, these diets provide valuable frameworks for making healthful dietary choices.

Exercise: The Cornerstone of Health and Well-being

Regular physical activity is a crucial element in maintaining overall health. It plays a significant role in managing weight, bolstering the cardiovascular system, and supporting mental health.

1. Maintaining a Healthy Weight:

Energy Balance: Exercise helps in maintaining a healthy weight by burning calories, contributing to the energy expenditure needed to balance the calories consumed through food.

Metabolism: Regular physical activity increases muscle mass, which in turn boosts metabolic rate, making it easier to maintain or lose weight.

2. Strengthening the Cardiovascular System:

Heart Health: Exercise strengthens the heart muscle, improving its ability to pump blood efficiently. This reduces the risk of heart diseases, including hypertension, coronary artery disease, and heart failure.

Circulation and Cholesterol: Physical activity improves blood circulation and can help in reducing levels of bad cholesterol (LDL) while increasing good cholesterol (HDL).

3. Enhancing Mental Health:

Mood Improvement: Exercise stimulates the release of endorphins, often known as 'feel-good' hormones, which can elevate mood and reduce feelings of depression and anxiety.

Cognitive Function: Regular physical activity has been linked to improved cognitive function, including enhanced memory and critical thinking skills. It also helps in reducing the risk of cognitive decline with aging.

World Health Organization Recommendations:

The World Health Organization (WHO) provides guidelines on the minimum levels of activity for different age groups:

Children and Adolescents (5-17 years): Should do at least 60 minutes of moderate to vigorous-intensity physical activity daily. Activities should be varied and include exercises to strengthen muscles and bones at least 3 days a week.

Adults (18-64 years): Should do at least 150–300 minutes of moderate-intensity aerobic physical activity, or at least 75–150 minutes of vigorous-intensity aerobic physical activity, or an equivalent combination of moderate- and vigorous-intensity activity throughout the week. Muscle-strengthening activities should be done involving major muscle groups on 2 or more days a week.

Older Adults (65 years and above): Should follow the adult guidelines, but also include activities that emphasize balance and coordination to prevent falls.

Incorporating regular physical activity into daily life is essential for maintaining a healthy weight, ensuring cardiovascular health, and supporting mental well-being. It is important for individuals to choose activities they enjoy and can sustain long-term. The WHO's guidelines provide a helpful framework, but any amount of physical activity is better than none. Starting with small goals.

Mental Health: A Pillar of Overall Well-Being

The importance of mental health in maintaining a holistic sense of well-being cannot be overstated. It is intrinsically linked to physical health, with each influencing the other significantly.

1. The Interconnection of Mental and Physical Health:

Bi-directional Relationship: Poor mental health can lead to an increased risk of physical health problems, just as chronic physical conditions can increase the risk of developing mental health issues.

Stress and Physical Health: Chronic stress, often a symptom of poor mental health, can contribute to a range of physical health problems, including heart disease, digestive issues, and a weakened immune system.

2. Stress Reduction Techniques:

Regular Exercise: Physical activity is a potent stress reliever. It not only helps to burn off energy and tension but also boosts the production of endorphins, the body's natural mood elevators.

Relaxation Techniques: Activities such as deep breathing, progressive muscle relaxation, and guided imagery can help calm the mind and reduce stress.

Adequate Sleep: Good sleep hygiene is crucial for stress management. Establishing a regular sleep routine and creating a restful environment can enhance sleep quality.

3. Benefits of Mindfulness and Meditation:

Mindfulness: This involves being fully present and engaged in the moment, aware of your thoughts and feelings without distraction or judgment. Regular mindfulness practice can reduce stress, improve attention, decrease emotional reactivity, and enhance mental resilience.

Meditation: Meditation practices, such as mindfulness meditation, guided meditation, or yoga, can help in achieving a state of calm and relaxation. Meditation has been linked to a variety of health benefits, including stress reduction, improved attention, better memory, and even increased empathy and compassion.

Neurological Benefits: Research indicates that meditation and mindfulness can lead to changes in brain areas related to stress, emotional regulation, and self-awareness.

4. Impact of Good Mental Health on Physical Health:

Improved Immune Function: Positive mental health can boost immune function, leading to better overall health and reduced susceptibility to illness.

Better Lifestyle Choices: Good mental health often correlates with making healthier lifestyle choices, such as regular exercise, a balanced diet, and avoiding harmful habits like smoking.

Longevity and Quality of Life: There is evidence to suggest that strong mental health can contribute to a longer lifespan and a better quality of life.

Maintaining mental health is as crucial as maintaining physical health. The adoption of stress reduction techniques, mindfulness, and meditation can play a significant role in improving mental health and, by extension, physical health. In our fast-paced, often stressful world, prioritizing mental well-being is not just beneficial; it is essential. A holistic approach to health that incorporates both mental and physical aspects can lead to a more balanced, healthier, and fulfilling life.

Importance of Regular Health Screenings and Early Detection:

Regular health screenings and early detection of diseases are critical components of proactive health management. They play a vital role in identifying health issues before they become more serious, improving the chances of effective treatment and better health outcomes.

1. Screening Guidelines for Various Populations:

Breast Cancer:

Women aged 40 to 44 are advised to start annual breast cancer screening with mammograms if they wish to do so.

Women 45 to 54 should get mammograms every year.

Women 55 and older can switch to mammograms every 2 years or continue yearly screening.

Colon Cancer:

Screening for colon cancer is recommended for both men and women starting at age 50, continuing until age 75.

Various tests are used for screening, including colonoscopy every 10 years, or stool-based tests annually.

Hypertension:

Adults should have their blood pressure checked at least every 2 years if they have never had high readings or other risk factors for heart disease.

Those with risk factors or previous high readings should have more frequent monitoring.

Diabetes:

Adults over age 45 are recommended to have a blood glucose screening. Younger adults with risk factors such as obesity or a family history of diabetes should also be screened.

Regular screenings are crucial for those with prediabetes, as lifestyle changes can prevent or delay the onset of type 2 diabetes.

Prostate Cancer:

Men should talk to their doctor about the potential benefits and harms of prostate cancer screening starting at age 50, or earlier for those with risk factors like a family history of prostate cancer.

2. The Importance of Early Detection:

Improved Outcomes: Many diseases, such as cancer, have significantly better treatment outcomes when detected early. For instance, early-stage cancers are often less aggressive and more responsive to treatment.

Prevention of Disease Progression: Regular screenings for conditions like hypertension and diabetes can help in managing these diseases early on, preventing complications and progression to more severe stages.

Cost-Effectiveness: Early detection and treatment are often more cost-effective than treating advanced diseases, reducing the financial burden on both individuals and healthcare systems.

Regular health screenings and early detection are indispensable tools in maintaining good health. They enable individuals to take timely and often less invasive actions to manage their health. Healthcare professionals play a crucial role in educating patients about the appropriate screenings based on their age, gender, family history, and overall health risk factors. Adhering to recommended screening guidelines is a proactive step towards a healthier, more informed life.

Personalized Screening Approaches in Modern Medicine

The evolution of healthcare towards personalized medicine has significantly impacted screening protocols, tailoring them to individual risk factors like family history, age, and genetic predispositions. This approach enhances the effectiveness of screenings by identifying those at higher risk and ensuring they receive timely and appropriate care.

1. Tailoring Screenings to Individual Risk Factors:

Family History: Individuals with a family history of certain diseases, such as breast or colon cancer, may require earlier and more frequent screenings. For instance, a person with a family history of breast cancer might begin mammograms before the typically recommended age.

Age: Age is a critical factor in determining the risk for various conditions. Screening guidelines often vary based on age groups, acknowledging the increased risk for diseases like cancer, diabetes, and cardiovascular issues as one ages.

Genetic Predispositions: Advances in genetics have enabled the identification of specific genes that increase the risk for certain diseases. Genetic testing can guide personalized screening schedules for diseases like cancer. For example, individuals with BRCA1 or BRCA2 gene mutations have a higher risk of developing breast and ovarian cancer and thus require more vigilant and early screening.

2. The Role of Predictive Analytics:

Predictive Modeling: With the integration of big data and AI in healthcare, predictive modeling can analyze various risk factors, including lifestyle and environmental factors, to determine personalized screening needs.

Risk Stratification: This approach classifies individuals based on their risk levels, allowing for more targeted and frequent screenings for high-risk groups, while reducing unnecessary screenings for low-risk individuals.

3. Benefits of Personalized Screening Approaches:

Improved Detection Rates: Personalized screening leads to earlier detection of diseases in high-risk individuals, improving treatment outcomes and survival rates.

Preventive Healthcare: By understanding individual risk factors, healthcare providers can also offer personalized advice on lifestyle changes to mitigate these risks.

Resource Optimization: Tailoring screening schedules based on individual risk ensures optimal use of healthcare resources, avoiding over-screening for low-risk individuals and focusing resources where they are most needed.

4. Challenges and Considerations:

Accessibility and Cost: Genetic testing and personalized screening approaches can be costly and are not always covered by insurance. There's also the challenge of ensuring equitable access to these advanced screening methods.

Ethical Considerations: The use of genetic information for screening purposes raises privacy and ethical questions, including concerns about genetic discrimination in employment and insurance.

The shift towards personalized medicine in screening represents a significant advancement in healthcare, offering more targeted and efficient approaches to disease prevention and early detection. By considering individual risk factors such as family history, age, and genetic predispositions, healthcare providers can deliver more precise and effective care. However, it is crucial to balance these advancements with considerations of accessibility, cost, and ethical use of genetic information.

Preventive Measures in Health Management

Preventive healthcare measures, including vaccinations and other strategies, play a critical role in maintaining health and preventing disease. These measures are fundamental in reducing the risk of various illnesses and improving the overall health of populations.

1. Vaccinations:

Essential for Preventing Infectious Diseases: Vaccinations are one of the most effective ways to prevent infectious diseases. They work by stimulating the immune system to recognize and combat pathogens, such as bacteria or viruses, without causing the disease itself.

Routine Vaccinations: Include immunizations against diseases like measles, mumps, rubella (MMR), diphtheria, tetanus, whooping cough (pertussis), polio, hepatitis B, and influenza. The specific schedule for these vaccines varies by age and country.

Travel Vaccinations: Depending on the destination, additional vaccines such as yellow fever, typhoid, or Japanese encephalitis may be recommended for travelers.

COVID-19 Vaccination: The emergence of COVID-19 has underscored the importance of vaccinations in controlling pandemics. COVID-19 vaccines have been crucial in reducing the severity and spread of the disease.

2. Regular Health Check-Ups:

Early Detection: Regular health check-ups with a healthcare provider can help in the early detection of diseases like hypertension, diabetes, and some cancers.

Personalized Advice: These visits also provide an opportunity for healthcare providers to offer personalized advice on lifestyle modifications for disease prevention.

3. Lifestyle Measures:

Healthy Diet: A balanced diet rich in fruits, vegetables, whole grains, lean proteins, and healthy fats can prevent a range of chronic diseases.

Physical Activity: Regular exercise is key in preventing obesity, heart disease, type 2 diabetes, and mental health disorders.

Avoiding Tobacco and Limiting Alcohol: Smoking cessation and moderate alcohol consumption are critical in preventing various cancers, liver diseases, and respiratory disorders.

4. Mental Health Care:

Stress Management: Techniques such as mindfulness, meditation, and regular physical activity can help manage stress, a significant risk factor for many physical and mental health issues.

Seeking Professional Help: Timely consultation with mental health professionals for symptoms of mental disorders is a vital preventive measure.

5. Environmental and Occupational Health:

Safe Practices at Work and Home: Understanding and adhering to safety protocols in the workplace and using protective equipment when necessary can prevent injuries and exposure to harmful substances.

Sun Protection: Using sunscreen and wearing protective clothing can prevent skin cancer.

Preventive measures in healthcare are fundamental in

mitigating the risk of diseases and promoting long-term health. They encompass a range of strategies from vaccinations, regular health screenings, lifestyle choices, mental health care, to environmental safety practices. Integrating these preventive measures into daily life and healthcare practices is key to maintaining health and well-being at both individual and community levels.

Case Studies of Successful Proactive Health Management:

Case Study: Managing Type 2 Diabetes Through Lifestyle Changes

Background:

Meet Sarah, a 52-year-old school teacher diagnosed with Type 2 diabetes. Her initial diagnosis came as a shock, leading to feelings of anxiety about her health and future. Sarah's family history of diabetes and her sedentary lifestyle contributed to her condition. At the time of diagnosis, her HbA1c level was 8.5%, well above the recommended range.

The Challenge:

Sarah faced several challenges in managing her diabetes. She struggled with a diet high in processed foods and sugars, minimal physical activity, and a demanding work schedule that often led to stress eating.

Intervention:

Sarah's journey began with education. She consulted with a

diabetes educator and a dietitian who helped her understand the importance of diet and exercise in managing blood sugar levels.

Dietary Changes:

Sarah switched to a diet rich in fiber, whole grains, lean proteins, and plenty of fruits and vegetables.

She significantly reduced her intake of processed foods, sugars, and unhealthy fats.

Smaller, more frequent meals were adopted to regulate her blood sugar levels throughout the day.

Physical Activity:

Sarah started with brisk walking for 30 minutes, five days a week.

As her fitness improved, she incorporated strength training and yoga into her routine.

Her exercise regimen was tailored to fit her schedule, making it sustainable in the long term.

Stress Management:

Mindfulness and meditation were introduced to manage stress.

She attended a weekly yoga class, which helped in reducing stress and improving her overall well-being.

Results:

After six months of these lifestyle changes, Sarah's HbA1c levels dropped to 6.4%. She also experienced weight loss, improved energy levels, and a reduction in the need for medication. Her doctor was pleased with the progress and encouraged her to continue with her lifestyle modifications.

We can conclude that Sarah's case is a testament to the power of lifestyle changes in managing chronic health conditions like Type 2 diabetes. By altering her diet, incorporating regular exercise, and adopting stress reduction techniques, she was able to significantly improve her health markers and overall quality of life. This case highlights that with the right guidance, education, and commitment, individuals can effectively manage diabetes and reduce their dependence on medication.

Corporate Wellness Program Success Story: TechForward Inc.

Background:

TechForward Inc., a mid-sized technology company, recognized the importance of employee health and wellness as a key factor in productivity and job satisfaction. The company launched a comprehensive wellness program aimed at improving the overall health and well-being of its employees.

The Challenge:

Before the program, the company faced high levels of employee stress, frequent sick leaves, and a generally sedentary workplace environment. There was a noticeable impact on employee morale and productivity.

Intervention:

TechForward's wellness program, named "HealthFirst," was a multifaceted initiative:

Health Assessments and Personalized Plans:

The program began with voluntary health assessments for all employees, including evaluations of fitness levels, stress, nutrition, and overall health.

Based on these assessments, employees were offered personalized wellness plans, which included dietary recommendations, exercise routines, and stress management techniques.

On-Site Fitness Facilities and Classes:

TechForward set up an on-site gym and offered various fitness classes, such as yoga, Pilates, and circuit training, to cater to different interests.

The company also formed running and walking clubs for employees, encouraging group activities that also fostered team building.

Nutritional Services:

The company cafeteria started offering healthy meal options, with nutritional information displayed for all items.

Monthly workshops on nutrition, cooking demonstrations, and consultations with a dietitian were provided.

Mental Health Support:

Stress management workshops and mindfulness sessions were introduced.

The company provided access to counseling services and established a quiet room for relaxation and meditation.

Incentivizing Participation:

TechForward incentivized participation in the program through a points system, where employees earned points for engaging in healthy activities, redeemable for health-related products or extra vacation days.

Results:

After one year of the HealthFirst program:

There was a 25% reduction in employee sick days.

Employee surveys indicated a 40% improvement in overall job satisfaction.

A notable increase in productivity was reported, with a 15% decrease in reported stress levels.

70% of participating employees reported improved physical health, and 65% reported better mental health.

TechForward's HealthFirst program illustrates the positive impact a well-rounded corporate wellness program can have on employee health outcomes. By investing in the physical and mental well-being of their employees, TechForward not only enhanced the quality of life for their team but also achieved tangible benefits in productivity and employee engagement. This success story serves as a model for other companies looking to implement effective wellness programs in their workplace.

Community Health Initiative: The Greenway Fitness Project

Background:

The Greenway Fitness Project was a community health initiative launched in the city of Brooksville. Aimed at promoting physical activity and healthy living, the project was a response to rising levels of obesity and sedentary lifestyles among the city's population.

The Challenge:

Brooksville faced a challenge common to many urban areas: high rates of obesity, heart disease, and diabetes, exacerbated by a lack of physical activity and poor dietary habits among its residents.

Fast-Track A&E

Intervention:

The Greenway Fitness Project was a multifaceted initiative involving various stakeholders, including the local government, healthcare providers, and community organizations.

Installation of Fitness Stations:

The city installed outdoor fitness stations along popular walking and biking trails. These stations included equipment for cardiovascular, strength, and flexibility exercises, accessible for free to the public.

Community Fitness Challenges:

The project organized city-wide fitness challenges, such as '10,000 Steps a Day' and 'Cycle the City' weekends, encouraging residents to increase their physical activity.

Local businesses sponsored these events, offering incentives and prizes for participants.

Health and Nutrition Workshops:

In collaboration with healthcare providers, the project hosted workshops on nutrition, healthy cooking, and lifestyle changes to reduce the risk of chronic diseases.

These workshops were held in community centers, schools, and even online platforms to maximize reach.

Collaboration with Schools:

The project partnered with local schools to promote physical education and healthy eating habits among children. This included setting up school gardens, nutrition education, and after-school fitness programs.

Regular Health Fairs:

Health fairs offering free screenings for blood pressure, cholesterol, and diabetes were conducted. These fairs also provided information on smoking cessation, mental health resources, and preventive healthcare.

Results:

Two years after the implementation of the Greenway **Fitness Project:**

A survey showed a 30% increase in the number of residents engaging in regular physical activity. There was a measurable decrease in average BMI scores and obesity rates in the community. Local schools reported increased participation in physical activities and better nutrition choices among students. The health fairs saw a consistent increase in attendance, indicating heightened community awareness and engagement in health matters.

The Greenway Fitness Project stands as a testament to the power of community-based initiatives in improving public health. By creating an environment that supports and encourages healthy lifestyles and by involving various sectors of the community, Brooksville was able to foster a culture of health and wellness, leading to improved health outcomes for its residents. This initiative serves as an inspiring model for other communities facing similar public health challenges.

Healthy and Balanced Nutrition

Healthy Mind in a Health Body

Chapter 3:

Effective Communication with Healthcare Professionals

1. Overcoming Language and Cultural Barriers:

The Importance of Cultural Competence:

In an increasingly diverse world, the ability of healthcare providers to understand and respect cultural differences in health beliefs and practices is not just beneficial – it's essential. Cultural competence in healthcare involves recognizing the diverse values, beliefs, and behaviours that patients bring to the healthcare setting and responding to these differences with respect and understanding.

Key Aspects of Cultural Competence:

1. **Awareness and Respect for Diversity:**
   - Healthcare professionals should be aware of the cultural diversity of the populations they serve. This includes understanding various cultural norms, health beliefs, and practices.
   - Showing respect for different cultures can be demonstrated through simple actions like asking about and using preferred names and pronouns, or understanding cultural norms around personal space and eye contact.
2. **Training and Education:**
   - Ongoing training in cultural competence for healthcare workers is crucial. This can include workshops, seminars, and other forms of education that focus on understanding and effectively interacting with people from different cultural backgrounds.

- Training should also cover implicit bias – the unconscious attitudes or stereotypes that can affect understanding and decision-making in a healthcare setting.

3. **Effective Communication:**
    - Clear communication is a cornerstone of cultural competence. This includes being mindful of language barriers and providing interpreter services when necessary.
    - Healthcare providers should also be trained to use plain language and avoid medical jargon, ensuring that explanations of diagnoses and treatments are understandable regardless of the patient's cultural or educational background.

4. **Patient-Cantered Care:**
    - Culturally competent care is patient-centred. It involves considering the patient's cultural, religious, and linguistic needs in the treatment plan.
    - This approach might include accommodating dietary restrictions, integrating traditional practices with conventional medicine (where safe and appropriate), or respecting religious beliefs in the treatment process.

5. **Building Trust and Collaboration:**
    - Establishing trust with patients from diverse backgrounds involves showing empathy and understanding towards their cultural needs.
    - Collaboration with community leaders and organizations can also enhance cultural competence and provide insights into the specific needs and preferences of different cultural groups.

Cultivating cultural competence is not just about avoiding misunderstandings or miscommunications; it's about providing high-quality, empathetic care that respects and honours the diverse cultural backgrounds of patients. As the healthcare landscape becomes increasingly multicultural, cultural competence becomes an indispensable skill for healthcare professionals, leading to more effective, respectful, and personalized care.

Use of Language Services in Healthcare Settings

Essential Role of Language Services:

Effective communication is a fundamental right in healthcare settings. Ensuring that patients who are not fluent in the primary language have access to interpreter services is crucial for delivering accurate and equitable medical care. Families and relatives could always be useful but for the sake of transparency, safeguarding and unbiased decision making, private translators shall always be most favourable than family and friends.

Implementation of Language Services:

1. **Availability of Interpreters:**
    - Hospitals and clinics should have a system for providing interpreter services, either in-person or through remote technologies like phone or video calls. These services should be readily available for patient consultations, medical procedures, and any situation where clear communication is essential.

- It's important that these interpreters are trained in medical terminology and understand the nuances of healthcare communication.
2. **Written Materials in Multiple Languages:**
   - Essential healthcare documents, including consent forms, informational brochures, treatment plans, and discharge instructions, should be available in multiple languages. This ensures that all patients have access to understandable and accurate information about their care.
   - The selection of languages for these materials should reflect the linguistic diversity of the community the healthcare facility serves.
3. **Training Staff in the Use of Language Services:**
   - Healthcare professionals should receive training on how to effectively utilize interpreter services. This includes understanding when to call for an interpreter and how to communicate effectively through an interpreter.
   - Staff should also be educated on the legal rights of patients to language services and the importance of these services in providing high-quality care.
4. **Cultural Sensitivity:**
   - Language services should be provided in a manner that is culturally sensitive. Interpreters must be aware of cultural nuances that might affect communication and understand the cultural context of the patients they are assisting.
5. **Quality Control and Feedback:**
   - Regular assessments of the language services provided should be conducted to ensure quality and effectiveness. Patient feedback can be an invaluable part of this process, highlighting areas for

improvement and ensuring that the services meet their needs.

The provision of language services in hospitals and clinics is not just a logistical or legal requirement; it is a vital aspect of patient-centered care. By ensuring that patients who are not fluent in the primary language receive accurate and comprehensible information, healthcare providers can significantly improve patient outcomes, satisfaction, and trust. This commitment to language access is a clear demonstration of respect for the diversity and dignity of all patients.

Encouraging Openness: Respecting Cultural Beliefs in Healthcare

The Value of Openness in Healthcare Settings:

Encouraging patients to share their cultural beliefs and practices is an essential aspect of delivering culturally competent and respectful healthcare. Understanding a patient's cultural background can significantly impact healthcare outcomes and patient satisfaction.

Strategies for Encouraging Openness:

1. **Creating a Welcoming Environment:**
   - Healthcare settings should be designed to be welcoming and inclusive to people from diverse backgrounds. This can be achieved through multilingual signage, diverse staff, and culturally sensitive decor.

- Ensuring that the healthcare environment feels safe and respectful encourages patients to open up about their cultural needs and practices.
2. **Building Trust through Communication:**
    - Healthcare providers should initiate conversations about cultural beliefs and practices in a respectful and non-judgmental manner.
    - Open-ended questions like, "Are there any cultural or religious practices or beliefs that we should consider in your care?" can invite patients to share relevant information.
3. **Educating Healthcare Providers:**
    - Training in cultural sensitivity and communication skills can equip healthcare providers to engage effectively with patients from various cultural backgrounds.
    - This training should include understanding the impact of cultural beliefs on health behaviours and decision-making.
4. **Respecting Patient Autonomy:**
    - Acknowledging and respecting a patient's cultural beliefs and practices, even when they differ from mainstream medical opinions, is crucial. This respect, however, should be balanced with the need to provide safe and effective medical care.
    - In cases where cultural practices may conflict with medical advice, a collaborative approach should be taken to find a mutually acceptable solution.
5. **Involving Family and Community:**
    - In many cultures, family and community play a significant role in healthcare decisions. Understanding and involving these support networks can be beneficial in providing holistic care.

- Healthcare providers might consider arranging meetings with family members or community leaders, when appropriate, to discuss care plans and cultural considerations.

Encouraging openness about cultural beliefs and practices in healthcare settings fosters an environment of mutual respect and understanding. It enables healthcare providers to deliver care that is not only clinically effective but also culturally sensitive. Such an approach enhances patient-provider communication, builds trust, and ultimately leads to improved health outcomes and patient satisfaction.

2. Strategies for Effective and Assertive Communication: Active Listening

Active Listening in Healthcare Communication:

Active listening is a critical component of effective communication in healthcare settings. It involves fully concentrating on the speaker, understanding their message, responding thoughtfully, and remembering what was said. This skill is essential for both healthcare providers and patients to ensure clear and efficient communication.

Implementing Active Listening:

1. **Full Attention to the Speaker:**
    - In a healthcare setting, distractions are common. Active listening requires giving undivided attention to the speaker. This means putting aside paperwork, turning away from computer screens, and minimizing interruptions during consultations.

- For patients, this involves focusing attentively on the healthcare provider's advice and instructions, without letting distractions interfere.

2. **Non-Verbal Cues:**
    - Non-verbal cues like nodding, maintaining eye contact, and appropriate facial expressions demonstrate engagement and understanding.
    - These cues are important for both parties; they convey empathy and reassure the speaker that their message is being received.

3. **Reflecting and Clarifying:**
    - Reflecting involves paraphrasing or summarizing what the speaker has said to ensure understanding. For instance, a doctor might say, "So, you're saying that the pain intensifies in the evenings?"
    - Clarifying is asking questions to clear up any confusion about what has been said. Patients should feel comfortable asking for clarification on medical jargon or treatment plans.

4. **Acknowledging Concerns:**
    - Active listening is not just about hearing words; it's about understanding the emotions and concerns behind them. Acknowledging a patient's worries or a healthcare provider's recommendations validates their feelings and fosters a supportive environment.
    - Simple statements like "I understand why that would be worrying" or "That makes sense" can be very effective.

5. **Thoughtful Responses:**
    - Responses should be thoughtful and relevant to what the speaker has just said. This shows that their message has been heard and considered.

- In healthcare, this could mean a provider offering solutions based on the patient's expressed concerns or a patient giving honest feedback about their ability to follow a treatment plan.

Active listening is a powerful tool in healthcare communication. It not only ensures that information is accurately exchanged but also builds trust and rapport between patients and healthcare providers. By practicing active listening, both parties can contribute to more effective, empathetic, and patient-cantered healthcare communication.

3. Assertiveness Training in Healthcare Communication

The Role of Assertiveness in Patient Communication:

Assertiveness is a key communication skill, particularly in healthcare settings. It involves expressing one's thoughts and feelings confidently and directly while respecting the rights and beliefs of others. For patients, being assertive can lead to more satisfying and effective interactions with healthcare providers, ensuring their needs and concerns are adequately addressed.

Developing Assertiveness Skills:

1. **Understanding Assertiveness:**
   - Assertiveness is the balance between passive and aggressive communication. It means expressing your views and needs openly and honestly, but without

being confrontational or disregarding others' perspectives.
   - It's about being self-assured and respectful, allowing for a two-way, honest, and respectful dialogue between patient and healthcare provider.
2. **Expressing Needs Clearly:**
   - Patients should practice stating their needs and concerns clearly and directly. For example, saying, "I need more information about the side effects of this medication" is an assertive way to seek information.
   - It's important to use "I" statements, such as "I feel" or "I think," to communicate personal feelings and thoughts without blaming or attacking others.
3. **Active Participation in Healthcare Decisions:**
   - Being assertive also means taking an active role in healthcare decisions. Patients should feel empowered to ask questions, discuss treatment options, and express preferences or concerns.
   - For instance, a patient might say, "I would like to explore alternative treatments. What options do we have?"
4. **Setting Boundaries:**
   - Assertiveness involves setting healthy boundaries and saying no when necessary. Patients should feel comfortable declining treatments or procedures they are not comfortable with after understanding the implications.
   - A patient might assertively say, "I'm not ready to make a decision about surgery today. Can we discuss this further?"

5. **Practicing Assertiveness:**
    - Role-playing exercises with a therapist or in support groups can be an effective way to practice assertiveness skills.
    - Patients can also practice assertiveness in everyday situations to build confidence, which can then be transferred to healthcare settings.
6. **Seeking Support if Needed:**
    - Patients who struggle with assertiveness may benefit from counselling or assertiveness training courses. These resources can provide strategies and practice opportunities in a supportive environment.

Assertiveness training is invaluable for patients navigating the healthcare system. It enables them to communicate more effectively with healthcare providers, leading to better healthcare experiences and outcomes.

4. Use of Open-Ended Questions in Healthcare Communication

Open-ended questions are a vital tool for healthcare professionals in eliciting detailed and meaningful responses from patients. Unlike closed-ended questions that limit answers to a simple 'yes' or 'no,' open-ended questions encourage patients to elaborate on their symptoms, feelings, and concerns.

Effective Implementation of Open-Ended Questions:

1. **Encouraging Detailed Responses:**
    - Open-ended questions allow patients to provide more information than what the healthcare provider might

anticipate. For example, asking "Can you describe your symptoms?" instead of "Do you have pain?" gives the patient an opportunity to provide a comprehensive description of their experience.

2. **Building a Complete Picture:**
   - These questions help in gathering a thorough history and understanding the full scope of the patient's condition. For instance, "What were you doing when you first noticed the problem?" can yield insights into potential causes or triggers of the condition.

3. **Fostering Patient Engagement:**
   - When patients are encouraged to speak more freely about their symptoms and concerns, they become more engaged in the diagnostic process. This engagement can lead to a greater understanding and acceptance of the treatment plan.

4. **Enhancing Patient-Provider Relationship:**
   - The use of open-ended questions demonstrates that healthcare providers are genuinely interested in the patient's perspective, fostering a sense of trust and rapport.

5. **Identifying Emotional and Psychological Factors:**
   - Such questions can also uncover emotional or psychological aspects related to the patient's physical health. Asking "How has this condition affected your daily life?" can reveal the emotional impact and guide more comprehensive care.

6. **Tailoring the Healthcare Experience:**
   - Responses to open-ended questions can provide healthcare professionals with the insights needed to tailor their approach to each individual patient, accommodating their unique needs and preferences.

In Practice: Healthcare professionals should integrate open-ended questions throughout the patient interaction, from initial history taking to discussing treatment options. This approach ensures a more patient-cantered and holistic approach to healthcare delivery.

5. Articulating Symptoms and Concerns Clearly

Preparing for Appointments:

Effective communication during medical appointments is crucial for accurate diagnosis and treatment planning. One of the best ways patients can contribute to this process is by coming well-prepared to their appointments.

1. **Making a List of Symptoms:**
   - Patients should jot down all symptoms they're experiencing, no matter how minor they may seem. This list should include details about the nature of the symptoms (e.g., sharp or dull pain), when they began, and any patterns or triggers noticed.
2. **Maintaining a Symptom Diary:**
   - Keeping a symptom diary can be particularly helpful for chronic or intermittent issues. In this diary, patients can record the time, duration, and intensity of symptoms, as well as any potential contributing factors like food, activities, or stressors.
3. **Gathering Medical History:**
   - It's beneficial for patients to have a comprehensive understanding of their medical history. This includes past diagnoses, treatments, surgeries, and any known allergies or adverse reactions to medications.

4. **Listing Current Medications:**
    - Patients should prepare a current list of all medications, including prescription drugs, over-the-counter medications, and supplements. This helps to avoid potential drug interactions and allows for a holistic view of the patient's treatment regimen.
5. **Identifying Key Concerns and Questions:**
    - Prior to the appointment, patients should think about what they want to get out of the visit. Writing down key concerns and questions ensures that these important points are addressed during the consultation.
6. **Bringing Relevant Documents:**
    - If applicable, bringing along previous test results, records from other doctors, or any relevant health documents can provide valuable information to the healthcare provider.

Describing Symptoms:

Effectively communicating symptoms to healthcare providers is crucial for accurate diagnosis and appropriate treatment. Patients play a vital role in this process by clearly and specifically describing their symptoms.

Key Elements in Describing Symptoms:

1. **Onset of Symptoms:**
    - Patients should describe when the symptoms first started. Pinpointing the exact time or event associated with the onset can provide critical diagnostic clues.

2. **Duration:**
   - It is important to communicate how long the symptoms have been present. Whether they are constant or intermittent can significantly affect the diagnostic process.
3. **Intensity and Nature:**
   - Describing the severity of the symptoms is essential. Patients should explain the intensity on a scale (e.g., on a scale of 1-10) and the nature of the symptoms (e.g., sharp pain, dull ache, throbbing sensation).
4. **Aggravating and Alleviating Factors:**
   - Identifying what makes the symptoms worse or better can help in understanding the underlying cause. This includes activities, foods, medications, or environmental factors.
5. **Associated Symptoms:**
   - Often, other symptoms may accompany the primary complaint. Patients should mention any additional symptoms, even if they seem unrelated, as they can provide valuable context.
6. **Effect on Daily Activities:**
   - Describing how the symptoms impact daily activities, like sleeping, eating, working, or physical activity, can give healthcare providers insight into the severity and practical implications of the health issue.

Effective Communication Tips:

- **Be Specific:** Instead of saying "I feel sick," describe specific symptoms like "I have a headache and feel nauseous."

- **Avoid Medical Jargon:** Patients should describe their symptoms in their own words, avoiding self-diagnosis or medical terms they are not sure about.
- **Chronological Order:** If there are multiple symptoms or a progression of symptoms, describing them in the order they appeared can be helpful.

Discussing Concerns with Healthcare Providers

Open and honest communication about concerns related to treatment, side effects, or lifestyle changes is essential for patients to ensure they receive the best possible care. Addressing these concerns can lead to more personalized and effective treatment plans.

Key Aspects of Discussing Concerns:

1. **Voicing Treatment Concerns:**
   - Patients should feel comfortable discussing any apprehensions or questions they have about recommended treatments. This might include concerns about the nature of the treatment, the expected outcomes, or alternative treatment options.
   - For instance, a patient might say, "I'm worried about the side effects of this medication. Are there other treatments available?"
2. **Understanding Side Effects:**
   - It is crucial for patients to understand potential side effects of medications or treatments. Discussing these concerns can help healthcare providers offer advice on managing side effects or consider alternative therapies.

- A patient could ask, "What are the common side effects of this medication, and how can I manage them if they occur?"
-

3. **Lifestyle Changes and Adaptations:**
   - When treatments require lifestyle changes, such as dietary adjustments or increased physical activity, patients should discuss how these can be integrated into their daily lives.
   - Patients might need guidance on practical aspects of these changes, like "How can I adjust my diet to better manage my diabetes?"

4. **Clarifying Instructions and Expectations:**
   - Patients should seek clarification on any aspect of their treatment plan that is unclear. This includes understanding the correct way to take medications, follow-up appointments times, or the expected timeline for recovery.
   - Asking questions like "Can you explain how and when I should take these medications?" is vital for effective treatment.

5. **Expressing Personal Constraints:**
   - It's important for patients to discuss any personal or logistical constraints that might impact their ability to follow a treatment plan. This could include financial limitations, work schedules, or family responsibilities.
   - For example, "I have difficulty coming for weekly appointments due to my work schedule. Can we consider a different plan?"

Chapter 4:
Pain Management

Introduction to Pain Management

In the realm of healthcare, pain management stands as a crucial yet intricate domain, deeply entwined with the fabric of human experience. It is a universal phenomenon, transcending age, race, and socioeconomic boundaries, and yet it is profoundly personal. The experience of pain, influenced by a complex interplay of biological, psychological, cultural, and social factors, varies significantly from one individual to another. This diversity in the experience and expression of pain necessitates an equally diverse approach to its management.

At its core, pain management is not merely about alleviating physical discomfort; it is about enhancing the quality of life. It requires a keen understanding of the multifaceted nature of pain and an appreciation for the unique ways in which each individual experiences and communicates it. In this pursuit, healthcare providers must navigate a labyrinth of challenges, balancing the need for effective intervention with the imperative to address the holistic needs of the patient.

This chapter delves into the realm of pain management, exploring the rich tapestry of strategies that encompass both the time-honored wisdom of cultural practices and the cutting-edge advancements of modern medicine. From the ancient art of acupuncture to the latest in pharmacological therapies, from the gentle touch of a therapeutic massage to the precision of interventional techniques, pain management is an ever-evolving field that stands at the crossroads of art and science.

We will explore how cultural perspectives shape the understanding and approach to pain, the role of medical and alternative therapies in pain relief, and the powerful testimonials of those who have journeyed through the landscape of pain and emerged empowered. By weaving together these diverse threads, the chapter aims to provide a comprehensive overview of pain management, offering insights and guidance to those seeking relief and to the professionals dedicated to providing it. In doing so, we affirm the fundamental right of every individual to live a life free from the constraints of pain, a journey that, while challenging, is replete with hope and possibility.

1. Cultural Approaches to Pain Understanding and Management:

Diverse Perceptions:

The way pain is perceived, expressed, and managed varies significantly across different cultures. These variations are not merely superficial differences but are deeply rooted in cultural beliefs, practices, and social norms.

- **Perception of Pain as a Sign of Strength or Weakness:** In some cultures, enduring pain without expressing it is seen as a sign of strength, resilience, or spiritual endurance. For example, in certain traditional societies, rituals involving endurance of pain are a rite of passage. In contrast, other cultures encourage open expression of pain, viewing it as a natural, human response requiring empathy and care.
- **Role of Stoicism:** Cultures that value stoicism might encourage individuals to bear pain silently. This attitude can affect how individuals within these cultures report

pain to healthcare providers, often underplaying their discomfort.
- **Expression and Communication:** In more expressive cultures, individuals are likely to describe their pain vividly and expect a more empathetic response from their caregivers and healthcare providers.
- **Influence on Healthcare Seeking Behaviour:** Cultural attitudes towards pain can influence how and when individuals seek medical help. In cultures where pain expression is discouraged, individuals might delay seeking treatment, leading to chronic pain conditions.
- **Holistic View of Pain:** Many cultures adopt a holistic approach to pain, considering it an interplay of physical, emotional, and spiritual factors. This perspective often leads to the use of traditional healing practices alongside or in place of conventional medical treatments.

Impact on Clinical Practice:

- **Healthcare Provider Awareness:** It is crucial for healthcare providers to be aware of these cultural nuances in pain perception and expression. This awareness can guide more effective communication strategies and pain assessment techniques.
- **Tailored Pain Management Approaches:** Understanding a patient's cultural background can help healthcare professionals tailor their pain management approaches. For instance, a patient from a culture that values stoicism might require different communication techniques to elicit an accurate description of their pain.
- **Respect for Traditional Practices:** Healthcare providers should respect and, where appropriate, integrate traditional and cultural practices in pain management. This

integration can enhance patient satisfaction and adherence to treatment plans.

Recognizing and respecting the cultural dimensions of pain is a critical component in the effective management of pain. It requires healthcare providers to not only consider the physiological aspects of pain but also the cultural context in which their patients experience and communicate their discomfort.

Cultural Practices in Pain Management:

Cultural practices have long been integral to managing pain in various societies around the world. Two prominent examples are acupuncture in traditional Chinese medicine and Ayurveda in Indian culture. These practices, deeply rooted in centuries-old philosophies and beliefs, offer alternative approaches to pain management that continue to be relevant and widely used today.

Acupuncture in Chinese Medicine:

- **Background:** Acupuncture, a key component of traditional Chinese medicine, is based on the concept of Qi (pronounced "chee"), which is believed to be a vital life force flowing through the body. Pain and illness are thought to result from blockages or imbalances in Qi.
- **Technique:** Acupuncture involves the insertion of thin needles into specific points on the body, known as acupuncture points. These points are situated along pathways called meridians, which correspond to different organ systems.

- **Effectiveness:** By stimulating these points, acupuncture aims to restore the flow of Qi and balance the body's energy, leading to pain relief and improved health. It is commonly used for a variety of pain conditions, including chronic pain, headaches, and arthritis.
- **Scientific Perspective:** Modern research suggests that acupuncture can be effective in pain relief, possibly by triggering the release of endorphins (the body's natural painkillers) and affecting the way pain signals are processed by the brain and spinal cord.

Ayurveda in Indian Culture:

- **Holistic Approach:** Ayurveda, the traditional system of medicine in India, takes a holistic approach to health and well-being, emphasizing the balance between body, mind, and spirit.
- **Pain Management:** In Ayurveda, pain is seen as a manifestation of an imbalance within the body. Treatment focuses on restoring balance through a combination of dietary modifications, herbal remedies, massage, yoga, and meditation.
- **Personalized Treatments:** Ayurvedic pain management is highly personalized. Practitioners consider an individual's unique constitutional type (or "dosha") – Vata, Pitta, or Kapha – when prescribing treatments.
- **Herbal Remedies:** A variety of herbs and spices used in Ayurveda, such as turmeric, ginger, and ashwagandha, are known for their anti-inflammatory and analgesic properties.

Integrating Cultural Practices in Modern Healthcare:

- **Complementary Approaches:** Both acupuncture and Ayurveda can be used alongside conventional medical treatments, offering a complementary approach to pain management.
- **Acceptance and Research:** These practices have gained wider acceptance in Western countries, with ongoing research exploring their mechanisms and efficacy.

In essence, cultural practices like acupuncture and Ayurveda contribute significantly to the diverse landscape of pain management. They embody the understanding that managing pain often requires more than just addressing physical symptoms; it involves considering the intricate interplay of mental, emotional, and spiritual factors.

Impact on Treatment: Recognizing Cultural Nuances in Pain Management

The impact of cultural nuances on pain management is profound, necessitating healthcare providers to adopt a more inclusive and sensitive approach to treatment. Recognizing and respecting these differences is not only a matter of cultural competence but also a key factor in providing effective and personalized care.

Understanding Cultural Influences:

- **Communication Styles:** Cultural background can influence how patients describe their pain and respond to questions. Some patients may be more expressive, while others may be more reserved. Healthcare providers should adapt their

communication style accordingly to ensure they are effectively assessing the patient's pain.
- **Perceptions of Pain Treatment:** Different cultures may have varying beliefs about certain medications or interventions. For instance, some patients might be wary of using pain medications due to concerns about addiction or side effects, preferring natural or holistic remedies.
- **Use of Traditional Remedies:** Patients from certain cultural backgrounds may use traditional remedies or practices as part of their pain management. Healthcare providers should inquire about these practices to avoid potential interactions with conventional treatments and to integrate them safely into the patient's care plan.

Incorporating Cultural Sensitivity into Pain Management:

- **Building Trust:** Showing respect and openness to a patient's cultural background can build trust, making them more likely to share important information about their pain and adhere to treatment plans.
- **Educational Materials:** Providing educational materials and instructions in the patient's preferred language and in a culturally appropriate format can enhance understanding and compliance.
- **Collaborative Decision-Making:** Involving patients in the decision-making process, considering their cultural and personal preferences, can lead to more effective pain management strategies.
- **Training for Healthcare Providers:** Ongoing training in cultural competence can equip healthcare professionals with the skills to recognize and respect cultural differences in pain perception and management.

Effective pain management requires a nuanced understanding of cultural influences. By acknowledging and adapting to these cultural variations, healthcare providers can offer more empathetic, respectful, and effective care. This approach not only improves patient satisfaction and comfort but also enhances the overall quality of pain management strategies.

2. Medical Pain Relief Methods:

Medications:

Medications play a crucial role in the management of pain, ranging from mild discomfort to severe chronic pain. The use of these medications, however, requires careful consideration regarding their effectiveness, potential side effects, and the risk of dependency, particularly with long-term use.

- **Over-the-Counter (OTC) Pain Relievers:**
  - Common OTC pain relievers include nonsteroidal anti-inflammatory drugs (NSAIDs) like ibuprofen and naproxen, as well as acetaminophen (paracetamol).
  - These medications are effective for mild to moderate pain and are often used for headaches, muscle aches, and minor injuries.
  - It is important for patients to adhere to the recommended dosages to avoid side effects such as gastrointestinal issues (with NSAIDs) or liver damage (with excessive use of acetaminophen).
- **Prescription Medications:**
  - For more severe or chronic pain, doctors may prescribe stronger painkillers, including opioids like morphine, oxycodone, and hydrocodone.

- While opioids are effective in managing severe pain, they come with significant risks, including the potential for addiction and overdose. Therefore, their use is typically closely monitored by healthcare providers.
- Other prescription medications used in pain management might include muscle relaxants, antidepressants (for neuropathic pain), and anticonvulsants (for seizure disorders and some types of nerve pain).
- **Topical Pain Relievers:**
  - Topical analgesics, available in creams, gels, and patches, can be applied directly to the skin over painful areas. Examples include lidocaine and capsaicin creams.
  - These are particularly useful for localized pain and can minimize some of the systemic side effects associated with oral medications.

Monitoring and Managing Risks:

- **Regular Review and Monitoring:** Especially with the use of opioids, regular review and monitoring are essential. This may involve assessing the effectiveness of the medication, monitoring for signs of dependency, and adjusting the treatment as necessary.
- **Patient Education:** Patients should be educated about the potential risks and side effects of their medications, signs of dependency, and the importance of adhering to prescribed dosages.
- **Balancing Pain Relief and Risks:** Healthcare providers must balance the need for effective pain relief with the potential risks, considering factors like the patient's

medical history, the nature of their pain, and their response to previous pain.

Medications are a fundamental aspect of pain management, offering relief and improving quality of life for those suffering from pain. However, their use requires a careful, individualized approach that considers the potential benefits against the risks, with ongoing monitoring and patient education to ensure safe and effective treatment.

3. Physical Therapy in Pain Management:

Physical therapy is a cornerstone in the non-pharmacological management of pain, especially effective for musculoskeletal conditions. It encompasses a range of techniques and practices aimed at alleviating pain, improving function, and facilitating recovery.

- **Exercise Therapy:**
    - Tailored exercise programs are central to physical therapy for pain management. These exercises help in strengthening muscles, improving flexibility, and enhancing joint mobility.
    - For chronic pain conditions like arthritis or back pain, specific exercises can reduce pain intensity and increase range of motion.
    - Exercise routines may include aerobic exercises, muscle-strengthening activities, and stretching exercises, customized to the patient's specific condition and physical capability.
- **Stretching Techniques:**
    - Stretching is vital in managing pain, particularly for conditions that involve muscle stiffness or spasms.

- Regular stretching helps in improving flexibility, reducing muscle tension, and enhancing blood circulation to the affected areas, which can aid in pain relief.
- Stretching should be done gently and within comfort limits, and it's often more effective when combined with other physical therapy techniques.
- **Manual Therapy and Massage:**
  - Manual therapy involves hands-on techniques to manipulate or mobilize soft tissues and joints. It can alleviate pain, improve movement, and encourage tissue healing.
  - Massage therapy can help in reducing muscle tension, improving circulation, and promoting relaxation, which can be particularly beneficial for patients with chronic pain.
- **Heat and Cold Therapy:**
  - The application of heat or cold can be a simple yet effective part of pain management. Heat therapy can relax and soothe muscles and heal damaged tissue, while cold therapy can reduce inflammation and numb sore areas.
  - The choice between heat and cold therapy depends on the type of pain and the underlying condition.
- **Education and Self-Management:**
  - Physical therapists also provide education on pain management, posture, body mechanics, and strategies for pain prevention.
  - Empowering patients with knowledge and self-management techniques is crucial for long-term pain management and prevention of future injuries.

Physical therapy offers a dynamic and patient-cantered approach to pain management, addressing the underlying causes of pain rather than just its symptoms. By incorporating a variety of techniques and emphasizing patient education, physical therapists play a crucial role in helping patients manage their pain, improve their function, and enhance their overall quality of life.

Interventional Procedures in Pain Management:

For certain types of chronic pain, especially when conventional therapies like medications and physical therapy have not provided adequate relief, interventional procedures can be effective. These procedures, typically performed by pain management specialists, involve minimally invasive techniques that target specific areas of pain.

- **Nerve Blocks:**
  - Nerve blocks involve the injection of anaesthetic, anti-inflammatory, or steroid medications near specific nerves or nerve clusters to block pain signals.
  - Commonly used for conditions such as neuropathic pain, severe headaches, and spinal pain, nerve blocks can provide temporary to long-lasting pain relief.
- **Spinal Injections:**
  - Epidural steroid injections are a common procedure for spinal pain, particularly for conditions like herniated discs, spinal stenosis, and radiculopathy.
  - The injection, usually a combination of a corticosteroid and a local anaesthetic, is administered into the epidural space of the spine to reduce inflammation and alleviate pain.

- **Radiofrequency Ablation:**
  - This procedure uses radiofrequency waves to create heat that selectively destroys nerve fibers carrying pain signals.
  - It is often used for chronic back and neck pain and can provide pain relief that lasts for several months or even years.
- **Spinal Cord Stimulation:**
  - Spinal cord stimulation involves the implantation of a device that sends electrical impulses to the spinal cord. These impulses interfere with the transmission of pain signals to the brain.
  - This method is beneficial for chronic pain conditions that have not responded to other treatments, such as complex regional pain syndrome or intractable back pain.
- **Intrathecal Pump Implants:**
  - These devices deliver pain medication directly into the spinal fluid, reducing the need for oral pain medications.
  - Intrathecal pumps are used for severe chronic pain conditions, including cancer-related pain.
- **Joint Injections:**
  - For pain originating in joints, such as the knee or hip, corticosteroid injections can provide relief from inflammation and pain.

Safety and Efficacy:

- **Risk-Benefit Assessment:** While these procedures can be highly effective, they come with certain risks. It is important for both the patient and the doctor to weigh the potential benefits against the risks.

- **Post-Procedure Care:** Proper care and follow-up after the procedure are crucial for ensuring the best outcomes and managing any potential side effects.

Interventional procedures offer significant pain relief for many patients suffering from chronic pain, particularly when other treatments have failed. By directly targeting the source of pain, these techniques can improve the quality of life for patients, enabling them to engage more fully in daily activities and regain a sense of normalcy.

Alternative Pain Relief Methods:

Acupuncture and Acupressure:

As part of the holistic approach to pain management, traditional Chinese medicine offers unique methods like acupuncture and acupressure. These techniques, rooted in ancient practices, have gained widespread recognition and use in modern pain relief strategies.

- **Acupuncture:**
  - **Principle:** Acupuncture is based on the principle of Qi (chi), the flow of energy along pathways in the body known as meridians. Pain is believed to be a result of disruptions in this energy flow.
  - **Technique:** The procedure involves inserting very thin needles into specific acupuncture points on the body. This process is thought to rebalance the Qi, thereby alleviating pain.
  - **Conditions Treated:** Acupuncture is used for a variety of pain conditions, including chronic back pain, neck pain, osteoarthritis, headaches, and menstrual pain.

- **Scientific Understanding:** From a Western medical perspective, acupuncture is thought to stimulate nerves, muscles, and connective tissue. This stimulation boosts the body's natural painkillers and increases blood flow.
- **Acupressure:**
  - **Technique:** Similar to acupuncture, acupressure involves the stimulation of specific points, but it uses gentle pressure from the fingers or hands instead of needles.
  - **Self-Application:** One of the advantages of acupressure is that it can be taught to patients for self-application, making it a convenient and non-invasive option for managing pain.
  - **Benefits:** Acupressure can help in reducing muscle tension, improving circulation, and enhancing relaxation, thereby contributing to pain relief.

Integration with Other Therapies:

- **Complementary Use:** Acupuncture and acupressure can be used in conjunction with other medical treatments. They are often integrated into a comprehensive pain management plan that includes medications, physical therapy, and lifestyle changes.
- **Patient Preference and Response:** The choice to use these methods often depends on patient preference, the specific condition being treated, and the individual's response to these therapies.

Acupuncture and acupressure are increasingly supported by modern research, to provide valuable options for individuals seeking relief from various pain conditions.

Mind-Body Techniques in Pain Management:

Mind-body techniques such as yoga, meditation, and tai chi have gained prominence as effective tools for pain management. These practices emphasize the connection between the mind and body and utilize this relationship to alleviate pain.

- **Yoga:**
  - **Holistic Approach:** Yoga combines physical postures, breathing exercises, and meditation. It enhances flexibility, strength, and balance, and its meditative aspect can help in managing pain.
  - **Pain Relief:** Regular yoga practice has been shown to relieve various types of pain, including lower back pain, arthritis, and migraine. It does so by improving muscle strength, enhancing flexibility, and reducing stress, which is often a contributing factor to chronic pain.
- **Meditation:**
  - **Stress Reduction:** Meditation, particularly mindfulness meditation, helps in reducing stress and anxiety, which can exacerbate pain.
  - **Altering Pain Perception:** By focusing on the present moment and developing an awareness of the body, meditation can change the way pain is perceived. It encourages a non-judgmental acknowledgment of pain, which can reduce the emotional response to it.
- **Tai Chi:**
  - **Gentle Movements:** Tai chi involves slow, gentle movements combined with deep breathing and mental focus. It is particularly suitable for those with chronic

pain who may be unable to perform more vigorous exercises.
- **Improving Physical Function:** Tai chi has been effective in reducing pain and improving physical function in conditions like osteoarthritis and fibromyalgia. It also enhances balance, which can prevent falls and related injuries.

Benefits of Mind-Body Techniques:

- **Accessibility:** These practices can often be done at home with minimal equipment, making them accessible to a wide range of people.
- **Enhanced Well-being:** Beyond pain relief, these techniques contribute to overall well-being, improving sleep, mood, and quality of life.
- **Empowering Self-Care:** Mind-body practices empower individuals to actively participate in their pain management, providing a sense of control over their health.

Mind-body techniques offer valuable tools for managing pain, emphasizing the powerful connection between mental and physical health. Through these, individuals can benefit from a holistic approach that addresses both the physical and emotional aspects of pain.

Herbal Remedies and Supplements in Pain Management:

In the quest for effective pain management strategies, many turn to herbal remedies and dietary supplements. These natural products, renowned for their therapeutic properties, offer an alternative or complementary approach to conventional pain treatments.

- **Turmeric:**
  - **Active Compound:** The active ingredient in turmeric is curcumin, known for its potent anti-inflammatory and antioxidant properties.
  - **Pain Relief:** Turmeric is particularly effective in managing pain related to inflammation, such as arthritis and muscle soreness. It can reduce the production of inflammatory compounds in the body.
  - **Usage:** Turmeric can be incorporated into the diet or taken as a supplement. However, when taken as a supplement, it's often combined with black pepper to enhance absorption.
- **Ginger:**
  - **Natural Anti-Inflammatory:** Ginger contains gingerols and shogaols, compounds with anti-inflammatory and analgesic (pain-relieving) properties.
  - **Versatility:** It is used to alleviate various types of pain, including menstrual pain, arthritis pain, and muscle pain following exercise.
  - **Forms of Consumption:** Ginger can be consumed in several forms – fresh, dried, powdered, or as an extract. It's also commonly used as a tea.
- **Omega-3 Fatty Acids:**
  - **Source:** Omega-3 fatty acids are found in high concentrations in fish oil and certain plant oils. They are essential fats that the body cannot produce on its own.
  - **Anti-Inflammatory Effect:** These fatty acids play a significant role in reducing inflammation in the body,

which can help alleviate pain, particularly in inflammatory conditions like rheumatoid arthritis.
- **Heart Health:** In addition to pain relief, omega-3 fatty acids have cardiovascular benefits, reducing the risk of heart diseases.

Considerations in Using Herbal Remedies and Supplements:

- **Consultation with Healthcare Providers:** It's important to consult with a healthcare provider before starting any herbal remedy or supplement, especially for individuals taking other medications, to avoid potential interactions.
- **Quality and Purity:** The quality and purity of herbal supplements can vary. Opting for reputable brands and products with certified purity is recommended.
- **Dosage and Side Effects:** Adhering to recommended dosages is crucial, as excessive intake can lead to side effects. While generally considered safe, some individuals may experience mild side effects from these natural products.

Herbal remedies and supplements offer a natural avenue for pain relief, particularly beneficial for those seeking alternatives to traditional pharmaceuticals. With their anti-inflammatory and analgesic properties, substances like turmeric, ginger, and omega-3 fatty acids can play a significant role in a holistic pain management plan. However, their use should be approached with an understanding of their effects and in consultation with healthcare professionals.

Multidisciplinary Approach in Pain Management:

Combining Techniques:

A multidisciplinary approach to pain management recognizes that pain is a complex condition that can be best addressed through a combination of various therapeutic methods. This approach often involves a team of healthcare professionals working together to create a comprehensive pain management plan.

- **Integrating Medical and Alternative Methods:**
    - Combining traditional medical treatments (such as medications and physical therapy) with alternative approaches (like acupuncture, massage, or herbal remedies) can address different aspects of pain.
    - For instance, while medications may alleviate the physical sensation of pain, alternative therapies can address underlying issues such as muscle tension or inflammation and improve overall well-being.
- **Inclusion of Psychological Support:**
    - Chronic pain is not just a physical experience; it has emotional and psychological dimensions. Including psychological support through counselling or therapy can help patients cope with the mental and emotional impact of chronic pain.
    - Techniques like cognitive-behavioural therapy (CBT) can be particularly effective in teaching pain coping skills, addressing negative thought patterns, and improving pain-related anxiety or depression.
- **Role of Nutrition and Lifestyle:**

- Diet and lifestyle also play a critical role in managing pain. Nutritional counselling and lifestyle modifications, such as regular exercise and stress management techniques, can significantly contribute to pain relief and overall health.
- A balanced diet, adequate sleep, and stress reduction practices can enhance the body's natural healing processes and pain tolerance levels.
- **Customized Treatment Plans:**
    - A multidisciplinary approach allows for the creation of customized treatment plans that cater to the individual's specific pain condition, lifestyle, and preferences.
    - Regular assessments and adjustments to the treatment plan are essential to ensure its continued effectiveness and to adapt to any changes in the patient's condition.

A multidisciplinary approach to pain management, which combines various medical, alternative, and psychological strategies, offers a comprehensive solution to managing pain. By addressing the multifaceted nature of pain, this approach can significantly improve treatment outcomes, enhance quality of life, and provide patients with the tools and support they need to manage their pain effectively.

Patient-Centered Care in Pain Management:

Tailoring Strategies to Individual Needs:

Patient-cantered care is a fundamental aspect of effective pain management, emphasizing the importance of tailoring treatment strategies to suit each individual's unique needs, preferences, and cultural background. This approach recognizes that pain is a subjective experience and what works for one person may not be effective for another.

- **Understanding Individual Needs:**
  - Healthcare providers should take the time to understand the patient's specific pain experience, medical history, lifestyle, and any underlying conditions. This understanding is crucial for developing an effective pain management plan.
  - For instance, a treatment plan for a young athlete might differ significantly from that for an elderly patient, even if they present with similar pain symptoms.
- **Respecting Patient Preferences and Values:**
  - Incorporating the patient's preferences and values into the treatment plan is essential. This may include their willingness to try certain medications, openness to alternative therapies, and their views on pain and pain management.
  - For example, some patients may prefer to avoid strong medications and opt for physical therapy or acupuncture instead.
- **Cultural Considerations:**
  - Being mindful of cultural beliefs and practices is also key in patient-cantered care. Understanding a patient's cultural background can help in providing pain management strategies that are both respectful and effective.
  - This can include integrating traditional practices or being sensitive to cultural beliefs about pain and medical interventions.

- **Empowering the Patient:**
    - Patient-centered care also involves empowering the patient through education and encouraging active participation in their own care. This includes providing information about their condition, treatment options, and self-management strategies.
    - Encouraging patients to voice their concerns, ask questions, and be a part of decision-making processes ensures that they are fully engaged in their treatment.

In patient-centered pain management, the focus shifts from treating pain as a standalone symptom to treating the patient as a whole. By tailoring pain management strategies to individual needs, preferences, and cultural backgrounds, healthcare providers can offer more effective, compassionate, and holistic care. This approach not only alleviates pain but also enhances the patient's overall well-being and quality of life.

Chapter 5:
When to Seek Emergency Care

Identifying Real Emergencies: Symptoms and Signs to Watch For

Understanding and recognizing life-threatening symptoms is a vital skill that can significantly impact the outcome of medical emergencies. Quick response and timely medical intervention are often crucial in these scenarios. Here's an expanded look at various life-threatening symptoms:

- **Chest Pain Suggestive of a Heart Attack:**
    - Symptoms can include a heavy, squeezing, or crushing sensation in the chest, often radiating to the jaw, neck, or arm.
    - Symptoms might include shortness of breath, sweating, nausea, or light-headedness.
    - Heart attack symptoms can vary, especially in women, who might experience more subtle symptoms like fatigue or indigestion.
- **Difficulty Breathing:**
    - This can manifest as gasping for air, wheezing, or not being able to take deep breaths.
    - It can be associated with conditions like severe asthma attacks, pulmonary embolism, or heart failure.
- **Severe Allergic Reactions (Anaphylaxis):**
    - Symptoms include hives, swelling (especially of the face, lips, or tongue), difficulty breathing, and a sudden drop in blood pressure.
    - Anaphylaxis is a rapid onset condition and can be life-threatening without immediate treatment.
- **Signs of a Stroke:**
    - The FAST acronym (Face drooping, Arm weakness, Speech difficulty, Time to call emergency services) helps in remembering the key symptoms.

- o Sudden vision problems, confusion, severe headache, or dizziness are also signs of a stroke.
- **Uncontrolled Bleeding:**
  - o This can be external or internal. External is visible bleeding that doesn't stop with direct pressure, while internal might present as blood in urine or stool, or coughing up blood.
  - o Severe internal bleeding can lead to shock, characterized by weakness, cold clammy skin, and rapid heartbeat.
- **Severe Burns:**
  - o Third-degree burns (where the burn penetrates through every layer of skin) or burns that cover a large area of the body should be treated as emergencies.
  - o Inhalation injury from smoke or toxic fumes should also be considered serious.
- **Major Trauma:**
  - o This includes injuries from major accidents like car crashes or falls from a significant height.
  - o Symptoms include severe pain, inability to move a body part, or obvious deformity.

Acute Symptoms Requiring Prompt Attention

In addition to life-threatening emergencies, there are acute symptoms that, while not immediately life-threatening, still require prompt medical attention. These symptoms can indicate serious health issues that might worsen without timely care.

Fast-Track A&E

- **High Fever with Stiff Neck (Possible Meningitis):**
  - A high fever accompanied by a stiff neck, especially when it occurs suddenly, can be a sign of meningitis, an inflammation of the membranes surrounding the brain and spinal cord.
  - Other symptoms of meningitis may include severe headache, sensitivity to light, confusion, and in some cases, a rash. Meningitis is a medical emergency that requires immediate attention.
- **Intense Abdominal Pain:**
  - Severe abdominal pain can have various causes, ranging from digestive issues to more serious conditions like appendicitis or an abdominal aortic aneurysm.
  - If the pain is sudden, sharp, and progressively worsening, it's important to seek medical care promptly to determine the cause and receive appropriate treatment.
- **Sudden Severe Headache:**
  - A sudden, severe headache, often described as a "thunderclap" headache, can be a sign of serious conditions such as a brain aneurysm, stroke, or arterial dissection.
  - Immediate medical evaluation is crucial, especially if the headache is accompanied by other symptoms like visual changes, slurred speech, or weakness.
- **Loss of Consciousness or Significant Disorientation:**
  - Any loss of consciousness, even brief, or significant disorientation (confusion, difficulty understanding or speaking, or altered behaviour) warrants immediate medical attention.
  - These symptoms can be indicative of various serious conditions, including stroke, seizure, or head injury.

Recognizing and responding quickly to these acute symptoms can prevent complications and improve outcomes. It's important to err on the side of caution; if you or someone you're with experiences any of these symptoms, seek medical care immediately. Quick action in such situations can be critically important.

Paediatric Emergencies: Recognizing Urgent Symptoms in Children

Children, particularly infants, may not always be able to communicate their discomfort or pain effectively. Recognizing the signs of a paediatric emergency is crucial for parents, caregivers, and educators. Here are key symptoms that should prompt immediate medical attention:

- **High Fever in Infants:**
    - Infants, especially those under three months, with a high fever (100.4°F or 38°C and above) require immediate medical evaluation. Their immune systems are not fully developed, making them more vulnerable to serious infections.
    - In older children, a high fever that persists despite fever-reducing medication or is accompanied by symptoms like lethargy, irritability, or difficulty waking should also be treated as an emergency.
- **Rash Combined with Fever:**
    - A rash that appears alongside a fever can be a sign of several serious conditions, such as meningitis or measles. Particular attention should be paid if the rash is purplish, does not fade when pressed (the 'glass test'), or is accompanied by other symptoms like drowsiness or irritability.

- **Difficulty Breathing:**
    - Signs of respiratory distress in children include fast breathing, flaring nostrils, grunting with breathing, the skin between the ribs sucking in with each breath (retractions), and a blue tint around lips or face.
    - Conditions like asthma, bronchiolitis, or severe allergic reactions can cause breathing difficulties and require immediate medical attention.
- **Seizures:**
    - A seizure in a child who has never had one before is a medical emergency. This can manifest as convulsions, uncontrolled shaking, or temporary loss of consciousness.
    - Even if the seizure stops on its own, it's important for the child to be evaluated by a healthcare professional as soon as possible.
- **Unresponsiveness or Altered Mental Status:**
    - If a child is not responding to external stimuli, is unusually drowsy, disoriented, or suddenly confused, it could indicate a serious problem like a head injury, infection, or intoxication.
    - Immediate medical evaluation is necessary to determine the cause and begin treatment.

In paediatric emergencies, acting quickly can be critical. Parents and caregivers should trust their instincts; if something seems seriously wrong with a child, it's better to seek medical help immediately. Being aware of these signs can enable faster response times and potentially life-saving intervention.

Global Guidelines and Application in Various Scenarios:

International Protocols for Identifying Emergencies:

In the realm of emergency care, certain protocols and guidelines have gained international acceptance and are utilized globally to identify medical emergencies quickly and effectively. These protocols are designed to be simple yet comprehensive, enabling both medical professionals and the public to recognize critical symptoms.

- **FAST Test for Stroke:**
  - The FAST test is a widely recognized method for identifying the signs of a stroke.
  - **Face:** Check if one side of the face droops when asked to smile.
  - **Arms:** Observe if one arm drifts downward or is weak when asked to raise both arms.
  - **Speech:** Listen for slurred or strange speech when asked to repeat a simple sentence.
  - **Time:** If any of these signs are present, it's time to call emergency services immediately.
- **ABCDE Protocol for Trauma Assessment:**
  - This protocol is another example, commonly used in assessing trauma patients:
  - **Airway:** Ensuring the airway is clear.
  - **Breathing:** Checking if the person is breathing adequately.
  - **Circulation:** Looking for signs of major bleeding.
  - **Disability:** Assessing neurological function, such as level of consciousness.

- **Exposure:** Examining for other injuries while preventing hypothermia.
- **CPR Guidelines:**
  - Cardiopulmonary resuscitation (CPR) guidelines, often taught in first-aid courses, are standardized across many countries. They provide instructions for people and professionals on how to perform chest compressions and rescue breathing.

Application in Various Scenarios:

- **Universal Applicability:** These protocols are designed to be universally applicable, regardless of the healthcare system or location. This standardization is crucial for travellers, expatriates, and professionals working in international settings.
- **Public Awareness Campaigns:** Many health organizations run public awareness campaigns to educate people on these protocols, to enhance community readiness to respond to emergencies.
- **Adaptation to Specific Environments:** In some scenarios, such as remote or resource-limited settings, these guidelines might be adapted to fit the available resources and immediate healthcare capabilities.

Global guidelines and protocols play a vital role in the rapid identification and initial management of emergencies. The have saved many lives over the years.

Cultural and Systemic Variations in Emergency Services:

The functioning and scope of emergency services can vary significantly across different countries and cultures. These variations are influenced by factors such as healthcare infrastructure, cultural norms, resource availability, and systemic healthcare policies. Understanding these differences is crucial, especially for individuals traveling or living abroad.

- **Variations in Emergency Room Use:**
    - In some countries, emergency rooms (ERs) are primarily reserved for acute, life-threatening conditions. However, in others, ERs may function as a catch-all for a wider range of health issues, including less critical medical problems.
    - This difference often reflects the overall structure of the country's healthcare system. For instance, in places with limited access to primary care or walk-in clinics, people might be more inclined to visit the ER for non-emergency medical issues.
- **Cultural Perceptions of Emergencies:**
    - Cultural attitudes towards health and illness can influence what is considered an emergency. In some cultures, certain symptoms might prompt an immediate visit to the ER, while in others, the same symptoms might be initially addressed with home remedies or a wait-and-see approach.
    - Public education about health emergencies and the appropriate use of ER services can vary, affecting how people respond to potential emergencies.
- **Access to Emergency Services:**

- o The accessibility of emergency services also varies. In some regions, advanced emergency medical services (EMS) are readily available with quick response times, while in others, geographical, infrastructural, or resource limitations can impact the accessibility and timeliness of emergency care.
  - o In many rural or remote areas, reaching an ER in time can be challenging, necessitating local adaptations in emergency response.
- **Emergency Numbers and Hotlines:**
  - o The emergency contact numbers differ across countries (like 911 in the USA, 999 in the UK, 112 in many European countries). Travelers and expatriates need to be aware of the local emergency numbers.
  - o Some countries also offer specific hotlines for different types of emergencies, including poison control or mental health crises.

Cultural and systemic variations in emergency services underscore the importance of understanding the local healthcare landscape, especially for those living or traveling in a foreign country. This knowledge can aid in making informed decisions about when and how to seek emergency care, ensuring appropriate and timely medical attention.

When in Doubt: Erring on the Side of Caution in Potential Emergencies

In situations where it's unclear whether a medical condition is an emergency, the safest approach is to err on the side of caution and seek immediate medical attention. This principle is critical in ensuring timely care for potentially serious health issues.

Fast-Track A&E

- **Importance of Prompt Action:**
    - In many medical emergencies, time is of the essence. Delaying medical care in cases like heart attacks, strokes, or severe injuries can have significant consequences, including long-term impairment or even fatality.
    - Symptoms that are ambiguous or seem minor can sometimes indicate more serious underlying conditions.
- **Guidance from Medical Professionals:**
    - If in doubt, individuals are encouraged to contact a healthcare provider or an emergency hotline for guidance. Many health systems have phone lines staffed by medical professionals who can help assess the situation and advise whether an ER visit is necessary.
    - In some cases, telemedicine or virtual consultations can also provide quick assessments and recommendations.
- **Using Available Resources:**
    - Many health information websites and mobile apps offer guidelines for assessing emergencies. While these tools are not a substitute for professional medical advice, they can be helpful in making an initial assessment.
    - Basic first-aid courses often provide information on how to recognize and respond to emergencies, equipping individuals with knowledge that can be crucial in moments of uncertainty.
- **Avoiding Self-Diagnosis and Delay:**
    - While self-diagnosis through internet research is common, it can lead to either underestimating a serious condition or unnecessary anxiety over a minor

issue. Professional medical assessment is always more reliable.
- Concerns about overburdening healthcare facilities or incurring medical costs should not deter individuals from seeking care in potentially serious situations.

In emergency medicine, it's better to be cautious than to risk the consequences of delayed care. Individuals should be encouraged to seek medical attention when unsure about the severity of a health issue. This approach not only safeguards individual health but also contributes to a more proactive and preventive healthcare culture.

Real-Life Examples of Emergency Room Visits:

Understanding when to appropriately use emergency room (ER) services can be elucidated through real-life examples. These scenarios highlight situations where an ER visit is not only justified but could be life-saving.

- **Suspected Heart Attack or Stroke:**
    - A person experiencing chest pain, shortness of breath, or symptoms of a heart attack should immediately go to the ER. Similarly, symptoms of a stroke, such as sudden numbness, confusion, trouble speaking, or severe headache, necessitate urgent medical attention.
    - Delay in these cases can lead to severe complications or be life-threatening.
- **Severe and Sudden Pain:**
    - Acute, intense pain, such as sudden abdominal pain or a severe headache, might indicate a serious underlying

condition like appendicitis or a brain aneurysm, requiring immediate evaluation and treatment.
- **Accidents Involving Head Injuries:**
  - Any accident that results in a head injury, especially if it involves loss of consciousness, confusion, vomiting, or changes in behaviour, should be evaluated in the ER. Head injuries can sometimes lead to internal bleeding or concussions that are not immediately apparent.
- **Deep Wounds Requiring Stitches:**
  - Deep cuts or wounds that won't stop bleeding or are gaping open likely need stitches and should be treated in the ER. Such wounds are at risk of infection and may require more complex care than what can be provided in a non-emergency setting.
- **High Fevers in Infants:**
  - Infants, particularly those under three months old, with a high fever should be taken to the ER. High fever in infants can be a sign of a serious infection since their immune systems are not fully developed.

Inappropriate Emergency Room Visits:

While the emergency room (ER) is crucial for life-threatening situations and serious medical conditions, there are scenarios where a visit to the ER may not be the most appropriate choice. Understanding what constitutes an inappropriate ER visit can help in better utilization of healthcare resources and ensure that ER services are available for those in dire need.

- **Mild Flu-Like Symptoms:**
  - Common cold and mild flu symptoms, such as a runny nose, mild fever, or sore throat, typically do

not require ER attention. These can often be effectively managed with rest, over-the-counter medications, and home remedies or through a visit to a primary care physician.
- The ER should be reserved for severe flu cases, such as those with difficulty breathing, chest pain, persistent high fever, or signs of severe dehydration.
- **Minor Cuts and Bruises:**
  - Minor injuries like small cuts, scrapes, or bruises that don't involve significant bleeding or deep wounds can usually be treated at home or in a primary care setting.
  - The ER should be considered if there's uncontrollable bleeding, the wound is deep or large, or if there's a possibility of a fracture or serious internal injury.
- **Routine Prescription Refills:**
  - The ER is not the right place for routine prescription refills. Such needs should be addressed with one's primary care provider or specialist.
  - Using the ER for prescription refills can divert resources from more urgent cases and may not be effective, as ER doctors typically do not refill long-term medications without a comprehensive evaluation.
- **Non-Severe, Chronic Complaints:**
  - Chronic conditions like back pain, mild arthritis, and stable, long-term health issues are best managed by a primary care doctor or a relevant specialist.
  - The ER should be reserved for exacerbations of these conditions that are severe, sudden, or unmanageable.

Chapter 6:

Mental Health and Its Role in Physical Well-being

Introduction

In today's fast-paced and often stress-laden world, the importance of mental health has never been more pronounced. Mental health, an integral component of overall well-being, profoundly influences not just our thoughts, emotions, and behaviours, but also our physical health. This chapter aims to unravel the complex, yet often overlooked, interplay between mental and physical health, underscoring the criticality of nurturing mental wellness in our pursuit of a healthy, balanced life.

The intricate connection between the mind and the body suggests that what affects one, affects the other. Stress, anxiety, and depression, prevalent in modern society, are not just states of mind but can manifest physically, impacting every aspect of health. Conversely, physical ailments can lead to mental distress, creating a cyclical interdependence that demands a holistic approach to health and wellness.

This chapter delves deeper into how mental health disorders can exacerbate or even contribute to the development of chronic physical conditions, like heart disease, diabetes, and obesity. It explores how psychological stress can impair the immune system, disrupt sleep patterns, and affect appetite and digestion, thereby affecting physical health. Moreover, it examines how physical illnesses can have a profound impact on mental health, often leading to anxiety and depression, which can further complicate the healing process.

In exploring strategies for maintaining mental well-being, this chapter emphasizes the power of lifestyle choices, therapeutic interventions, and societal support systems in fostering mental resilience. It highlights how regular physical activity, a balanced diet, adequate sleep, mindfulness practices, and social connections can not only bolster mental health but also enhance physical well-being.

Furthermore, the chapter takes a global lens to understand the varying perceptions of mental health across different cultures and societies. It discusses the global burden of mental health disorders, the disparities in mental health care, and the ongoing efforts to integrate mental health more comprehensively into public health policies and practices worldwide.

In conclusion, this chapter aims to provide a comprehensive understanding of the pivotal role mental health plays in physical well-being. By weaving together insights from various disciplines, personal anecdotes, and global perspectives, it seeks to advocate for the harmonious balance of mental and physical health, essential for achieving optimal health and living a fulfilling life.

Connection Between Mental and Physical Health:

Bi-directional Relationship:

The relationship between mental and physical health is not linear but bi-directional, indicating that each can significantly influence the other. This interconnection highlights the need for a holistic approach to health and well-being.

- **Impact of Mental Health on Physical Health:**
  - **Chronic Stress and Physical Illness:** Chronic stress, a common feature of many mental health conditions, can lead to a range of physical health problems. It can disrupt hormonal balances, weaken the immune system, and increase the risk of conditions like heart disease, diabetes, and gastrointestinal disorders.
  - **Behavioural Factors:** Mental health conditions can affect an individual's behaviour, leading to poor lifestyle choices such as inadequate nutrition, lack of exercise, and substance abuse, all of which have detrimental effects on physical health.
  - **Psychosomatic Symptoms:** Psychological distress can manifest as physical symptoms – a phenomenon known as psychosomatic illness. For instance, anxiety and depression can contribute to chronic pain, fatigue, and digestive issues.
- **Effect of Physical Health on Mental Health:**
  - **Chronic Illness and Mental Well-being:** Living with a chronic physical health condition can significantly impact an individual's mental health. Conditions like cancer, stroke, or chronic pain are often associated with an increased risk of depression, anxiety, and other mental health disorders.
  - **Disability and Psychological Impact:** Physical disabilities or limitations can lead to social isolation, loss of independence, and changes in self-perception, which can have profound psychological repercussions.
  - **Medication Side Effects:** Some medications used for physical health conditions can have side effects that impact mental health, such as mood swings, depression, or anxiety.

Understanding the bi-directional relationship between mental and physical health is crucial for comprehensive healthcare. It underscores the importance of considering both aspects in diagnosis and treatment. This approach not only helps in effectively addressing the root cause of health issues but also in developing more integrated and personalized treatment plans. It is a reminder that mental and physical health are not separate entities but interconnected aspects of overall well-being.

Stress and Physical Health:

Chronic Stress as a Contributor to Physical Health Problems:

Chronic stress, a prevalent mental health issue in today's fast-paced world, has profound and far-reaching effects on physical health. Its persistent nature means that the body's stress response, which is designed to handle short-term threats, is activated over an extended period, leading to various physical health problems.

- **Cardiovascular Diseases:**
    - **Increased Risk:** Chronic stress is a known risk factor for cardiovascular diseases. It can lead to high blood pressure, arterial damage, and irregular heart rhythms.
    - **Mechanisms:** Stress hormones such as cortisol and adrenaline, when released persistently, can strain the heart and blood vessels, increasing the risk of hypertension, heart attacks, and strokes.
- **Weakened Immune System:**

- **Lowered Immune Response:** Chronic stress can weaken the immune system, making the body more susceptible to infections and illnesses. It may slow down the healing process and can exacerbate autoimmune conditions.
  - **Impact on Inflammation:** Stress can also increase systemic inflammation, potentially worsening conditions like rheumatoid arthritis and other inflammatory diseases.
- **Chronic Pain:**
  - **Tension and Pain:** Prolonged stress often leads to muscular tension and can contribute to chronic pain conditions, such as tension headaches, migraines, and musculoskeletal disorders.
  - **Pain Sensitivity:** Chronic stress can also heighten pain sensitivity, making existing pain conditions worse or contributing to the development of conditions like fibromyalgia.
- **Other Physical Health Impacts:**
  - **Gastrointestinal Issues:** Stress can affect the gastrointestinal system, leading to conditions like gastritis, irritable bowel syndrome (IBS), and acid reflux.
  - **Weight Fluctuations:** Stress can affect appetite and metabolism, leading to weight gain or weight loss. It often results in unhealthy eating behaviours.

The impact of chronic stress on physical health underscores the importance of stress management in maintaining overall well-being. Addressing stress not only involves managing the psychological aspects but also adopting lifestyle changes, therapeutic interventions, and, in some cases, medical treatment to mitigate its physical health repercussions.

Recognizing and managing stress is a key component of a holistic approach to health.

Psychosomatic Symptoms: The Physical Manifestation of Mental Health Conditions

Understanding Psychosomatic Symptoms:

Psychosomatic symptoms are physical symptoms that have a mental or emotional origin. These symptoms are very real and can cause significant distress and impairment, often leading to a cycle where psychological distress exacerbates physical symptoms, which in turn worsen the mental health condition.

- **Common Psychosomatic Symptoms:**
    - **Fatigue:** One of the most common psychosomatic symptoms, fatigue can be a physical manifestation of depression, anxiety, and stress. It's more than just feeling tired; it's a pervasive sense of exhaustion that doesn't improve with rest.
    - **Headaches:** Tension headaches and migraines can be triggered or worsened by stress and mental health disorders. The pain can range from mild to debilitating and can also exacerbate the stress, creating a vicious cycle.
    - **Gastrointestinal Disturbances:** Conditions like irritable bowel syndrome (IBS), indigestion, and acid reflux can be linked to or exacerbated by mental health issues. Stress and anxiety can alter gut motility and sensitivity, leading to these symptoms.
    -

- **The Mind-Body Connection:**
  - **Neurological Influence:** The brain and the body are interconnected through complex neural pathways. Mental health conditions can trigger physical reactions and changes in the body, leading to various symptoms.
  - **Stress Response:** The body's response to stress involves numerous physiological changes, including in the digestive, immune, and neurological systems, which can manifest as physical symptoms.
- **Diagnosis and Treatment:**
  - **Challenges in Diagnosis:** Psychosomatic symptoms can be challenging to diagnose as they often mimic symptoms of other physical diseases. A thorough medical evaluation is necessary to rule out other causes.
  - **Holistic Approach to Treatment:** Treatment should address both the mental and physical aspects of the symptoms. This may include psychotherapy, stress management techniques, medication for the mental health condition, and treatment for the physical symptoms.

Recognizing these symptoms as valid and treatable is essential in the management of both mental and physical health. A comprehensive, multidisciplinary approach that encompasses both psychological and physical care, is needed, affirming the importance of treating mental health conditions not just for emotional well-being but also for overall physical health.

Strategies for Maintaining Mental Well-being

Maintaining mental well-being is a multifaceted endeavour, requiring attention to various aspects of lifestyle and behaviour. Here are expanded strategies, along with additional ones, to support mental health:

1. **Regular Exercise:**
   - **Endorphin Release:** Exercise stimulates the release of endorphins, the body's natural mood lifters. It can also serve as a distraction, allowing you to find some quiet time to break out of the cycle of negative thoughts that feed depression and anxiety.
   - **Types of Exercise:** Activities like brisk walking, running, swimming, or cycling are particularly beneficial. Even low-impact exercises like yoga or tai chi can have significant mental health benefits.
2. **Healthy Diet:**
   - **Brain Food:** Certain nutrients are particularly important for mental health, such as omega-3 fatty acids, antioxidants, and vitamins. Foods like fatty fish, nuts, seeds, fruits, and vegetables are rich in these nutrients.
   - **Avoiding Harmful Substances:** Reducing caffeine, sugar, and processed foods can also positively impact mood and anxiety levels.
3. **Adequate Sleep:**
   - **Sleep Hygiene:** Good sleep hygiene practices include maintaining a regular sleep schedule, creating a restful environment, and avoiding caffeine and electronics before bedtime.

- **Impact on Mood and Cognition:** Quality sleep is crucial for mood regulation and cognitive processes, including thinking, problem-solving, and memory.
4. **Mindfulness and Meditation:**
    - **Reducing Stress:** Practices like mindfulness meditation can help lower stress levels, reduce symptoms of anxiety and depression, and improve overall emotional well-being.
    - **Enhancing Awareness:** Mindfulness helps in cultivating a greater awareness of the present moment, which can shift attention away from stressors and negative thought patterns.
5. **Seeking Professional Help:**
    - **Therapy and Counselling:** Professional mental health care, like psychotherapy or counselling, provides a safe space to explore feelings, thoughts, and behaviours, and to develop coping strategies.
    - **Medication:** In some cases, especially for clinical depression, anxiety disorders, or other mental health conditions, medications like antidepressants can be beneficial.
6. **Social Connections:**
    - **Support Systems:** Maintaining strong relationships with family and friends provides emotional support and a sense of belonging and purpose.
    - **Community Engagement:** Participating in community activities or groups can provide a network of support and decrease feelings of loneliness.
7. **Stress Management Techniques:**
    - **Relaxation Techniques:** Activities such as deep breathing exercises, progressive muscle relaxation, or visualization can help manage stress.

- **Time Management:** Prioritizing tasks, setting boundaries, and taking breaks can prevent burnout and reduce stress levels.

8. **Creative Outlets:**
   - **Artistic Expression:** Engaging in creative activities like painting, writing, or music can be therapeutic and offer a means of expressing emotions and reducing stress.

Incorporating these strategies into daily life can lead to significant improvements in mental well-being. It's important to recognize that maintaining mental health is an ongoing process, and what works for one person may not work for another. Therefore, it's crucial to find a personal balance and a set of strategies that suit individual needs and lifestyles.

Global Perspective on Mental Health's Impact on Physical Health:

Cultural Differences in Mental Health Perception:

The perception and treatment of mental health issues vary significantly around the world, influenced by cultural, social, and economic factors. These differences can have a profound impact on the way mental health problems are addressed and managed.

1. **Variability in Stigma and Acceptance:**
   - **Stigmatization:** In many cultures, mental health issues are stigmatized, often seen as a sign of weakness or as a taboo subject. This stigma can lead to underreporting, misdiagnosis, and a reluctance to seek help, exacerbating the physical health

consequences associated with mental health disorders.
- **Acceptance and Understanding:** Conversely, some societies have a more open and accepting attitude towards mental health, encouraging discussion, support, and treatment. These attitudes can lead to better mental health outcomes and a greater understanding of the connection between mental and physical health.

2. **Impact of Socioeconomic Factors:**
   - **Resource Allocation:** The availability of mental health resources, including trained professionals and treatment facilities, varies significantly. In many low- and middle-income countries, resources for mental health are limited, affecting the quality of care and access to treatment.
   - **Economic Stress:** Socioeconomic stressors, including poverty, unemployment, and social inequality, can exacerbate mental health issues, leading to a higher incidence of both mental and physical health problems.

3. **Cultural Approaches to Treatment:**
   - **Traditional Practices:** In some cultures, traditional healing practices and holistic approaches play a significant role in treating mental health issues. These methods may sometimes be more culturally acceptable or accessible than conventional Western medicine.
   - **Integration of Practices:** There's a growing trend towards integrating traditional and Western medical approaches to provide a more comprehensive treatment that respects cultural beliefs while addressing mental health needs effectively.

4. **Global Health Initiatives:**
    - **International Focus:** Global health initiatives increasingly recognize the importance of mental health. Organizations like the World Health Organization (WHO) advocate for integrating mental health into primary healthcare and developing policies that address the global impact of mental health issues.
    - **Awareness and Education:** International campaigns and World Mental Health Day are examples of efforts to raise awareness, reduce stigma, and promote a global dialogue about mental health.

The global perspective on mental health's impact on physical health highlights the need for cultural sensitivity, resource allocation, and a balanced approach that combines traditional and modern practices. Recognizing the cultural nuances in mental health perception and treatment is vital in developing effective strategies to address the mental health needs of diverse populations worldwide. This approach not only improves mental health outcomes but also enhances overall physical health and well-being.

Global Burden of Mental Health:

The impact of mental health disorders extends far beyond the individual, affecting societies and economies on a global scale. The burden of these disorders is significant, both in terms of human suffering and economic costs.

1. **Prevalence and Disability:**
    - **Widespread Impact:** Mental health disorders, including depression, anxiety, bipolar disorder, and schizophrenia, are among the leading causes of

disability worldwide. Millions of people are affected, with conditions often starting at a young age and persisting throughout life.
   - **Impact on Daily Life:** These disorders can severely impair an individual's ability to function in daily life, affecting their ability to work, study, and maintain relationships.
2. **Economic Burden:**
   - **Healthcare Costs:** The treatment and management of mental health disorders require significant healthcare resources. In many cases, the costs are exacerbated by late diagnosis and inadequate treatment.
   - **Productivity Loss:** Mental health disorders can lead to decreased productivity, increased absenteeism, and premature retirement, posing a substantial economic burden on societies.
3. **Impact on Healthcare Systems:**
   - **Strain on Services:** The high prevalence of mental health issues places a considerable strain on healthcare systems, many of which are already under-resourced and facing challenges in meeting the demand for mental health care.
   - **Need for Integration:** There is a growing recognition of the need to integrate mental health services into primary healthcare settings to make treatment more accessible and reduce the stigma associated with seeking help.
4. **Quality of Life and Societal Impact:**
   - **Personal Suffering:** Beyond the economic impact, mental health disorders profoundly affect individuals' quality of life, often leading to social isolation, stigmatization, and decreased life satisfaction.

- **Broader Societal Issues:** Mental health issues are often intertwined with broader societal issues, such as poverty, violence, and social inequality, creating a cycle that can perpetuate these conditions.
5. **Global Response and Challenges:**
    - **Awareness and Advocacy:** Despite growing awareness, mental health still often receives less attention and funding compared to physical health conditions.
    - **Global Initiatives:** Efforts like the WHO's Mental Health Action Plan and various non-governmental organizations aim to address the global burden of mental health by promoting mental well-being, preventing mental disorders, providing care, and enhancing recovery, advocacy, and research.

The global burden of mental health is a multifaceted issue requiring a concerted effort from governments, healthcare providers, communities, and individuals. Addressing this burden effectively not only improves the lives of those directly affected but also benefits societies and economies at large. It calls for an integrated approach that acknowledges mental health as a key component of overall health and human development.

Public Health Policies and Mental Health:

The approach to mental health within public health policies varies significantly across different countries, reflecting diverse healthcare systems, cultural attitudes, and resource allocations. However, there is a growing global movement toward the integration of mental health care into primary healthcare settings, recognizing the importance of mental health as a fundamental component of overall health.

1. **Varied National Approaches:**
   - **High-Income Countries:** Often have more resources allocated to mental health, with policies that support a range of services including inpatient care, community-based programs, and counselling services. However, even in these countries, mental health can be under-prioritized compared to physical health.
   - **Low- and Middle-Income Countries:** Typically face challenges due to limited resources, lack of mental health professionals, and sometimes, cultural stigmas. Mental health care in these countries might rely more on community-based approaches and integration into primary health care.
2. **Global Movement for Integration:**
   - **Primary Health Care Integration:** There is a worldwide push to integrate mental health services into primary health care. This approach helps in early detection and intervention, makes mental health care more accessible, and can reduce stigma.
   - **WHO's Leadership:** The World Health Organization advocates for the integration of mental health into primary care and has developed resources and guidelines to support countries in this endeavour.
3. **Policy Challenges and Opportunities:**
   - **Stigma and Discrimination:** Many public health policies aim to address stigma and discrimination against people with mental health issues, recognizing that these social barriers can be as debilitating as the illnesses themselves.

- **Funding and Resource Allocation:** Adequate funding is a persistent challenge. There is a need for increased investment in mental health services, training for health care providers, and public health campaigns.

4. **Innovative Models and Community Involvement:**
   - **Community Mental Health:** Innovative models involving community mental health services have shown promise, particularly in areas with scarce resources. These models often involve training community members to provide support and basic mental health care.
   - **Digital and Telehealth Services:** The use of digital platforms for mental health care, including teletherapy and mobile health apps, has been growing, offering new ways to provide support, especially in remote or underserved areas.

5. **Education and Awareness:**
   - **Public Awareness Campaigns:** Many countries run public awareness campaigns to increase knowledge about mental health, reduce stigma, and encourage people to seek help.
   - **Education in Schools:** Incorporating mental health education in schools is increasingly viewed as an important strategy to promote early awareness and resilience.

Mental health is a critical aspect of public health policy, requiring attention, resources, and innovative approaches to ensure effective and accessible care. The integration of mental health into primary healthcare settings, the reduction of stigma, and the provision of adequate resources are essential steps towards improving mental health care globally.

Your Mental Health Is Our Responsibility

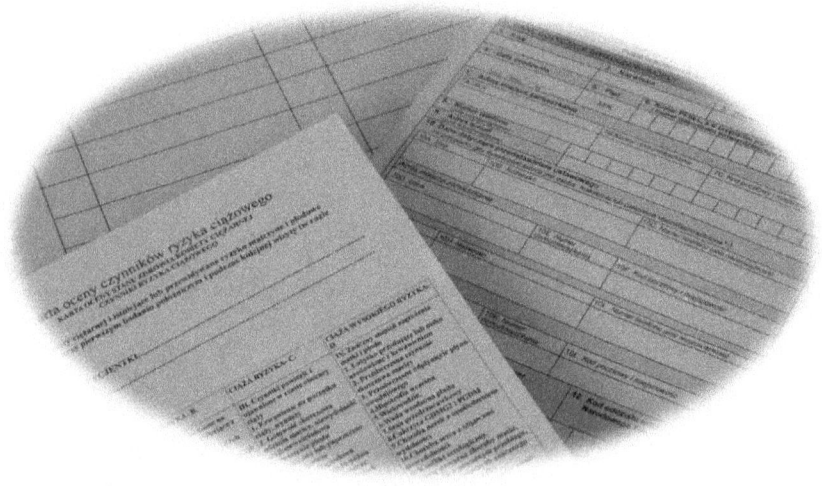

Health Policies Must Evolve With Time.

Fast-Track A&E

Chapter 7:

Dealing with Specific Conditions

Introduction:

In the intricate landscape of healthcare, understanding the nuances of specific conditions that frequently lead to Accident and Emergency (A&E) visits is pivotal. This chapter delves into a detailed exploration of such conditions, unraveling the complexities behind their high incidence in emergency settings across the globe. By shining a light on these prevalent health issues, the chapter endeavors to arm readers with crucial knowledge that spans prevention, early detection, and management.

The focus extends beyond mere recognition of symptoms. It encompasses a comprehensive approach that intertwines preventative strategies with actionable steps for early intervention. The objective is to equip individuals with the knowledge to not only identify these conditions early but also to understand the lifestyle choices and healthcare decisions that can reduce the likelihood of their escalation to emergencies.

Incorporating personal narratives and case studies, the chapter aims to bridge the gap between clinical information and real-life experiences. These stories serve multiple purposes - they provide a human touch to medical facts, enhance the learning experience, and offer relatable insights. From the heart-wrenching tales of emergency encounters to the inspiring stories of preventative triumphs, these accounts are selected to resonate with readers, providing both cautionary tales and beacons of hope.

Moreover, the chapter seeks to underscore the importance of a proactive stance towards health. It emphasizes that many emergency visits can be prevented through informed choices, regular health screenings, and a keen awareness of one's own body and health conditions. The intention is to foster a mindset where individuals are encouraged to take charge of their health, understanding the critical role they play in the prevention and early detection of serious health issues.

This chapter is not just a compilation of medical facts and guidelines; it is a comprehensive guide designed to empower readers with the tools and knowledge necessary to navigate the often-daunting world of healthcare emergencies. Through a blend of scientific information, practical advice, and personal anecdotes, it aims to enhance understanding and promote a proactive approach to dealing with specific health conditions.

Cardiovascular Emergencies: Detailed Insights and Preparedness

Cardiovascular emergencies encompass a range of urgent medical conditions that demand immediate attention. Understanding the nuances of these emergencies, including patient experiences and ways to prepare, is vital for effective response and management.

1. **Heart Attacks:**
    - **Risk Factors:** Include smoking, high blood pressure, high cholesterol, obesity, sedentary lifestyle, diabetes, and family history of heart disease.
    - **Common Signs:** Intense chest pain or discomfort (often described as pressure, squeezing, or fullness), pain radiating to the shoulder, arm, back, neck, or jaw, shortness of breath, nausea, and cold sweats.

- **Immediate Actions:** Call emergency services immediately. If available and not contraindicated, administer aspirin. It's crucial for the patient to rest and avoid any physical exertion.
- **Detailed Symptoms:** Patients often describe the chest pain during a heart attack as a pressure, squeezing, fullness, or pain in the canter of the chest that lasts for more than a few minutes. This pain can radiate to the arms, back, neck, jaw, or stomach. Other symptoms may include shortness of breath, cold sweat, nausea, or light-headedness.
- **Patient Experience:** The intensity of symptoms can vary, and some people, especially women, may experience more subtle symptoms like shortness of breath, fatigue, and a general sense of unease.
- **Preparedness:** Those at risk should be educated about their condition, the importance of timely medication, and lifestyle modifications. Keeping emergency contact numbers handy and informing family members about the condition and what to do in an emergency is crucial.

2. **Strokes:**
   - **Risk Factors:** Include smoking, high blood pressure, high cholesterol, obesity, sedentary lifestyle, diabetes, and family history of heart disease.
   - **Common Signs:** Intense chest pain or discomfort (often described as pressure, squeezing, or fullness), pain radiating to the shoulder, arm, back, neck, or jaw, shortness of breath, nausea, and cold sweats.
   - **Immediate Actions:** Call emergency services immediately. If available and not contraindicated, administer aspirin. It's crucial for the patient to rest and avoid any physical exertion.

- **Detailed Symptoms:** In addition to the FAST symptoms, patients might experience sudden confusion, trouble seeing in one or both eyes, trouble walking, dizziness, loss of balance or coordination, and a sudden, severe headache with no known cause.
- **Patient Experience:** The onset of a stroke can be frightening. Victims might suddenly find themselves unable to speak clearly or move parts of their body. Prompt recognition of these symptoms is essential for a fast response.
- **Preparedness:** Individuals with risk factors such as hypertension should regularly monitor their blood pressure and adhere to prescribed treatments. Awareness of the nearest stroke treatment canter can also be lifesaving.

3. **Hypertensive Crises:**
   - **Risk Factors:** Include smoking, high blood pressure, high cholesterol, obesity, sedentary lifestyle, diabetes, and family history of heart disease.
   - **Common Signs:** Intense chest pain or discomfort (often described as pressure, squeezing, or fullness), pain radiating to the shoulder, arm, back, neck, or jaw, shortness of breath, nausea, and cold sweats.
   - **Immediate Actions:** Call emergency services immediately. If available and not contraindicated, administer aspirin. It's crucial for the patient to rest and avoid any physical exertion.
   - **Detailed Symptoms:** Symptoms of a hypertensive crisis can include severe chest pain, severe headache, accompanied by confusion and blurred vision, nausea and vomiting, severe anxiety, shortness of breath, seizures, and unresponsiveness.

- **Patient Experience:** Patients may experience overwhelming anxiety and a sense of impending doom. The severity of symptoms can escalate quickly, necessitating immediate medical intervention.
- **Preparedness:** Patients with a history of hypertension should regularly monitor their blood pressure, understand their medication regimen, and be aware of the warning signs of a hypertensive crisis. Having a home blood pressure monitor and emergency medications (as advised by a doctor) can be crucial.

Cardiovascular emergencies are serious medical conditions characterized by distinct symptoms that patients are likely to experience. Individuals at risk, as well as their families and caregivers, should be well-informed about these signs and symptoms, and the immediate actions to take. Being prepared, both in terms of knowledge and practical steps, can significantly impact the outcome in such emergencies. Regular check-ups, lifestyle changes, and medication adherence are key preventive measures.

Respiratory Conditions: Asthma Attacks and COPD Exacerbations

Understanding and Managing Respiratory Emergencies:

Respiratory conditions, particularly asthma attacks and Chronic Obstructive Pulmonary Disease (COPD) exacerbations, are common reasons for emergency department visits. Recognizing early warning signs and understanding management strategies are crucial for patients and caregivers.

Fast-Track A&E

1. **Asthma Attacks:**
   - **Symptoms and Patient Experience:** An asthma attack can involve severe wheezing, unrelenting coughing, rapid breathing, and tightness in the chest. The inability to speak in full sentences or the blueness of lips or fingernails are severe symptoms. Patients might experience a sense of panic due to difficulty in breathing.
   - **Management Strategies:** Patients should have an asthma action plan developed with their healthcare provider, which typically includes the use of rescue inhalers, recognizing triggers, and understanding when to seek emergency medical help. Keeping a peak flow meter at home to monitor lung function can be helpful.
   - **Preparedness:** Regular use of controller medication (if prescribed), avoidance of known triggers, and having a written asthma action plan are key. Patients and families should know the location of the nearest emergency facility and have a plan for getting there quickly if an attack is severe.
2. **COPD Exacerbations:**
   - **Symptoms and Patient Experience:** COPD exacerbations involve a significant increase in shortness of breath, coughing, wheezing, and production of phlegm. The symptoms are more intense than the usual day-to-day variations and can be disabling. Patients may experience fatigue, swelling in the ankles or legs, and a decreased ability to perform daily activities.
   - **Management Strategies:** COPD patients should be educated about their condition, including the importance of taking maintenance medications as

prescribed. Pulmonary rehabilitation and regular exercise can help improve endurance and breathing capacity. In an exacerbation, the use of rescue inhalers and supplemental oxygen (if prescribed) is vital.
- **Preparedness:** Patients with COPD should have regular follow-ups with their healthcare provider to monitor their condition and adjust treatments as needed. They should also be vigilant about flu and pneumonia vaccinations, as respiratory infections can exacerbate COPD.

Both asthma and COPD are chronic respiratory conditions that can lead to life-threatening emergencies if not properly managed. Patients with these conditions should work closely with healthcare providers to develop comprehensive management plans that include medication regimens, lifestyle modifications, and emergency response strategies. Education, self-monitoring, and regular healthcare engagement are key components of effective management, helping to reduce the frequency and severity of emergency visits.

Trauma and Accidents: Understanding and Prevention

Comprehensive Overview of Physical Trauma:

Trauma and accidents, encompassing a wide range of incidents from road traffic accidents to falls and workplace injuries, are significant contributors to emergency department visits. Understanding their common causes and implementing preventive measures are essential steps in reducing their occurrence and severity.

1. **Road Traffic Accidents:**
    - **Common Causes and Experience:** Major causes include speeding, driving under the influence of alcohol or drugs, distracted driving (like using a cell phone), and not wearing seat belts. Victims may experience a range of injuries, from minor cuts and bruises to severe, life-threatening conditions like head injuries and internal bleeding.
    - **Prevention Strategies:** Adhering to traffic rules, avoiding impaired or distracted driving, and using seat belts and appropriate child car seats are critical. Awareness campaigns and strict law enforcement can also play a significant role in prevention.
2. **Falls:**
    - **Common in the Elderly:** Falls are especially common among the elderly and can lead to serious injuries such as hip fractures or head trauma. In younger individuals, falls often occur in active settings like sports or playgrounds.
    - **Prevention Strategies:** For the elderly, fall prevention includes regular physical activity to maintain strength and balance, making living spaces safer (e.g., removing tripping hazards, installing grab bars), and regular vision and hearing checks. In workplaces and sports, ensuring safety protocols and using protective gear are vital.
3. **Workplace Injuries:**
    - **Varied Nature:** Workplace injuries can range from repetitive strain injuries to acute incidents like machinery accidents. The nature of these injuries often depends on the occupation and workplace environment.

- **Prevention Strategies:** Adherence to safety protocols, proper training, use of protective equipment, and ergonomic workplace design can significantly reduce the risk of injuries. Employers play a crucial role in creating a safe work environment.
4. **Preparation for Emergency Situations:**
    - **Education:** Basic first aid training and emergency response education for the public can be invaluable. Knowing how to respond in the immediate aftermath of an accident can sometimes make a life-saving difference.
    - **Emergency Services:** Quick access to emergency services and well-equipped emergency departments are essential for handling trauma cases effectively.

The impact of trauma and accidents on individuals and healthcare systems is profound. While not all accidents can be prevented, understanding their common causes and implementing effective prevention strategies can significantly reduce their frequency and severity. From policy-making and public education to individual actions, a multifaceted approach is necessary to tackle the challenge of physical trauma. It's about creating safer environments, encouraging responsible behaviours, and being prepared for emergency situations.

Infectious Diseases: Emergency Management and Response

Navigating Infectious Disease Emergencies:

Infectious diseases, ranging from common illnesses like the flu to global health crises like COVID-19, can lead to critical emergencies requiring immediate medical attention. Understanding how to identify severe cases and respond appropriately is crucial for effective management and containment.

1. **Severe Cases of Flu:**
   - **Symptoms and Risks:** While many cases of influenza are mild, severe cases can occur, especially in vulnerable populations like the elderly, young children, and those with chronic health conditions. Symptoms of a severe flu case may include difficulty breathing, persistent chest pain, severe weakness, and high fever.
   - **Preventative Measures:** Annual flu vaccines, good hygiene practices, and avoiding close contact with sick individuals are key preventative measures.
   - **When to Seek Emergency Care:** If symptoms rapidly worsen or if high-risk individuals show any signs of severe illness, immediate medical attention is necessary.
2. **Pneumonia:**
   - **Recognizing Severity:** Pneumonia can become life-threatening if not treated promptly, especially in high-risk groups. Symptoms of severe pneumonia include difficulty breathing, chest pain, persistent fever, and confusion or delirium in older adults.

- **Preventative Strategies:** Vaccinations (like pneumococcal vaccine), maintaining a healthy lifestyle, and good hygiene can reduce the risk of pneumonia.
- **Treatment:** Severe cases often require hospitalization, where patients may receive oxygen therapy, antibiotics, and fluids.

3. **COVID-19:**
   - **Identifying Emergency Signs:** COVID-19, caused by the novel coronavirus SARS-CoV-2, can lead to severe respiratory illness. Emergency warning signs include trouble breathing, persistent chest pain or pressure, new confusion, inability to stay awake, and bluish lips or face.
   - **Prevention and Containment:** Key strategies include vaccination, mask-wearing, social distancing, and frequent hand washing. Testing and contact tracing are also crucial in managing the spread.
   - **Managing Severe Cases:** Treatment for severe COVID-19 may involve hospitalization, oxygen therapy, and in some cases, mechanical ventilation. Antiviral treatments and steroids have also been used in treatment protocols.

Infectious disease emergencies, such as severe flu, pneumonia, and COVID-19, demand prompt and effective medical intervention. Understanding the signs of severe illness and knowing when to seek emergency care are vital for patient outcomes and public health. Alongside this, preventive measures like vaccinations and hygiene practices play a crucial role in reducing the incidence and severity of these infections. The global experience with COVID-19 has underscored the importance of rapid response and adaptability in managing infectious disease emergencies.

Sepsis: A Critical Global Health Concern

Understanding and Responding to Sepsis Emergencies:

Sepsis is a life-threatening condition resulting from the body's response to infection, leading to tissue damage, organ failure, and potentially death. It's a global health concern due to its high mortality rate and the speed at which it can progress. Recognizing the early signs of sepsis and ensuring prompt medical treatment are key to improving outcomes.

1. **Identifying Sepsis:**
    - **Early Symptoms:** Sepsis often presents with fever, chills, rapid breathing, and a high heart rate. It may start with an infection in any part of the body, such as the lungs, urinary tract, skin, or gastrointestinal tract.
    - **Severe Sepsis:** As it progresses, symptoms can include severe weakness, dizziness, decreased urination, mental confusion, and a significant drop in blood pressure, leading to septic shock.
    - **High-Risk Groups:** While anyone can develop sepsis, the risk is higher in the very young, the elderly, those with chronic diseases, and individuals with a weakened immune system.
2. **Preventative Measures:**
    - **Infection Control:** Preventing infections through proper hygiene, wound care, and vaccinations is a primary strategy in reducing the risk of sepsis.

- **Prompt Treatment of Infections:** Early and effective treatment of infections is crucial to prevent their progression to sepsis.

3. **When to Seek Emergency Care:**
   - **Time-Sensitive Condition:** Sepsis is a medical emergency. If sepsis is suspected, especially if the person has an infection and begins to display any of the severe symptoms, immediate medical attention is necessary.
   - **Public Awareness:** Increasing public awareness about sepsis, its signs, and the urgency it requires is crucial in improving outcomes.

4. **Treatment of Sepsis:**
   - **Rapid Intervention:** Treatment involves rapid administration of antibiotics, intravenous fluids, and, in severe cases, vasopressors to maintain blood pressure and organ function.
   - **Comprehensive Care:** Patients may require intensive care, and support for failing organs, such as dialysis for kidney failure or mechanical ventilation for severe respiratory distress.

Sepsis represents a significant global health challenge due to its rapid progression and potential for severe complications. Early recognition and prompt medical intervention are crucial in the management of sepsis. Comprehensive strategies encompassing prevention, education, and emergency response are essential to combat this life-threatening condition.

Focus on Global Health Concerns with High A&E Incidence:

1. Cardiovascular Emergencies:

Cardiovascular emergencies are among the leading causes of visits to Accident and Emergency (A&E) departments worldwide. Timely recognition and intervention are crucial in these cases.

- **Heart Attacks (Myocardial Infarction):**
    - **Risk Factors:** Include smoking, high blood pressure, high cholesterol, obesity, sedentary lifestyle, diabetes, and family history of heart disease.
    - **Common Signs:** Intense chest pain or discomfort (often described as pressure, squeezing, or fullness), pain radiating to the shoulder, arm, back, neck, or jaw, shortness of breath, nausea, and cold sweats.
    - **Immediate Actions:** Call emergency services immediately. If available and not contraindicated, administer aspirin. It's crucial for the patient to rest and avoid any physical exertion.
- **Strokes:**
    - **Risk Factors:** High blood pressure, smoking, diabetes, high cholesterol, and obesity. Family history and age also play a role.
    - **Recognizing Symptoms:** Use the FAST acronym (Face drooping, Arm weakness, Speech difficulty, Time to call for help). Additional symptoms can include sudden confusion, trouble seeing, difficulty walking, dizziness, or severe headache.
    - **Immediate Actions:** Time is critical. Immediate medical attention is necessary for effective treatment and to minimize long-term damage.
- **Hypertensive Crises:**

- o **Risk Factors:** Poorly controlled high blood pressure, non-adherence to antihypertensive medication, and certain medical conditions.
- o **Signs:** Severe headache, shortness of breath, nosebleeds, severe anxiety, and symptoms of stroke or heart attack.
- o **Immediate Actions:** Hypertensive crises require urgent medical treatment to prevent a heart attack, stroke, or other life-threatening events. While waiting for emergency care, the patient should try to stay calm and avoid any physical activity.

Understanding the risk factors, signs, and immediate actions for cardiovascular emergencies is vital. These conditions represent a significant portion of global A&E visits and are often life-threatening. Public education, risk factor management, and quick, effective emergency response are essential components in reducing mortality and improving outcomes in cardiovascular emergencies.

Preventative Measures and Early Detection Strategies:

1. Lifestyle Modifications:

Lifestyle choices play a pivotal role in the prevention of various health conditions that commonly lead to A&E visits. This chapter section focuses on how adopting healthier habits can significantly reduce the risk of developing such conditions.

- **Diet:**
  - o **Balanced Nutrition:** A diet rich in fruits, vegetables, whole grains, lean proteins, and low in saturated fats, trans fats, cholesterol, salt (sodium), and added sugars can help prevent a range of diseases, including cardiovascular issues and diabetes.

- **Specific Dietary Plans:** The Mediterranean diet, DASH diet, and plant-based diets have been shown to reduce the risk of chronic illnesses.
  - **Hydration:** Adequate water intake is essential for overall health and can prevent conditions like kidney stones and urinary tract infections.
- **Exercise:**
  - **Regular Physical Activity:** Engaging in regular exercise such as walking, cycling, swimming, or strength training helps maintain a healthy weight, lowers blood pressure, improves cholesterol levels, and enhances overall heart health.
  - **Recommended Activity Levels:** The World Health Organization recommends at least 150 minutes of moderate-intensity aerobic physical activity or 75 minutes of vigorous-intensity activity per week, along with muscle-strengthening activities on two or more days a week.
- **Smoking Cessation:**
  - **Immediate Health Benefits:** Quitting smoking has immediate as well as long-term benefits, significantly reducing the risks of heart disease, stroke, and certain cancers.
  - **Support for Quitting:** Strategies include nicotine replacement therapy, medications, behavioural therapy, and support groups.
- **Alcohol Moderation:**
  - **Limiting Consumption:** Excessive alcohol use can lead to liver disease, heart problems, and accidents leading to trauma. Moderating alcohol intake can prevent these risks.
  - **Seeking Help for Addiction:** Professional help should be sought in cases of alcohol dependence.

- **Stress Management:**
  - **Reducing Stress:** Chronic stress can lead to a host of health problems, including mental health issues and heart disease. Techniques such as mindfulness, meditation, and counselling can be effective in managing stress.
- **Regular Health Screenings:**
  - **Early Detection:** Regular health check-ups and screenings can detect problems before they start or in the early stages when chances for treatment and cure are better.
  - **Screening Tests:** These may include blood pressure measurements, cholesterol level checks, diabetes screening, cancer screenings, and osteoporosis screenings.

Adopting healthier lifestyle choices is a powerful tool in preventing many of the conditions that lead to A&E visits. This section of the chapter highlights the importance of proactive health management through diet, exercise, smoking cessation, and regular health screenings, emphasizing that many emergencies can be prevented through these measures. The key message is that taking charge of one's health through lifestyle modifications can significantly reduce the risk of acute health crises.

2. Regular Health Screenings:

Regular health screenings are a critical component in the early detection and management of various conditions, such as hypertension, diabetes, and cancers. These screenings can often identify problems before symptoms become apparent.

- **Hypertension Screenings:**
  - **Frequency and Importance:** Regular blood pressure checks are essential, as hypertension often goes unnoticed due to its asymptomatic nature. Early detection can prevent complications like heart disease and stroke.
  - **At-Home Monitoring:** For those at risk or already diagnosed with high blood pressure, home monitoring can be a valuable tool in conjunction with regular healthcare visits.
- **Diabetes Screenings:**
  - **Risk Assessment:** Screening for diabetes typically involves blood sugar tests. It's especially important for individuals who are overweight, have a family history of diabetes, or have other risk factors like high cholesterol.
  - **Pre-Diabetes:** Identifying pre-diabetes can allow individuals to make lifestyle changes to prevent the progression to type 2 diabetes.
- **Cancer Screenings:**
  - **Types of Screenings:** Depending on age, gender, and risk factors, various screenings are recommended. These include mammograms for breast cancer, colonoscopies for colorectal cancer, Pap tests for cervical cancer, and skin examinations for skin cancer.
  - **Personalized Screening Plans:** The frequency and type of cancer screenings can vary based on individual risk factors, including family history and lifestyle. Discussions with healthcare providers can help determine the best screening plan.
- **Cholesterol Checks:**
  - **Heart Health Indicator:** High cholesterol is a significant risk factor for heart disease. Regular

cholesterol screenings are important for early detection and management.
- **Lipid Profile:** A lipid profile test measures various types of cholesterol and triglycerides in the blood.
- **Osteoporosis Screenings:**
  - **Bone Density Tests:** For older adults, especially postmenopausal women, bone density screenings can detect osteoporosis early, allowing for interventions to strengthen bones and reduce fracture risk.

Regular health screenings play a pivotal role in preventive healthcare. They allow for the early detection of conditions that might otherwise become serious or even life-threatening if left unnoticed. By undergoing routine screenings, individuals can take proactive steps to manage their health, leading to better outcomes and reduced A&E visits. This chapter segment emphasizes the need for regular check-ups and staying informed about which screenings are appropriate at different life stages.

3. Public Awareness and Education:

Enhancing public awareness and education about health conditions is essential in promoting timely medical interventions and can significantly reduce the incidence of emergency department visits. Educated individuals are more likely to recognize early warning signs and seek medical help promptly.

- **Developing Effective Information Campaigns:**
  - **Targeted Messaging:** Tailoring messages to specific demographics, considering factors like age, gender, and risk factors, can make education campaigns more effective.

- Utilizing Various Media Platforms: Leveraging social media, television, radio, and print media to disseminate information ensures a broader reach.
- **Focusing on Common and Serious Conditions:**
  - **Heart Disease and Stroke:** Campaigns should educate the public on recognizing signs of heart attacks and strokes, emphasizing the importance of immediate medical attention.
  - **Diabetes Awareness:** Information on recognizing early symptoms of diabetes, like increased thirst, frequent urination, and unexplained weight loss, along with the importance of regular screenings.
  - **Cancer Prevention and Early Detection:** Highlighting the importance of screenings such as mammograms, Pap tests, and colonoscopies, and educating on early signs of various cancers.
- **Incorporating Health Education in Schools:**
  - **Early Education:** Introducing basic health education in school curricula can instil awareness from a young age, covering topics like nutrition, exercise, and the importance of regular health check-ups.
- **Community Outreach Programs:**
  - **Local Events and Workshops:** Hosting community events, workshops, and health fairs to educate the public on various health issues and preventive measures.
  - **Collaboration with Healthcare Providers:** Partnering with local healthcare providers and clinics to offer educational sessions and free or low-cost screenings.
- **Training in Basic First Aid and CPR:**
  - **Community Training Programs:** Encouraging the public to participate in first aid, CPR, and AED (Automated External Defibrillator) training can be

lifesaving, especially in cases of heart attacks and accidents.
- **Mental Health Awareness:**
  - **Removing Stigma:** Campaigns that focus on destigmatizing mental health issues and providing information on recognizing and seeking help for mental health problems.
- **Using Survivor Stories and Testimonials:**
  - **Relatable Narratives:** Including stories from individuals who have experienced these conditions can make the impact of these diseases more tangible and relatable.

Public awareness and education are critical tools in the prevention and early detection of various health conditions. By increasing knowledge and understanding, individuals are empowered to take charge of their health, potentially reducing the need for emergency medical care. Well-informed individuals are more likely to engage in preventive behaviours, recognize when to seek medical help, and contribute to a healthier community overall.

Case Studies

1. Survivor Stories:

Personal narratives and survivor stories can be incredibly powerful in conveying the reality of acute health emergencies. They offer unique insights into recognizing symptoms, the importance of quick action, and the experience of navigating the healthcare system.

- **Heart Attack Survivors:**
  - **Real-Life Experiences:** Stories from heart attack survivors can highlight the variety of ways symptoms can present and the critical importance of acting quickly. For example, a survivor might recount how they mistook their symptoms for indigestion, only to realize the seriousness of their condition later.
  - **Lessons Learned:** These narratives often emphasize overlooked signs and the crucial role of immediate medical attention, potentially encouraging readers to not ignore similar symptoms.
- **Stroke Recovery Journeys:**
  - **Early Signs and Response:** Accounts from stroke survivors can illustrate the suddenness of symptom onset and the rapid progression of the condition. They can also shed light on the recovery process and the challenges faced during rehabilitation.
  - **Importance of Support Systems:** Many stroke survivors highlight the importance of support from family, friends, and healthcare professionals in their recovery journey.
- **COPD and Asthma Management:**
  - **Living with Chronic Conditions:** Personal stories from individuals managing COPD or asthma can provide valuable tips on recognizing and responding to exacerbations and the importance of adherence to treatment plans.
  - **Lifestyle Adjustments:** These stories often include insights into lifestyle changes that have helped in managing their condition, such as quitting smoking or avoiding triggers.

- **Sepsis Survival Accounts:**
  - **Recognizing the Unseen Enemy:** Sepsis survivors can recount their experiences of how quickly sepsis can escalate, often starting from a minor infection. These stories can be eye-opening in understanding the critical nature of this condition.
  - **Post-Sepsis Challenges:** Many sepsis survivors face long-term effects post-recovery. Sharing these experiences can bring awareness to the aftermath of sepsis and the need for comprehensive post-care.

Survivor stories serve as powerful educational tools, providing real-life context to medical information. They offer a human perspective that can resonate deeply with readers, making the lessons more memorable and impactful. These narratives not only help in understanding the importance of recognizing symptoms and seeking timely care but also provide comfort and support to those who might be going through similar health challenges.

2. Case Studies of Preventative Success:

Case studies of individuals who have successfully mitigated health risks through preventative measures can be highly instructive and motivating. These narratives underscore the impact of proactive health management and early detection on improving health outcomes.

- **Overcoming Heart Disease Risks:**
  - **Lifestyle Transformation:** A case study could focus on an individual who, after a mild heart attack, made significant lifestyle changes. This might include adopting a heart-healthy diet, regular exercise, and stress management, leading to improved

cardiovascular health and reduced risk of further cardiac events.
  - **Regular Monitoring:** The story might also emphasize the importance of regular health screenings and check-ups that helped in early detection and management of the condition.
- **Cancer Prevention through Screening:**
  - **Early Detection:** A narrative could detail the experience of someone who detected cancer at an early stage through routine screening, such as a mammogram or colonoscopy. The case study would highlight how early detection contributed to a more successful treatment outcome and a quicker return to health.
  - **Awareness and Advocacy:** The individual's story might also include how they became an advocate for regular screenings within their community.
- **Managing Diabetes Effectively:**
  - **Lifestyle and Medication Adherence:** A case study could describe someone diagnosed with pre-diabetes and how through dietary changes, increased physical activity, and medication adherence, they were able to prevent the progression to type 2 diabetes.
  - **Education and Support:** The narrative could also focus on how education about the disease and support from healthcare providers played a crucial role in managing the condition.
- **Asthma Control Success Story:**
  - **Environmental Modifications:** This case study might explore how an individual with asthma made environmental changes at home and work, along with lifestyle adjustments, to significantly reduce the frequency and severity of asthma attacks.

- **Regular Follow-ups:** Highlighting the role of regular follow-ups with healthcare providers in adjusting treatment plans and ensuring effective asthma control.

3. Learning from Mistakes: Cautionary Tales in Health Management

Learning from mistakes, especially in health-related matters, can be a potent tool for education and prevention. This section of the chapter will share stories where delayed action or misjudgement led to complications, emphasizing the critical importance of being proactive about health.

- **Ignoring Warning Signs of Heart Disease:**
  - **A Missed Opportunity:** A narrative might detail how ignoring or dismissing early signs like chest discomfort or shortness of breath led to a severe heart attack. The story can highlight how this delay resulted in more extensive heart damage or more complicated medical intervention than if it had been addressed promptly.
  - **Reflective Lesson:** The story can emphasize the importance of recognizing and acting on early symptoms, no matter how minor they may seem.
- **Underestimating the Severity of a Respiratory Condition:**
  - **Misjudging Symptoms:** This case study could describe a person with COPD or asthma who underestimated a worsening of symptoms, attributing them to less serious causes, leading to a severe respiratory crisis requiring emergency intervention.
  - **Consequences of Delay:** The focus would be on the ramifications of delaying medical consultation,

including prolonged recovery and increased risk of long-term complications.
- **Overlooking the Importance of Regular Screenings:**
    - **Delayed Diagnosis:** A personal story could illustrate how skipping routine health screenings, such as mammograms or colonoscopies, resulted in a later-stage diagnosis of cancer. The narrative would contrast the outcomes with what might have been if the cancer had been detected earlier.
    - **Awareness and Regret:** The individual's reflection on the importance of regular screenings and the wish that they had adhered to recommended guidelines could serve as a powerful message.
- **Not Adhering to Treatment Regimens:**
    - **Neglecting Medication:** A case study might recount how neglecting to take prescribed medication for a condition like hypertension led to a preventable stroke or heart failure.
    - **Lifestyle Complacency:** The story could also include aspects of lifestyle complacency, such as poor diet and lack of exercise, contributing to the health crisis.

These cautionary tales serve as stark reminders of the potential consequences of neglecting early warning signs, underestimating symptoms, and not adhering to recommended health screenings and treatment plans. By learning from these mistakes, readers can be motivated to take a more active and informed role in their health and well-being, potentially preventing similar situations in their own lives.

Fast-Track A&E

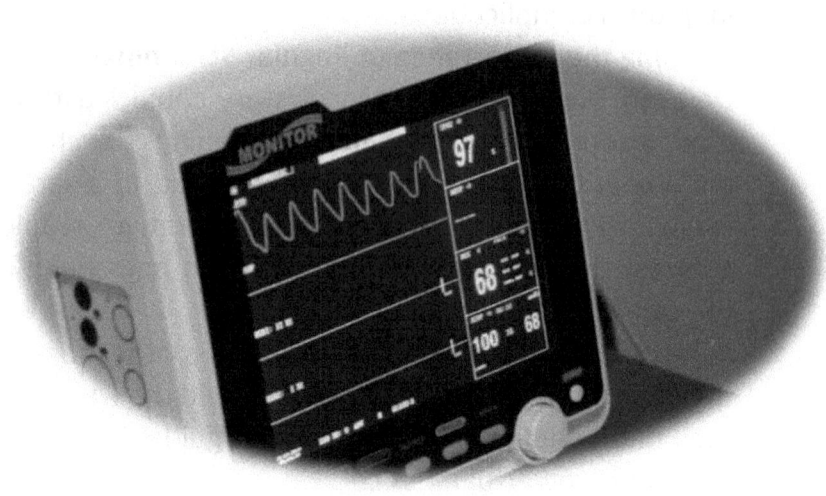

Keep The Heartbeat Off The Monitors By Being Active

Infections Need A Host, Don't' Be One.

Chapter 8:

Role of Telemedicine in Modern Healthcare

Technology and Healthcare

As we navigate through the 21st century, the fusion of technology and healthcare is not just inevitable but already well underway, reshaping the landscape of medical care. The advent of groundbreaking technological innovations has initiated a paradigm shift in how healthcare services are provided and received. This chapter aims to unravel the multifaceted role technology plays in modern healthcare, providing a window into a future where technology and health are inextricably linked.

The integration of technology in healthcare goes beyond mere convenience; it represents a fundamental transformation in tackling some of the most pressing healthcare challenges of our time. From remote villages to urban centers, technology is making healthcare more accessible, personalized, and efficient. This chapter delves deep into the realms of telemedicine, a field that has rapidly gained traction, democratizing access to healthcare by transcending geographical barriers.

Furthermore, the proliferation of health apps and online resources has empowered patients like never before, placing health management literally at their fingertips. These digital tools have opened new avenues for patient education, self-care, and disease management, fostering an era of informed and engaged healthcare consumers.

But this is just the beginning. The chapter also ventures into the exciting and rapidly evolving future of healthcare technology. From artificial intelligence (AI) and machine learning transforming diagnostics and patient care, to the advent of wearable health technology and 3D printing revolutionizing treatment and recovery processes, the possibilities are boundless. These advancements are not only changing the face of healthcare delivery but also challenging and expanding our very understanding of medicine.

1. Expanding Access to Care:

Remote Consultations and Telemedicine:

One of the most significant impacts of technology in healthcare is its ability to expand access to care through remote consultations and telemedicine. This section explores how these innovations are breaking down traditional barriers to healthcare access.

- **Remote Consultations:**
    - **Bridging Geographic Gaps:** Telemedicine allows patients in remote, rural, or underserved areas to receive medical consultations without the need for long-distance travel. This is particularly vital for communities where access to healthcare facilities is limited.
    - **Convenience and Efficiency:** Patients can receive medical advice from the comfort of their homes, saving time and resources. This is especially beneficial for individuals with mobility issues, chronic illnesses, or those requiring frequent follow-ups.
- **Enhancing Primary Care:**
    - **Ongoing Monitoring and Management:** Telemedicine enables continuous monitoring and management of chronic conditions, such as diabetes or hypertension,

through virtual consultations and digital monitoring tools.
    - **Preventive Care:** Regular virtual check-ups and health education via telemedicine can play a crucial role in preventive care, reducing the incidence of acute health emergencies.
- **Specialist Access:**
    - **Consultations with Specialists:** Patients can access specialists who may not be available in their local area, ensuring they receive expert advice for specific medical conditions.
    - **Second Opinions:** Telemedicine facilitates easy access to second opinions, which can be crucial in critical and complex medical cases.
- **Mental Health Services:**
    - **Overcoming Stigma:** Remote consultations for mental health services can help overcome stigma and privacy concerns, making it easier for individuals to seek help.
    - **Continuity of Care:** Telemedicine provides a platform for consistent and ongoing mental health care, which is essential for effective treatment.
- **Technology in Emergencies:**
    - **Immediate Response:** In emergency situations, telemedicine can provide immediate medical advice, guiding patients on necessary actions and whether an A&E visit is required.

Remote consultations and telemedicine are revolutionizing the way healthcare is delivered, offering numerous benefits in terms of accessibility, efficiency, and patient-cantered care. By enabling more people to access quality healthcare regardless of their location or mobility, telemedicine is playing a pivotal role in reducing health disparities and improving the overall health of populations. This section highlights how the integration of technology in healthcare is not just a convenience but a necessity in today's world, fostering a more inclusive and accessible healthcare system.

Managing Chronic Conditions Through Telemedicine:

Telemedicine has emerged as a vital tool in the management of chronic conditions, transforming the traditional model of care by enabling regular monitoring and management without the frequent need for in-person visits to healthcare facilities.

- **Regular Monitoring and Accessibility:**
    - **Remote Monitoring:** Patients with chronic conditions like diabetes, heart disease, or hypertension can use telemedicine platforms to regularly update their health status, share vital signs, and communicate symptoms with their healthcare providers.
    - **Ease of Access:** This approach is particularly beneficial for patients with mobility issues or those living in remote areas, making it easier to manage their conditions without the burden of frequent travel.
- **Improved Patient Engagement:**
    - **Self-Management:** Telemedicine encourages patients to take an active role in managing their health. Digital tools and apps can aid in medication adherence, lifestyle changes, and self-monitoring of vital parameters.
    - **Education and Support:** Telemedicine provides opportunities for patient education, helping them

understand their condition better and the importance of adherence to treatment plans.
- **Personalized Care Plans:**
  - **Tailored Treatment:** Healthcare providers can offer more personalized care plans based on the data collected through telemedicine platforms, adjusting treatments as needed based on real-time information.
  - **Collaborative Care:** Telemedicine facilitates a team-based approach, allowing for easier collaboration between different healthcare providers involved in a patient's care.
- **Reduced Hospital Readmissions:**
  - **Early Intervention:** With regular monitoring, healthcare providers can identify potential issues before they become severe, potentially reducing the need for hospital readmissions.
  - **Continuity of Care:** Continuous care and monitoring through telemedicine can lead to better overall management of chronic conditions, improving patient outcomes.
- **Mental Health and Chronic Illness:**
  - **Addressing Psychological Aspects:** Chronic conditions can have a significant psychological impact. Telemedicine allows for easy access to mental health professionals, helping address depression, anxiety, and other mental health issues that may accompany chronic illnesses.

The management of chronic conditions through telemedicine represents a significant advancement in healthcare delivery. By facilitating regular monitoring, personalized care, and patient engagement, telemedicine is not just enhancing the quality of care for chronic conditions but also making it more accessible and efficient. This approach is particularly beneficial in improving long-term health outcomes and quality of life for patients with chronic illnesses, marking a shift towards more patient-cantered and proactive healthcare models.

2. Enhancing Convenience and Efficiency:

Time and Cost Savings through Telemedicine:

Telemedicine not only transforms the delivery of healthcare services but also introduces significant efficiencies and cost savings for both patients and healthcare systems. This aspect of telemedicine is crucial in a world where time and resources are increasingly valued.

- **Reduced Travel Time and Expenses:**
    - **For Patients:** Telemedicine eliminates the need for patients to travel to healthcare facilities for routine consultations, saving significant time and transportation costs, especially for those living in remote areas.
    - **Broader Impact:** The reduction in travel is not just a matter of convenience; it also means less time off work or away from other responsibilities, which can be particularly beneficial for people with chronic conditions requiring regular monitoring.
- **Efficiency in Healthcare Delivery:**
    - **For Healthcare Providers:** Telemedicine can streamline the consultation process, allowing healthcare providers to see more patients in a shorter amount of time. This efficiency can lead to cost savings

for healthcare facilities by reducing overhead costs and optimizing resource allocation.
  - **Reduced Hospital Stays and Readmissions:** By facilitating ongoing monitoring and follow-up care, telemedicine can help reduce the length of hospital stays and prevent unnecessary readmissions, leading to significant cost savings for healthcare systems.
- **Minimizing Missed Appointments:**
  - **Decreased No-Shows:** Telemedicine reduces the rate of missed appointments, as patients can attend consultations from anywhere. Missed appointments are a significant cost factor for healthcare providers and can delay care for other patients.
  - **Flexible Scheduling:** The flexibility in scheduling and attending appointments via telemedicine can lead to better patient adherence to treatment plans and follow-up schedules.
- **Impact on Insurance and Healthcare Costs:**
  - **Lower Healthcare Costs:** Many insurance companies and national health services recognize the cost-effectiveness of telemedicine and are increasingly covering telemedicine services, reflecting its potential to lower overall healthcare costs.
  - **Preventive Care Savings:** By facilitating early intervention and ongoing management of chronic diseases, telemedicine can reduce the incidence of severe health emergencies, which are typically more costly to treat.

Telemedicine's role in saving time and reducing costs is a testament to its potential as a transformative force in healthcare. By enhancing convenience and efficiency, telemedicine not only improves patient experiences but also contributes to more sustainable and cost-effective healthcare systems. This aspect of technology in healthcare represents a win-win for patients, healthcare providers, and insurers, highlighting the synergy between technological advancement and healthcare optimization.

Integration with Traditional Care:

Complementing Conventional Healthcare with Telemedicine:

The integration of telemedicine into traditional healthcare models represents a significant advancement in the medical field. This hybrid approach combines the best of both worlds, enhancing the quality and continuity of patient care.

- **Blended Care Models:**
    - **Seamless Integration:** Telemedicine is not a replacement but a complement to traditional in-person healthcare services. It offers an additional, flexible layer of care that works alongside conventional methods.
    - **Holistic Patient Care:** By integrating telemedicine, healthcare providers can offer a more holistic approach, ensuring patients receive the right care in the right setting. For example, follow-up appointments and routine check-ups can be conducted virtually, while more complex cases can be managed in person.
- **Enhanced Accessibility and Continuity:**
    - **Continuous Monitoring:** For chronic conditions, telemedicine allows for continuous monitoring and

management, enhancing the continuity of care between in-person visits.
    - **Accessible Specialist Care:** Telemedicine provides easier access to specialists who may not be available locally, ensuring patients receive expert care without geographical limitations.
- **Personalized Healthcare:**
    - **Tailored Treatment Plans:** The data collected through telemedicine can be used to tailor treatment plans more effectively, taking into account the patient's lifestyle, environment, and real-time health status.
    - **Patient Engagement:** This model encourages active patient participation in their health management, leading to increased patient engagement and satisfaction.
- **Efficient Use of Healthcare Resources:**
    - **Resource Optimization:** Telemedicine can help optimize healthcare resources, reducing the burden on overtaxed healthcare systems, especially in emergency and primary care settings.
    - **Reduced Healthcare Costs:** By preventing unnecessary hospital visits and readmissions, telemedicine can contribute to overall cost savings in healthcare.
- **Improving Healthcare Outcomes:**
    - **Early Intervention:** Timely virtual consultations can lead to earlier interventions, potentially preventing conditions from worsening.
    - **Quality of Care:** The integration of telemedicine has been shown to maintain, and in some cases improve, the quality of care provided to patients.

The integration of telemedicine into traditional healthcare models is a testament to the evolving nature of medical care. It represents a paradigm shift towards a more connected, accessible, and patient-cantered healthcare system. This complementary approach not only makes healthcare more efficient and effective but also brings care into the modern digital age, meeting patients' growing needs for flexibility and convenience. As telemedicine continues to grow and develop, its role in enhancing patient care within the broader healthcare ecosystem becomes increasingly significant.

Overview of Helpful Health Apps and Online Resources:

1. Health Monitoring Apps:

In the digital age, health monitoring apps have become valuable tools for individuals looking to maintain a healthy lifestyle. These apps, accessible on smartphones and other devices, offer a range of functionalities to track various health metrics.

- **Fitness and Nutrition Trackers:**
  - **Activity Tracking:** Many apps are designed to track physical activities, such as walking, running, cycling, and more. They often use the device's built-in sensors to monitor steps taken, distance travelled, and calories burned.
  - **Personalized Fitness Goals:** These apps allow users to set and track fitness goals, offering tailored recommendations based on individual health data and progress.

- **Nutritional Insights:** Nutrition tracker apps help users monitor their food intake, providing insights into the nutritional value of the foods they consume. They can track calories, macronutrients (proteins, fats, carbohydrates), and micronutrients (vitamins and minerals).
    - **Diet Planning:** Some apps also offer features like meal planning, recipe suggestions, and grocery lists, making it easier for users to maintain a balanced diet.
    - **Integration with Wearable Devices:** Many fitness and nutrition apps can sync data from wearable health devices, providing a more comprehensive overview of the user's health and activity levels.
- **Benefits of Fitness and Nutrition Trackers:**
    - **Encouraging Healthy Habits:** By making users more aware of their activity levels and dietary habits, these apps can encourage healthier lifestyle choices.
    - **Data-Driven Decisions:** The ability to track and analyse personal health data empowers users to make informed decisions about their fitness and nutrition.
    - **Motivation and Engagement:** Features like goal setting, progress tracking, and social sharing can provide motivation and increase user engagement with their health goals.

Health monitoring apps, particularly those focused on fitness and nutrition, play a significant role in promoting and maintaining a healthy lifestyle in today's tech-centric world. By providing tools for tracking, analysing, and managing health-related data, these apps empower individuals to take charge of their health and well-being. As technology continues to advance, we can expect these apps to become even more sophisticated, offering more personalized and interactive health management experiences.

Chronic Disease Management through Health Apps:

Health apps designed for chronic disease management are transforming how patients with long-term health conditions like diabetes or hypertension manage their health. These apps offer functionalities tailored to specific diseases, assisting in monitoring vital statistics and facilitating disease management.

- **Diabetes Management Apps:**
    - **Blood Sugar Tracking:** Apps for diabetes patients often include features for logging blood sugar levels, which can be crucial for monitoring the condition and making necessary adjustments in medication or diet.
    - **Insulin Dosage and Medication Reminders:** They can provide reminders for insulin doses or other medications, ensuring adherence to treatment schedules.
    - **Dietary Management:** Many diabetes apps also offer tools for tracking carbohydrate intake, which is vital for blood sugar control, and may provide nutritional advice and diabetic-friendly recipes.
    - **Trend Analysis:** Advanced apps may analyse data over time to identify trends and patterns in blood sugar levels, which can be useful for patient-doctor discussions.

- **Hypertension Management Apps:**
  - **Blood Pressure Monitoring:** These apps allow patients to record and track their blood pressure readings, which is essential for managing hypertension.
  - **Lifestyle Advice:** They often include features to help manage factors that affect blood pressure, such as diet, exercise, and stress management.
  - **Medication Tracking:** Reminders for taking antihypertensive medications can help maintain effective treatment regimens.
- **Other Chronic Conditions:**
  - **Condition-Specific Features:** There are apps available for a variety of chronic conditions, each providing specific features suited to the management of that condition. For example, apps for asthma might include a symptom diary and peak flow tracking.
  - **Integration with Medical Devices:** Some apps can synchronize with medical devices like blood pressure monitors or glucose meters for automatic data capture.
- **Health Data Sharing:**
  - **Sharing with Healthcare Providers:** Many chronic disease management apps offer the option to share health data with healthcare providers, enabling more informed discussions during medical consultations and better-personalized care plans.
- **Educational Resources:**
  - **Information and Support:** These apps often provide educational resources about the disease, tips for managing symptoms, and sometimes access to support groups or forums.

Health apps dedicated to chronic disease management are becoming increasingly sophisticated, offering comprehensive tools to assist individuals in managing their health conditions effectively. By enabling the tracking of vital health metrics, medication adherence, and lifestyle modifications, these apps are crucial in empowering patients to take an active role in managing their chronic conditions. As technology evolves, these apps are likely to become even more integral to chronic disease management, providing patients with greater control over their health and well-being.

Mental Health and Wellness Apps:

Mental Health Support through Digital Platforms:

The increasing prevalence and awareness of mental health issues have given rise to a variety of apps designed to offer support and improve mental well-being. These apps utilize techniques such as mindfulness, meditation, and cognitive behavioural therapy (CBT) to assist users in managing stress, anxiety, depression, and other mental health conditions.

- **Mindfulness and Meditation Apps:**
  - **Stress Reduction:** These apps typically offer guided meditation sessions, which can be an effective tool for reducing stress and anxiety. They often include a range of meditation styles and lengths to suit different preferences and schedules.
  - **Enhancing Focus:** Regular use of mindfulness apps can improve concentration and overall mental clarity, helping users to stay more present and engaged in their daily lives.

- **Sleep Improvement:** Many mindfulness apps also include sleep-focused meditations and sounds designed to improve sleep quality, which is closely linked to mental health.
- **Cognitive Behavioural Therapy (CBT) Apps:**
    - **Self-Managed Therapy:** CBT apps provide tools and exercises based on cognitive behavioural therapy, helping users to identify and challenge negative thought patterns and engage in healthier thinking habits.
    - **Accessible Psychological Tools:** These apps make psychological tools more accessible, allowing users to work on their mental health independently or as a supplement to traditional therapy.
- **Mental Health Tracking:**
    - **Mood Tracking:** Many mental health apps include features for tracking mood and emotional states over time, which can provide valuable insights into patterns and triggers.
    - **Symptom Management:** These insights can assist in managing symptoms and can be valuable information to share with mental health professionals during therapy sessions.
- **Community and Support:**
    - **Connecting with Others:** Some apps offer community features, allowing users to connect with others who are experiencing similar mental health challenges, fostering a sense of support and understanding.
    - **Anonymity and Privacy:** These platforms often provide a safe and anonymous space for individuals to discuss their mental health without fear of stigma or judgment.
- **Relaxation and Stress Management:**

- **Breathing Exercises:** Apps often include guided breathing exercises, which can be particularly helpful for managing acute stress and anxiety.
- **Relaxation Techniques:** Techniques such as progressive muscle relaxation and visualization exercises are also commonly featured.

Mental health and wellness apps are becoming an integral part of modern mental healthcare, offering tools and resources that are easily accessible and user-friendly. These apps provide valuable support for those looking to improve their mental health, whether as a stand-alone tool or in combination with traditional mental health treatments. As the field of digital mental health continues to grow, these apps will likely play an increasingly significant role in promoting mental wellness and resilience.

Stress and Sleep Management Through Apps:

In today's fast-paced world, managing stress and getting adequate sleep are essential for maintaining mental well-being. Apps focused on stress reduction and sleep improvement are gaining popularity, offering accessible solutions to help individuals enhance their mental health.

- **Stress Reduction Apps:**
  - **Guided Relaxation Techniques:** These apps often provide guided relaxation sessions, including deep breathing exercises, progressive muscle relaxation, and guided imagery, which can be effective in reducing stress levels.

- **Mindfulness-Based Stress Reduction:** Incorporating mindfulness practices, these apps teach users how to stay present and reduce rumination, a common contributor to stress.
- **Personalized Stress Management:** Some apps offer personalized stress management plans based on user input, tracking stress levels and providing tailored recommendations.
- **Sleep Improvement Apps:**
  - **Sleep Tracking:** Many apps monitor sleep patterns and provide insights into sleep quality, duration, and consistency. They can track movements and sounds during sleep to offer a comprehensive analysis of sleep cycles.
  - **Sleep-Friendly Audio Content:** Apps frequently feature a variety of sleep-friendly content, including white noise, nature sounds, sleep stories, and calming music designed to aid in falling asleep.
  - **Cognitive Behavioural Therapy for Insomnia (CBT-I):** Some advanced apps utilize CBT-I techniques to address thoughts and behaviours that contribute to sleep disturbances, offering structured programs to improve sleep habits.
- **Interactive Features:**
  - **Reminders and Notifications:** To assist with stress management and sleep routines, apps can send reminders for relaxation exercises, bedtime, or winding down activities.
  - **Journaling and Reflection:** Encouraging users to journal their thoughts and reflect on their stressors and sleep habits can increase self-awareness and promote positive changes.

- **Educational Resources:**
  - **Learning Modules:** These apps often include educational content on stress management techniques and sleep hygiene, helping users understand the science behind stress and sleep, and how to improve them.
- **Customization and User Experience:**
  - **Customizable Settings:** Many apps allow users to customize their experiences, whether it's choosing the type of relaxation audio, setting sleep goals, or tailoring the interface to their preferences.
  - **User-Friendly Design:** A well-designed user interface can enhance the app experience, making it easier and more enjoyable for users to engage with the app regularly.

Apps focusing on stress and sleep management are valuable tools in the realm of digital health, offering practical and accessible ways to enhance mental well-being. By providing users with the means to track, manage, and improve their stress levels and sleep patterns, these apps play a crucial role in promoting overall health and wellness. As technology continues to advance, these apps are likely to become even more sophisticated, offering increasingly personalized and effective solutions for managing stress and sleep.

3. Educational Resources:

Medical Information Platforms: Empowering Patients with Knowledge

In the digital age, access to medical information has become more democratized than ever. Websites and apps dedicated to providing reliable medical information play a crucial role in empowering patients by enhancing their knowledge about various health conditions, treatments, and wellness strategies.

- **Websites and Apps Offering Medical Information:**
    - **Accurate and Up-to-Date Content:** Many health information platforms are maintained by medical professionals and offer content that is accurate, current, and evidence-based. This includes information about diseases, conditions, medications, and health tips.
    - **Ease of Access:** The convenience of accessing this information through smartphones and computers allows individuals to easily find answers to their health-related questions.
- **Benefits of Informed Patients:**
    - **Improved Understanding of Health Conditions:** These resources enable patients to better understand their health conditions, including symptoms, causes, and treatment options.
    - **Enhanced Patient-Provider Communication:** Well-informed patients can have more productive consultations with their healthcare providers, leading to more personalized care and better health outcomes.
    - **Empowerment in Health Management:** Knowledge empowers patients to take an active role in managing their health, including making informed decisions about treatments and lifestyle changes.
- **Interactive Educational Tools:**
    - **Symptom Checkers:** Some platforms offer interactive tools like symptom checkers, which can provide initial

guidance on potential conditions based on the symptoms entered by the user.
- **Health Calculators and Assessments:** Tools such as BMI calculators, heart risk assessments, and mental health screenings can offer valuable insights and prompt discussions with healthcare providers.
- **Safety and Reliability Concerns:**
  - **Credible Sources:** It's important for users to rely on information from credible sources, such as reputable health organizations, hospitals, and government health departments, to ensure the accuracy of the information.
  - **Complement to Professional Advice:** While these resources are valuable, they should not replace professional medical advice, diagnosis, or treatment. Users should always consult healthcare professionals for personalized medical advice.
- **Patient Education and Chronic Disease Management:**
  - **Managing Chronic Conditions:** For those managing chronic diseases, these platforms can provide extensive information on disease management, including lifestyle tips, medication adherence, and symptom monitoring.
- **Multimedia Content for Enhanced Learning:**
  - **Videos and Illustrations:** Many platforms use multimedia content like explanatory videos, animations, and illustrations to make complex medical information more understandable and engaging.

The proliferation of medical information platforms has significantly contributed to patient education and empowerment. By providing easy access to reliable health information, these platforms enhance patients' ability to understand and manage their health conditions, fostering a more informed and engaged approach to healthcare. As technology evolves, these resources are poised to become even more interactive and personalized, further enhancing their role in patient education and health management.

Online Communities: Support and Information Sharing

Online communities, including forums and social networks dedicated to specific health conditions, have become vital resources for patients and caregivers. These platforms provide a space for sharing experiences, information, and support, creating a sense of community among individuals facing similar health challenges.

- **Forums for Specific Health Conditions:**
    - **Peer Support:** Online forums allow patients and caregivers to connect with others who are dealing with similar health issues. This peer support can be invaluable in coping with the emotional and practical aspects of managing a health condition.
    - **Information Exchange:** These forums often become hubs for exchanging information about treatments, medications, and personal experiences with different therapies, offering insights that might not be available through traditional medical channels.
- **Social Networks Focused on Health:**
    - **Building Connections:** Social networking sites dedicated to health create opportunities for individuals to build connections, share stories, and find encouragement and understanding from others who truly comprehend their struggles.

- o **Access to Diverse Experiences:** They provide access to a wide range of experiences and perspectives, which can be particularly helpful for rare or less-understood conditions.
- **Benefits of Online Health Communities:**
  - o **Reduced Isolation:** For many, these communities offer a sense of belonging and reduce feelings of isolation that often accompany health issues.
  - o **Empowerment Through Knowledge:** Engaging in discussions and reading about others' experiences can empower patients and caregivers with knowledge and confidence to advocate for their own or their loved one's care.
- **Navigating Online Communities Wisely:**
  - o **Evaluating Information:** While these communities can be excellent sources of support and information, it's important for users to evaluate the credibility of the information shared and to remember that it does not replace professional medical advice.
  - o **Privacy Considerations:** Users should be mindful of their privacy and the personal information they share in these online spaces.
- **Role in Chronic Disease Management:**
  - o **Ongoing Support:** For chronic conditions, ongoing support from peers who understand the day-to-day challenges can be as important as medical treatment in managing the disease.
- **Mental Health Support:**
  - o **Forums for Mental Health:** Online communities are also significant for mental health support, offering a platform for those who might not have access to traditional support systems or who prefer the anonymity of online forums.

Online communities and forums have become integral parts of the healthcare landscape, providing emotional support, practical advice, and a sense of community for those living with various health conditions. They complement traditional healthcare by offering a platform for connection and knowledge sharing that can positively impact patients' and caregivers' experiences. As these online communities continue to grow, they provide an increasingly important resource for support and information in the healthcare journey.

Potential Future Developments in Healthcare Technology:

1. Artificial Intelligence and Machine Learning:

The future of healthcare technology is increasingly intertwined with advancements in artificial intelligence (AI) and machine learning. These technologies hold immense potential to revolutionize various aspects of healthcare, from diagnostics to treatment planning.

- **Predictive Analytics in Healthcare:**
    - **Predicting Disease Patterns:** AI algorithms can analyse vast amounts of health data to identify patterns and trends that may predict the onset of diseases. This can enable earlier interventions and preventive measures, potentially reducing the incidence and severity of diseases.
    - **Risk Stratification:** AI can help in stratifying patients based on their risk of developing certain conditions, allowing for more targeted and effective preventive care.

- **Personalizing Treatment Plans:**
  - **Tailored Healthcare:** AI and machine learning can analyse individual patient data, including genetic information, lifestyle factors, and previous health records, to develop highly personalized treatment plans.
  - **Precision Medicine:** This approach is a cornerstone of precision medicine, which seeks to customize healthcare, with medical decisions and treatments tailored to the individual patient.
- **Assisting in Diagnosis and Treatment Decisions:**
  - **Diagnostic Assistance:** AI algorithms can assist doctors in diagnosing diseases by analyzing medical imaging, laboratory results, and patient history more quickly and accurately than traditional methods.
  - **Treatment Optimization:** AI can also suggest the most effective treatment options based on the analysis of similar cases and outcomes, potentially improving patient outcomes.
- **Enhancing Clinical Decision Making:**
  - **Decision Support Systems:** AI-driven decision support systems can provide healthcare professionals with evidence-based clinical guidelines and recommendations, helping them make more informed decisions.
  - **Error Reduction:** By providing accurate and up-to-date information, AI has the potential to reduce diagnostic and treatment errors.
- **Monitoring and Predictive Alerts:**
  - **Real-Time Monitoring:** AI systems can continuously monitor patient data in real-time, providing predictive alerts for conditions like sepsis or heart failure, which require immediate medical attention.

- **Wearable Technologies:** Integration with wearable technologies can facilitate continuous health monitoring outside of clinical settings, offering opportunities for early intervention.

Artificial Intelligence and machine learning are at the forefront of the next wave of healthcare innovations. Their potential to transform disease prediction, personalize treatment plans, and enhance diagnostic accuracy promises a future where healthcare is more proactive, personalized, and effective. As these technologies continue to evolve and integrate into healthcare systems, they will play an increasingly vital role in shaping the future of medical care and patient outcomes.

Robotics in Surgery: Enhancing Precision and Outcomes

The incorporation of robotics into surgery represents one of the most exciting and rapidly advancing areas in healthcare technology. Robotics are revolutionizing surgical procedures, offering enhanced precision, control, and outcomes.

- **Increased Precision in Surgical Procedures:**
    - **Fine Manipulation:** Robotic systems allow for incredibly precise movements in surgery, which can be particularly advantageous for complex or delicate procedures. These systems can perform intricate manoeuvres that are beyond the capabilities of the human hand.
    - **Minimally Invasive Techniques:** Robotics often enable minimally invasive surgery, resulting in

smaller incisions, less pain, and quicker recovery times for patients.
  o
- **Improved Outcomes and Reduced Complications:**
  o **Higher Accuracy:** The precision of robotic systems can lead to reduced risk of complications, less blood loss, and quicker healing.
  o **Consistency:** Robotics provide a level of consistency in surgical procedures, which can be particularly important in repetitive or particularly challenging surgeries.
- **Enhanced Visualization:**
  o **Advanced Imaging:** Robotic systems are often equipped with high-definition, 3D cameras that offer surgeons enhanced visualization of the surgical area, providing greater detail and depth perception than the human eye.
  o **Real-Time Feedback:** Many systems also offer real-time imaging and feedback, aiding surgeons in making immediate adjustments during the procedure.
- **Expanding Applications:**
  o **Diverse Surgical Fields:** The use of robotics is expanding across a wide range of surgical fields, including orthopaedics, neurosurgery, cardiology, and oncology.
  o **Customization for Individual Patients:** Robotics can be used to tailor surgical procedures to the specific anatomy and needs of individual patients, enhancing the effectiveness of surgeries.

- **Training and Skill Development:**
  - **Enhanced Training for Surgeons:** Robotics technology is also changing the way surgeons are trained, offering simulation-based training tools that provide a safe and controlled environment for learning and practicing surgical skills.
  - **Continuous Learning:** Robotic systems can store data from surgeries, which can be analysed for training purposes and to improve surgical techniques over time.
- **Patient-Cantered Care:**
  - **Reduced Recovery Time:** The minimally invasive nature of robotic surgery often results in shorter hospital stays and faster recovery times, improving the overall patient experience.
  - **Quality of Life:** By reducing recovery time and surgical complications, robotic surgery can significantly improve the quality of life for patients post-surgery.

Robotics in surgery is a groundbreaking development that is transforming the landscape of surgical care. With advancements in precision, visualization, and minimally invasive techniques, robotic surgery is setting new standards in patient care and surgical outcomes. As technology continues to advance, the role of robotics in surgery is expected to grow, further enhancing the capabilities of surgeons and the care received by patients.

Wearable Health Technology:

Continuous Monitoring and Its Advancements

Wearable health technology is rapidly evolving, offering sophisticated solutions for continuous monitoring of vital signs and health metrics. These devices are playing a pivotal role in transforming healthcare from reactive to proactive and personalized.

- **Sophistication in Wearable Devices:**
  - **Advanced Health Tracking:** Modern wearable devices go beyond basic fitness tracking. They are now equipped to monitor a range of vital signs such as heart rate, blood oxygen levels, blood pressure, and even glucose levels in some cases.
  - **Real-Time Health Data:** These devices provide real-time data, allowing both patients and doctors to monitor health metrics continuously. This constant stream of data can be crucial for managing chronic conditions and for early detection of potential health issues.
- **Enhanced Patient Engagement and Self-Management:**
  - **Empowering Patients:** By providing immediate feedback on their health status, wearable devices empower patients to take an active role in managing their health. They can track the impact of lifestyle changes and medications on their health metrics.
  - **Encouraging Healthy Behaviours:** Continuous monitoring can motivate individuals to adopt healthier lifestyle choices, such as increased physical activity and better sleep habits.
  -

- **Remote Patient Monitoring:**
  - **Facilitating Home-Based Care:** Wearable devices are integral in remote patient monitoring programs, allowing healthcare providers to monitor patients outside traditional clinical settings. This is especially beneficial for elderly patients, post-operative care, and individuals managing chronic diseases.
  - **Reducing Hospital Visits:** Continuous monitoring can help in identifying health issues before they require emergency care, potentially reducing hospital admissions and visits.
- **Data-Driven Clinical Decisions:**
  - **Informing Treatment Plans:** The data collected from wearable devices can be used to inform and tailor treatment plans. For instance, data can indicate the need for medication adjustments in chronic disease management.
  - **Predictive Analytics:** When combined with AI and machine learning, the data can be used for predictive analytics, potentially identifying health risks before they become apparent.
- **Interoperability and Integration:**
  - **Integration with Electronic Health Records (EHR):** Efforts are being made to integrate data from wearable devices with EHRs, enabling a more comprehensive view of a patient's health over time.
  - **Seamless Connectivity:** Advances in technology are improving the connectivity of these devices with smartphones and healthcare systems, allowing for seamless transmission and analysis of health data.

Wearable health technology represents a significant leap forward in continuous health monitoring, offering sophisticated tools that enhance patient engagement, self-management, and remote monitoring. As these devices become more advanced, they not only provide invaluable data for individuals to manage their own health but also equip healthcare providers with detailed, real-time insights to make data-driven decisions. The future of wearable technology in healthcare is bright, with potential impacts that could redefine how health and wellness are monitored and maintained.

Predictive Health Alerts in Wearable Technology:

The future of wearable health technology is not just in monitoring but also in predicting potential health events. Advanced wearables are being developed to provide predictive health alerts, which could significantly enhance preventive healthcare and emergency response.

- **Early Warning Systems:**
    - **Predicting Critical Health Events:** With advancements in sensor technology and data analysis, wearable devices are being developed to detect early signs of serious health events, such as heart attacks or seizures, before they occur.
    - **Real-Time Data Analysis:** These devices will continuously analyse health data in real-time, using sophisticated algorithms to identify patterns or changes that may precede a critical health event.
- **Integration with AI and Machine Learning:**
    - **Learning from Patterns:** By incorporating AI and machine learning, wearables can learn from vast amounts of health data, improving their ability to

predict potential health issues based on individual health patterns and histories.
- **Personalized Health Insights:** This technology can lead to highly personalized health insights, tailoring alerts to the specific risk factors and health profiles of individual users.
- **Enhancing Preventive Care:**
  - **Proactive Health Management:** Predictive alerts can enable users and healthcare providers to take proactive steps in managing health, potentially preventing serious events or mitigating their severity.
  - **Behavioural Modification:** These alerts can also motivate users to adopt healthier lifestyles and adhere more closely to treatment regimens.
- **Emergency Response Coordination:**
  - **Immediate Alerts to Emergency Services:** In the event of a predicted medical emergency, wearables could automatically alert emergency services, providing them with critical information, such as the user's location, medical history, and the nature of the predicted event.
  - **Family and Caregiver Notifications:** Wearables can also be programmed to notify family members or caregivers, ensuring immediate support and intervention.
- **Challenges and Considerations:**
  - **Accuracy and Reliability:** Ensuring the accuracy and reliability of predictive alerts is crucial to prevent false alarms and ensure user trust in the technology.
  - **Privacy and Data Security:** As these devices handle sensitive health data, robust privacy and data security measures will be essential.

The development of wearable technology capable of providing predictive health alerts represents a significant advancement in personal health monitoring. By offering early warnings of potential health crises, these devices have the potential to transform preventive healthcare and emergency medical response. As this technology continues to evolve, it promises to play an increasingly vital role in health management, offering users peace of mind and empowering them with timely, personalized health insights.

3D Printing in Medicine:

Customization and Innovation Through 3D Printing

3D printing technology, also known as additive manufacturing, is revolutionizing the field of medicine by enabling the creation of customized medical devices, prosthetics, and implants. This rapidly advancing field is offering new possibilities for personalized medical care and treatment.

- **Customized Prosthetics and Implants:**
  - **Tailored to the Patient:** 3D printing allows for the production of prosthetics and implants that are custom-fitted to the individual's specific anatomy, leading to improved comfort and functionality compared to traditional, off-the-shelf products.
  - **Innovative Design Possibilities:** The technology enables the creation of complex geometric structures that can be difficult or impossible to achieve with conventional manufacturing methods, offering new solutions for challenging medical problems.
  -

- **Benefits of Customization:**
    - **Improved Patient Outcomes:** Customized prosthetics and implants can lead to better integration with the body, reduced risk of rejection, and improved overall patient outcomes.
    - **Rapid Production:** 3D printing can significantly reduce the time it takes to produce medical devices, which is particularly crucial in emergency situations or when dealing with rapidly changing conditions, such as in paediatric care.
- **Advancements in Surgical Planning and Training:**
    - **3D Printed Anatomical Models:** Surgeons can use 3D printed models of patient-specific anatomy for pre-surgical planning and simulation. This can enhance the understanding of complex structures and facilitate more effective surgical interventions.
    - **Training Tools:** 3D printed models provide valuable tools for medical training, allowing students and surgeons to practice on anatomically accurate replicas.
- **Expanding Applications:**
    - **Bioprinting Tissues and Organs:** Research is ongoing into 3D bioprinting, which involves the layer-by-layer deposition of bioinks to create tissue-like structures and potentially organs for transplantation.
    - **Dental and Orthopaedic Applications:** 3D printing is increasingly used in dentistry for crowns, bridges, and orthodontic devices, and in orthopaedics for joint replacements and spinal implants.
- **Cost-Effectiveness and Accessibility:**
    - **Reducing Costs:** While the initial investment in 3D printing technology can be high, it has the potential to reduce the overall costs of medical devices and

prosthetics, making them more accessible to a broader range of patients.
- **Potential for Global Impact:** This technology could have a significant impact in low-resource settings, where traditional manufacturing and supply chain logistics are challenging.

3D printing in medicine is a field ripe with potential, offering groundbreaking possibilities in the customization of prosthetics, implants, and even the creation of tissues and organs. As the technology continues to evolve and become more accessible, its impact on personalized medicine and patient care is expected to be profound. This area of healthcare technology not only highlights the innovative spirit of medical science but also its commitment to improving patient care and quality of life.

Tissue and Organ Printing: The Frontier of 3D Bioprinting

The realm of 3D bioprinting, especially in the context of tissue and organ printing, represents one of the most exciting and potentially transformative areas of medical research and technology. This field holds the promise of revolutionizing transplant medicine by providing a solution to the shortage of donor organs and the challenges of transplant rejection.

- **3D Bioprinting Technology:**
  - **Layer-by-Layer Fabrication:** 3D bioprinting involves depositing layers of bio-inks – materials made of living cells, biomaterials, and growth factors – to build tissue-like structures.

- **Customization of Tissues:** This technology enables the creation of tissues customized to the specific needs of patients, potentially leading to more successful integration and function once transplanted.
- **Potential for Organ Printing:**
  - **Addressing Organ Shortage:** One of the most compelling aspects of 3D bioprinting is the potential to print whole organs for transplant, which could significantly alleviate the current shortage of donor organs.
  - **Reducing Transplant Rejection:** By using a patient's own cells, the printed organs would be biologically compatible, reducing the risk of rejection and the need for lifelong immunosuppression.
- **Current Progress and Challenges:**
  - **Research and Development:** While the printing of complex organs like kidneys or hearts is still in the research phase, significant progress has been made in printing simpler tissues, such as skin, cartilage, and bladders.
  - **Complexity of Organs:** The primary challenge lies in replicating the complex structure and function of organs, including the development of a functional vascular network to supply blood and nutrients to the printed tissues.
- **Clinical Applications and Trials:**
  - **Skin Grafts and Cartilage Repair:** Some of the first clinical applications of 3D bioprinting are likely to be in areas like skin grafts for burn victims and cartilage repair for joint injuries.
  - **Regulatory Approval:** As with any new medical technology, regulatory approval will be a critical step,

requiring extensive clinical trials to ensure the safety and efficacy of bio printed tissues and organs.
- **Ethical and Social Implications:**
    - **Ethical Considerations:** The development of bio printed organs raises various ethical questions, including issues of accessibility, cost, and the implications of creating human tissues.
    - **Public Perception and Acceptance:** Public education and engagement will be important in addressing any concerns and fostering acceptance of this groundbreaking technology.

3D bioprinting, particularly in the context of tissue and organ printing, offers a vision of the future where the challenges of organ shortage and transplant rejection could be significantly mitigated. While the field is still in its nascent stages, the potential it holds is enormous, not just for transplant medicine but for the broader realm of medical treatment and research. As technology advances and overcomes current limitations, 3D bioprinting could well become a cornerstone of regenerative medicine and a testament to the incredible possibilities at the intersection of biology and technology.

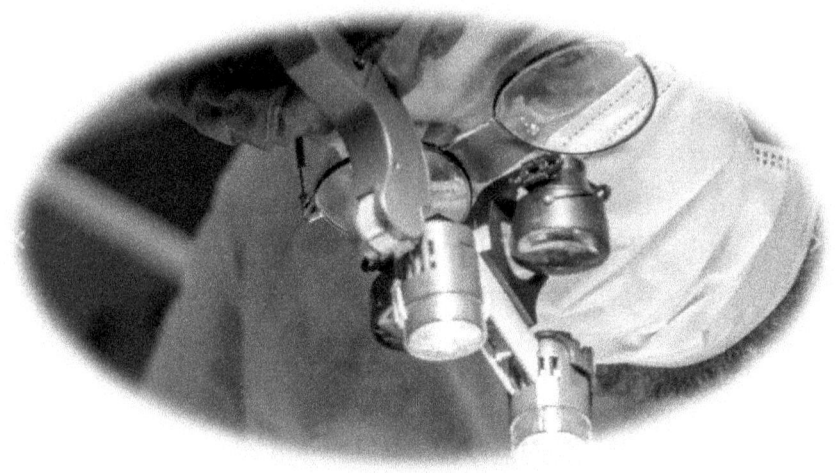

The Future Of Healthcare Is In Telemedicine.

Sleep Gives Us Peace Of Mind, Soul And Body.

Chapter 9:

Preparing for Hospital Visits

Fast-Track A&E

Introduction:

Hospital visits, irrespective of their nature, can often be overwhelming not only due to the health concerns involved but also because of the numerous logistical, financial, and emotional aspects associated with them. Whether one is facing a scheduled surgery, dealing with an unforeseen emergency, or preparing for a prolonged treatment period, the experience encompasses far more than just the medical procedure itself. This chapter is designed as a comprehensive guide to demystify and simplify the process of hospital visits, providing clarity and comfort to patients and their families during these challenging times.

Embarking on a hospital journey often begins long before setting foot in the hospital itself. It involves understanding the intricacies of insurance policies, navigating through the maze of healthcare costs, and often dealing with the paperwork and procedures that vary significantly across different countries and healthcare systems. This chapter delves into these critical financial and administrative aspects, offering insights and practical advice to ensure patients are well-prepared and informed.

Additionally, hospital visits do not occur in a cultural vacuum. They are deeply influenced by and situated within diverse cultural contexts. This aspect of hospital care is crucial as it impacts patient experience, communication with healthcare providers, and the overall comfort level during the stay. Recognizing and respecting cultural norms, dietary preferences, language needs, and religious practices play a significant role in the quality of care and patient satisfaction. This chapter provides guidance on navigating these cultural considerations, aiming to foster a respectful and sensitive environment for all patients.

Moreover, practical preparation for a hospital visit is equally essential. From what to pack for a stay to making arrangements for home and family during one's absence, these practicalities can significantly impact the ease and comfort of the experience. This chapter includes detailed checklists and tips, covering everything from essential items to bring along to making necessary arrangements for post-hospitalization care. It also offers advice on managing logistics like transportation and accommodation for family members, if needed.

The chapter further extends to preparing patients and their families for what to expect during the hospital stay, including interactions with healthcare professionals, understanding hospital routines, and navigating the hospital setting. It emphasizes the importance of effective communication, advocating for oneself or a loved one, and understanding patient rights and responsibilities.

Navigating Insurance and Healthcare Costs in Different Countries:

Understanding Insurance Coverage:

Navigating the maze of healthcare insurance is a critical step in preparing for a hospital visit, particularly given the variations in coverage policies and healthcare systems across different countries. Understanding the specifics of one's insurance policy can significantly impact the financial and logistical aspects of hospital care.

- **Policy Details:**
  - **Scope of Coverage:** Patients should be well-informed about the extent of their insurance coverage. This includes knowing which medical procedures, treatments, and medications are covered under their policy.
  - **Coverage Limits:** Understanding the limits of the policy, such as maximum coverage amounts and any caps on specific types of care, is essential to avoid unexpected expenses.
  - **Inclusions and Exclusions:** Being aware of what is specifically included and excluded in the policy can prevent surprises during billing. For instance, some policies might cover surgery costs but not postoperative rehabilitation.
- **Out-of-Pocket Costs:**
  - **Deductibles and Co-pays:** Patients need to be aware of any deductibles – the amount paid out of pocket before insurance coverage begins – and co-pays, which are fixed amounts for certain services.
  - **Hidden Costs:** It's also important to inquire about potential hidden costs that might not be immediately apparent, such as fees for specialist consultations or certain diagnostic tests.
- **Pre-Authorization Requirements:**
  - **Approval for Procedures:** Some insurance plans require pre-authorization for certain medical procedures or treatments. Understanding this process is crucial to ensure that the costs will be covered.
  - **Timelines and Documentation:** Patients should be aware of the timelines for obtaining pre-authorization and the necessary documentation required to avoid delays in treatment.

- **International and Travel Insurance:**
  - **Coverage in Different Countries:** For those traveling or living abroad, understanding how their insurance works in different countries is crucial. This includes knowing whether their policy provides international coverage or if additional travel health insurance is necessary.
  - **Repatriation and Emergency Services:** Especially for travel insurance, it's important to check if the policy includes emergency medical repatriation and evacuation services.

Pre-Authorization in Healthcare Insurance:

Pre-authorization, often a crucial step in the healthcare process, involves obtaining approval from an insurance provider before undergoing certain medical procedures or treatments. This process ensures that the insurance company will cover the costs associated with the care, thereby avoiding unexpected expenses for the patient.

- **Understanding the Pre-Authorization Process:**
  - **Identifying Requirements:** Patients should first determine whether their planned medical procedure or treatment requires pre-authorization. This information is typically available in the insurance policy documents or can be obtained directly from the insurance provider.
  - **Initiating Pre-Authorization:** The process usually involves the healthcare provider submitting a request to the insurance company, outlining the necessity of the procedure or treatment. It often includes clinical

information and justification for why the procedure is essential.
- **Timeliness and Coordination:**
    - **Allowing Sufficient Time:** Pre-authorization can be a time-consuming process. Patients and healthcare providers should initiate it well in advance of the scheduled procedure to avoid delays.
    - **Coordination Between Provider and Insurer:** Effective communication between the healthcare provider and the insurance company is vital to ensure all necessary documentation is submitted, and any queries are promptly addressed.
- **Understanding Denials and Appeals:**
    - **Handling Denials:** If pre-authorization is denied, patients have the right to know why. They should receive clear instructions on how to appeal the decision or explore alternative treatment options.
    - **Appeal Process:** Patients can appeal a denial, which usually involves submitting additional information or clarification regarding the medical necessity of the procedure.
- **Role of Healthcare Providers:**
    - **Provider Responsibility:** In many cases, healthcare providers handle much of the pre-authorization process, including submitting the necessary documentation and following up with the insurance company.
    - **Patient Advocacy:** Patients should actively engage with their healthcare providers to ensure the process is being handled and to understand their role in it, if any.

- **International Considerations:**
  - **Varied Policies:** For international patients or those traveling, it's important to understand how pre-authorization works in different countries and with different insurance providers, as practices may vary significantly.

Pre-authorization is a critical component of the healthcare journey, particularly when dealing with insurance companies. Understanding and efficiently navigating this process is key to ensuring that the necessary medical procedures are covered and to minimize financial stress. Patients should proactively engage with both their healthcare providers and insurance companies to facilitate a smooth pre-authorization process, thereby ensuring timely access to needed medical care.

Healthcare Systems Across Countries:

Understanding Global Healthcare Variations

The landscape of healthcare systems varies widely across the globe, with each country having its own unique approach to providing medical care to its citizens. This diversity in healthcare models can significantly impact how hospital visits, treatments, and insurance coverage are approached in different countries.

- **Public Healthcare Models:**
  - **Example: The NHS in the UK:** The National Health Service (NHS) in the United Kingdom is a publicly funded healthcare system. It provides most healthcare services free at the point of use for UK residents, funded through taxation.

- **Accessibility and Coverage:** Public healthcare systems generally offer a wide range of medical services, aiming to provide comprehensive care that is accessible to all citizens. However, there may be longer wait times for certain procedures and treatments.
- **Predominantly Private Healthcare Systems:**
  - **Example: The United States:** The healthcare system in the United States is primarily private, with care typically accessed through private health insurance, either purchased individually or provided by employers. Government programs like Medicare and Medicaid also play significant roles.
  - **Insurance-Driven Care:** In private healthcare systems, the type and extent of medical care are often closely tied to one's insurance coverage, making understanding and navigating insurance plans crucial.
- **Hybrid Models:**
  - **Combination of Public and Private:** Many countries employ hybrid models, where public healthcare is available but can be supplemented with private insurance for quicker access or broader coverage. Examples include Canada and Australia, where public healthcare covers a substantial part of medical care, but private insurance can cover additional services or reduce waiting times.
- **Universal Healthcare Systems:**
  - **Coverage for All Citizens:** Some countries, such as Canada and many in the European Union, have universal healthcare systems, aiming to provide healthcare access to all citizens, often funded through taxation.

- o **Balance of Quality and Accessibility:** Universal healthcare systems strive to balance quality of care with accessibility and affordability for the entire population.
- **Navigating Healthcare as a Foreigner or Traveler:**
  - o **Research and Preparation:** For those traveling or moving abroad, understanding the healthcare system in the destination country is vital. It's important to research how to access medical care as a non-resident and the role of travel or expatriate health insurance.
- **Cultural and Operational Differences:**
  - o **Varied Healthcare Practices:** Patients should also be aware of potential cultural and operational differences in healthcare practices, which can impact the patient experience and expectations in hospital settings.

Navigating healthcare systems in different countries can be challenging due to the wide spectrum of healthcare models and practices. Understanding the fundamental structure and principles of the healthcare system in a given country is crucial for anyone planning a hospital visit, whether as a resident or a visitor. This knowledge not only aids in planning and preparing for medical care but also helps in making informed decisions regarding treatments and managing expectations related to healthcare services.

Navigating Non-Resident Care:

Travelers and expatriates often face unique challenges when accessing healthcare services in foreign countries. Understanding the nuances of non-resident care and the role of specialized insurance is crucial in ensuring access to necessary medical services while abroad.

- **Access to Healthcare Services for Non-Residents:**
  - **Research Local Healthcare Systems:** Before traveling or relocating, it's important to research the healthcare system of the destination country. This includes understanding how non-residents can access medical services and any associated costs.
  - **Navigating Public and Private Sectors:** Some countries may allow non-residents to use public healthcare services, while others may require them to seek care only in private facilities. Knowing these distinctions can save time and confusion in emergency situations.
- **Travel and International Health Insurance:**
  - **Assessing Insurance Needs:** Travelers and expatriates should assess their health insurance needs based on the length of stay, the nature of their visit, and the healthcare system of the destination country.
  - **Coverage for International Care:** Standard health insurance policies may not cover medical services in other countries. Therefore, obtaining travel health insurance or international health insurance is essential. These policies are designed to cover healthcare costs incurred while abroad, including emergencies, routine care, and sometimes medical evacuation.
  - **Understanding Policy Details:** It is crucial to understand the specifics of the insurance policy, including coverage limits, exclusions, and the process for filing claims. Some policies may require upfront payment for services, with reimbursement to follow.
- **Emergency Medical Assistance Services:**
  - **Emergency Support:** Many travel and international health insurance plans offer emergency assistance

services, which can guide non-residents in finding local medical facilities and navigating language barriers.
    - **24/7 Hotlines:** Access to 24/7 support hotlines can be particularly helpful in urgent situations, providing immediate advice and assistance.
- **Preparation and Documentation:**
    - **Carrying Proof of Insurance:** Travelers and expatriates should carry proof of their health insurance and understand how to use it in the destination country.
    - **Health Records and Medications:** It's advisable to carry a copy of personal health records and a sufficient supply of any regular medications, along with prescriptions.

Navigating non-resident care requires careful preparation and an understanding of the specific healthcare and insurance landscapes of the destination country. By researching in advance and securing appropriate international health insurance coverage, travellers and expatriates can mitigate potential healthcare challenges and ensure access to necessary medical services while abroad. This section of the chapter provides essential guidance and tips for those seeking medical care outside their home country, ensuring they are well-prepared for any health-related eventualities during their travels or expatriate life.

Cultural Considerations in Hospital Settings:

1. Respecting Cultural Diversity:

In today's globalized world, hospitals are increasingly becoming melting pots of diverse cultures. Understanding and respecting this cultural diversity is crucial for both healthcare providers and patients to ensure that hospital experiences are comfortable, respectful, and effective.

- **Cultural Sensitivity in Healthcare:**

o   Recognizing Diversity: Hospitals must recognize and be prepared to cater to a wide range of cultural backgrounds. This involves understanding different cultural norms, values, beliefs, and practices that patients bring with them.

o   Training for Healthcare Providers: Providing cultural sensitivity training for healthcare staff can significantly improve patient care. This training should cover aspects such as communication styles, health beliefs, and practices that are common in different cultures.

- **Language Considerations:**

o   Overcoming Language Barriers: Language differences can be a major barrier to effective healthcare. Hospitals should provide access to interpreters or translation services to ensure clear communication between healthcare providers and patients.

o   Written Materials: Providing patient education materials in multiple languages can help in better understanding and compliance with medical advice and procedures.

- **Respecting Religious Practices:**

o   Accommodating Religious Needs: Healthcare providers should be aware of and accommodate, when possible, the religious needs of patients. This might include dietary restrictions, prayer requirements, or specific religious rituals.

o   Sensitivity During Treatment: Understanding how religious beliefs might impact treatment decisions is important for healthcare providers. This includes being aware of any religious concerns regarding medications, procedures, or examinations.

- **Dietary Preferences and Restrictions:**

o   Catering to Different Diets: Hospitals should strive to provide meal options that cater to various dietary requirements, such as vegetarian, kosher, halal, or allergen-free meals.

o   Understanding Cultural Nuances: Dietary needs can be deeply rooted in cultural practices. Being aware of these nuances can help in providing patient-centred care.

- **Culturally Competent Care:**

o   Building Trust: Culturally sensitive care can help in building trust between patients and healthcare providers, leading to better patient outcomes.

o   Patient-Centered Approach: Adapting care to meet the cultural needs and preferences of patients is an essential part of a patient-centered approach to healthcare.

Cultural considerations in hospital settings are not just about adherence to protocols; they are about fostering an environment of respect, understanding, and personalized care. By emphasizing cultural sensitivity, hospitals can ensure that they are not only treating illnesses but also caring for patients in a manner that respects their cultural identity and individual needs. This section of the chapter provides a guide for both healthcare providers and patients on navigating the multicultural landscape of modern hospitals, emphasizing the importance of cultural awareness in providing effective healthcare.

Language Challenges in Hospital Settings:

Effective communication is a cornerstone of quality healthcare. In multicultural hospital environments, language barriers can pose significant challenges, affecting everything from understanding medical information to expressing concerns and making informed decisions. Addressing these language challenges is essential for ensuring that all patients receive equitable and effective care.

- **Importance of Overcoming Language Barriers:**
    - **Ensuring Accurate Diagnosis and Treatment:** Miscommunication due to language differences can lead to misdiagnosis or inappropriate treatment. Clear communication is critical for accurate medical assessments.
    - **Informed Consent:** Patients must fully understand their condition, treatment options, and the risks involved to give informed consent. This is only possible when communication is clear and in a language the patient understands.
- **Access to Interpreters and Translation Services:**
    - **Professional Medical Interpreters:** Hospitals should provide access to professional medical interpreters who are trained in medical terminology and

confidentiality, ensuring accurate and sensitive translation.
- **On-Demand Interpretation Services:** Many hospitals use on-demand telephone or video interpretation services, which can provide immediate access to interpreters in a wide range of languages.
- **Written Materials:** Providing patient education materials, consent forms, and discharge instructions in multiple languages can significantly enhance understanding and compliance.

- **Training for Healthcare Providers:**
  - **Cultural Competence and Communication Skills:** Healthcare providers should receive training in working effectively with interpreters and in strategies for communicating with patients who have limited proficiency in the dominant language.
  - **Awareness of Non-Verbal Cues:** Non-verbal communication can vary significantly across cultures. Healthcare providers should be aware of these differences and how they might impact patient interactions.
- **Technology Aiding in Translation:**
  - **Digital Translation Tools:** The use of apps and digital tools for translation can aid in basic communication, although they should be used cautiously and never replace professional interpreters in critical or complex medical discussions.
- **Patient Empowerment:**
  - **Encouraging Patients to Request Assistance:** Patients should be encouraged and feel empowered to request language assistance services when needed. This can be facilitated by making information about such services visibly available in multiple languages.

Language challenges in hospital settings require thoughtful solutions and resources. By ensuring access to interpreters and translation services, hospitals can overcome language barriers, leading to better patient outcomes, higher satisfaction, and a more inclusive healthcare environment. This section of the chapter underscores the importance of clear communication in healthcare and provides practical advice for both healthcare providers and patients in navigating language challenges effectively.

Understanding Hospital Etiquette:

Navigating Cultural Norms and Practices in Hospital Settings

Hospital etiquette encompasses more than just manners; it involves understanding and adhering to the various cultural norms and practices that are prevalent in hospital settings across different countries and cultures. Recognizing these differences is crucial for patients, families, and healthcare providers to ensure a respectful and comfortable experience for everyone involved.

- **Global Differences in Hospital Etiquette:**
    - **Varied Visiting Hours and Policies:** Hospital visiting hours and policies on who can visit and when can differ significantly across countries. For instance, some hospitals may have more restrictive visiting hours compared to others that may offer more flexibility.
    - **Cultural Sensitivity in Interactions:** The way patients and healthcare providers interact can vary based on cultural norms. In some cultures, a more formal interaction style is preferred, while in others, a casual approach may be acceptable.

- **Expectations of Privacy:** Views on privacy and modesty in medical settings can differ, affecting everything from room sharing to the presence of family members during consultations.
- **Gift-Giving Practices:**
    - **Cultural Appropriateness:** In some cultures, it is common to bring gifts for healthcare providers or hospital staff as a gesture of gratitude, while in others, this may be frowned upon or even against hospital policy.
    - **Understanding Limits:** If gift-giving is customary, understanding what types of gifts are appropriate is important. Small, non-monetary tokens are generally more acceptable.
- **Dress Codes and Personal Conduct:**
    - **Appropriate Attire:** Some hospitals or cultures may have specific expectations regarding dress codes for visitors, which could range from modest clothing to specific hygiene-related apparel.
    - **Behaviour Within Hospital Premises:** Guidelines on behaviour, such as maintaining quiet in certain areas, using mobile phones, or eating and drinking, can vary and should be respected.
- **Religious and Spiritual Practices:**
    - **Accommodating Religious Needs:** Hospitals in multicultural settings often make provisions for religious and spiritual practices, including prayer rooms or chaplaincy services. Understanding how to access these facilities is important for patients and families.
- **Navigating Language and Communication:**

- **Communication Styles:** The preferred style of communication, whether direct or indirect, can vary culturally and impact interactions in hospital settings.
- **Language Assistance:** For non-native speakers, knowing how to access language assistance can be an important aspect of hospital etiquette.

Understanding and respecting hospital etiquette in different cultural and country contexts is a key component of a positive hospital experience. This section of the chapter provides insights into the diverse practices and norms associated with hospital visits around the world. By being aware of these differences, patients, families, and healthcare providers can foster a respectful, understanding, and comfortable environment for everyone involved in the healthcare process.

Preparing for Hospital Stays: Checklists and Tips:

1. What to Bring:

A well-prepared hospital bag can significantly enhance the comfort and ease of a hospital stay. Knowing what essential items to pack is crucial for ensuring that you have everything you need during your time in the hospital.

- **Essential Items Checklist:**
    - **Identification and Documentation:**
        - Personal identification (ID card, driver's license, or passport).
        - Health insurance information and cards.
        - Emergency contact information.

- Legal documents if applicable (e.g., advance directives, power of attorney).
  - **Medical Information:**
    - A list of current medications, including dosages and schedules.
    - Medical history, including any allergies and previous surgeries.
    - Contact information for your primary care doctor and any specialists.
  - **Medications:**
    - Prescribed medications in their original containers.
    - Over-the-counter medications you regularly use (e.g., pain relievers, antacids).
  - **Personal Care Items:**
    - Toiletries (toothbrush, toothpaste, deodorant, hairbrush, etc.).
    - Glasses, contact lenses with solution, or hearing aids with extra batteries.
    - Sanitary or incontinence products if needed.
  - **Clothing:**
    - Comfortable clothing, including pyjamas or a robe.
    - Non-slip slippers or comfortable shoes.
    - A lightweight sweater or jacket, as hospital rooms can be cool.
- **Comfort Items:**
  - **Entertainment and Relaxation:**
    - Books, magazines, or an e-reader.
    - Smartphone, tablet, or laptop with chargers.
    - Headphones or earbuds for listening to music or watching videos.
  - **Personal Touches:**
    - A small family photo, a comforting item like a pillow or a blanket.

- - Relaxation aids, such as a sleep mask, earplugs, or a small aromatherapy item (check hospital policy).
- **Additional Considerations:**
  - **Valuables:** It's advisable to leave valuables like jewellery and large amounts of cash at home.
  - **Snacks:** Non-perishable snacks, especially for patients with dietary preferences or restrictions (check with the hospital first).
  - **Childbirth:** For expecting mothers, additional items like a birthing plan, baby clothes, and infant car seat for the trip home.

Packing for a hospital stay requires thoughtful consideration of what you might need for both comfort and practicality. This checklist aims to cover the essentials and a few additional items to make your stay as comfortable as possible. Being well-prepared can help reduce stress and make your hospital experience more pleasant, allowing you to focus on your recovery and health.

Comfort Items for Hospital Stays:

While the primary focus of a hospital stay is medical care, personal comfort plays a significant role in the overall patient experience and can even impact recovery. Including comfort items in your hospital stay preparation can make a noticeable difference in your well-being during your time in the hospital.

- **Personalizing Your Space:**
  - **Photographs:** Bringing photographs of loved ones or favourite places can help personalize your hospital room and provide a sense of comfort and connection to your life outside the hospital.

- o **Favourite Blanket or Pillow:** A familiar blanket or pillow not only can make your hospital bed feel more comfortable but also provide a sense of home.
- **Entertainment and Relaxation:**
  - o **Books and Magazines:** Reading material can be a great way to pass the time and distract yourself from the hospital environment.
  - o **Music and Audio:** A playlist of your favourite music, audiobooks, or podcasts can be soothing and help to reduce stress. Don't forget to bring headphones to avoid disturbing others.
  - o **Puzzles and Games:** Crossword puzzles, sudoku, or small games can keep your mind engaged during your stay.
- **Stress-Relief Items:**
  - o **Stress Balls or Fidget Toys:** Items that you can fiddle with or squeeze can help manage anxiety or restlessness.
  - o **Aromatherapy:** Scented lotions or essential oil rollers (if allowed in the hospital) can provide a sense of relaxation. However, it's important to be considerate of any scent sensitivities of those around you.
- **Crafts and Hobbies:**
  - o **Knitting, Crocheting, or Drawing:** If you have a hobby that is easy to bring along, such as knitting or sketching, it can be a great way to keep occupied and feel productive.
- **Journaling:**
  - o **Notebook or Journal:** Writing about your hospital experience, thoughts, and feelings can be therapeutic and help process the experience.
- **Spiritual or Religious Items:**

- **Prayer Books or Religious Texts:** For those who find comfort in spirituality or religion, having a prayer book, rosary, or other spiritual items can be comforting during a hospital stay.

Comfort items play a crucial role in enhancing the hospital experience, providing emotional support, and promoting relaxation. They serve as a bridge between the hospital environment and the comforts of home, contributing positively to the patient's mental well-being. Incorporating these personal touches into your hospital preparation can make a significant difference in how you perceive and cope with your hospital stay.

Managing Logistics:

Arrangements for Home and Family Care

When planning for a hospital stay, managing the logistics of home and family care is as important as preparing for the medical aspects of the visit. Ensuring that everything at home is taken care of can provide peace of mind, allowing patients to focus on their health and recovery.

- **Arranging Family Care:**
    - **Children:** Arrange for childcare, whether it's with a partner, family member, friend, or a professional caregiver. Ensure they have a clear schedule of the children's routines, school or daycare details, and any special needs.
    - **Elderly Relatives:** If you are a caregiver for elderly relatives, arrange for someone to take over your responsibilities. Ensure that the temporary caregiver is

informed about medications, appointments, and daily routines.
- **Pet Care:**
    - **Pet Sitting:** Make arrangements for pets to be looked after, either by having someone stay at your home, placing pets with a family member or friend, or utilizing pet-sitting services.
    - **Care Instructions:** Provide detailed instructions on feeding, exercise routines, and any medication requirements for your pets.
- **Home Maintenance:**
    - **Security:** Ensure your home is secure during your absence. This might involve asking a neighbour to keep an eye on your house, setting up timed lighting systems, or ensuring all doors and windows are locked.
    - **Routine Tasks:** Arrange for routine tasks to be handled, such as lawn care, plant watering, mail collection, and garbage disposal.
- **Financial and Administrative Tasks:**
    - **Bill Payments:** Set up automatic payments for bills or arrange for someone to take care of any pending payments to avoid late fees.
    - **Important Documents:** Keep important documents (like insurance papers, medical documents, and legal paperwork) in an accessible and known location in case they are needed in your absence.
- **Communication Plan:**
    - **Staying in Touch:** Establish a plan for how and when you will communicate with family members during your hospital stay, especially if you have children who may need regular reassurance.
    - **Emergency Contacts:** Provide family members and caregivers with a list of emergency contacts, including

your doctors and someone who can make decisions on your behalf if needed.

Effectively managing the logistics of home and family care during a hospital stay is essential for minimizing stress and ensuring that your focus can be on recovery. By planning ahead and making comprehensive arrangements for children, elderly relatives, pets, and home maintenance, you can ensure that all aspects of your life are taken care of, allowing for a more peaceful and focused hospital experience.

Transportation and Accommodation Planning

Arranging transportation and accommodation is a critical aspect of hospital visit logistics, particularly for extended stays or when family members are involved. Adequate planning in these areas ensures smooth transitions to and from the hospital and provides comfort for both patients and their families.

- **Transportation Arrangements:**
    - **To and From the Hospital:** Plan how you will get to the hospital, especially if you are undergoing a procedure that prevents you from driving afterwards. Options may include asking a friend or family member to drive, using a taxi or rideshare service, or exploring any hospital-provided transportation services.
    - **Post-Procedure Transportation:** Post-surgery or treatment, you may require special transportation arrangements, particularly if you have mobility restrictions. Discuss these needs in advance with your healthcare provider.

- **Accommodation for Family Members:**
  - **Nearby Stays:** If family members are accompanying you and need to stay overnight, research nearby accommodation options such as hotels, motels, or guest houses. Some hospitals might have tie-ups with local hotels to provide discounted rates for patients' families.
  - **Hospital Facilities:** Inquire if the hospital offers any family-stay facilities or has partnerships with local accommodations for longer stays. Some hospitals may have family lounges or rest areas for short-term use.
- **Financial Considerations:**
  - **Budget Planning:** Consider the costs associated with transportation and accommodation in your budget planning. Look for cost-effective options and check if your insurance or any welfare organizations offer financial assistance for these expenses.
  - **Emergency Funds:** Keep some emergency funds or a credit card handy for unexpected transportation or accommodation costs.
- **Special Considerations for Non-Local Patients:**
  - **Traveling for Specialized Treatment:** If you are traveling to a non-local hospital for specialized treatment, the logistics can be more complex. Consider the broader aspects of long-distance travel, including air travel, long-term accommodation, and managing life away from home.
  - **Local Support Services:** Explore local support services or patient advocacy groups that can assist with accommodation and transportation needs in unfamiliar locations.

Careful planning of transportation and accommodation is a vital component of preparing for a hospital visit, particularly for those undergoing major procedures or with family members in attendance. By ensuring reliable transportation and comfortable accommodation for the duration of the hospital stay, patients and their families can alleviate additional stress, allowing them to focus on the primary concern of health and recovery. This section of the chapter provides practical advice and considerations to help in organizing these critical aspects of hospital visit logistics.

Medical and Health Information:

Organizing Essential Health Records

Properly organizing and having easy access to your medical and health information is crucial when preparing for a hospital stay. It ensures that healthcare providers have all the necessary details to offer the best possible care and make informed medical decisions.

- **Health Records:**
    - **Medical History:** Compile a comprehensive record of your medical history. This should include any chronic conditions, past illnesses, hospitalizations, and treatments you have received.
    - **List of Current Medications:** Maintain an up-to-date list of all medications you are taking, including prescriptions, over-the-counter drugs, and dietary supplements. Include dosages and frequency of use.
    - **Allergies:** Clearly document any allergies, particularly to medications, latex, or food, as this information is

critical for avoiding adverse reactions during your hospital stay.
- **Previous Surgeries:** Provide a list of any previous surgeries, including minor and major procedures, along with approximate dates. This information can be vital, especially if you are undergoing further surgical treatment.
- **Keeping Information Accessible:**
  - **Electronic Copies:** Consider keeping an electronic copy of your medical information on your smartphone or a portable USB drive. Many health apps and platforms also allow you to store and easily share this information.
  - **Hard Copies:** Have printed copies of your medical information, as they can be handy if electronic devices are not accessible or in areas with limited technology access.
- **Communication with Healthcare Providers:**
  - **Sharing Information:** Upon admission or during consultations, share your health records with your healthcare providers. Accurate and comprehensive information aids in diagnosing, planning, and providing appropriate care.
  - **Updates and Changes:** If there are any changes in your health or medication regimen close to your hospital visit, ensure that these are communicated to the healthcare team.
- **Advance Directives and Emergency Contacts:**
  - **Advance Directives:** If you have advance directives, such as a living will or healthcare proxy, bring copies to the hospital. These documents guide your care if you are unable to communicate your wishes.

- **Emergency Contacts:** Provide the hospital with a list of emergency contacts, including names, relationships, and contact information.

Organizing and providing easy access to your medical and health information is a vital step in preparing for a hospital stay. It empowers healthcare providers with the knowledge needed to offer personalized and effective care and ensures that your health needs are comprehensively addressed. This section of the chapter guides patients on how to efficiently compile and share their health records, enhancing communication with healthcare providers and contributing to a more streamlined and effective hospital experience.

Questions for Healthcare Providers:

Effectively communicating with healthcare providers is a key part of any hospital stay. Preparing a list of questions or concerns in advance can ensure that important aspects of your care are addressed and can help you feel more informed and involved in your healthcare decisions.

- **Developing a Question List:**
  - **Understanding Your Condition:** Prepare questions that help you understand your diagnosis, the nature of your illness or condition, and its potential causes.
  - **Treatment Options:** Ask about the different treatment options available, including their benefits, risks, and potential side effects.
  - **Procedure Details:** If you are undergoing a procedure or surgery, inquire about what it entails, the preparation required, the recovery process, and any associated risks.

- **Medication Inquiries:**
  - **Prescriptions and Uses:** For any new medications prescribed, ask about their purpose, how they should be taken, and possible side effects.
  - **Interactions with Current Medications:** Discuss how new medications might interact with your current medication regimen.
- **Managing Your Care:**
  - **Post-Hospitalization Care:** Ask about what care, follow-up appointments, or rehabilitation will be needed after you leave the hospital.
  - **Lifestyle Changes:** Inquire about any lifestyle changes that you might need to make for better management of your condition, including diet, exercise, and activity restrictions.
- **Concerns About Hospital Stay:**
  - **Daily Routine:** Ask about the daily routine in the hospital, including meals, tests, and visiting hours.
  - **Patient Services:** Inquire about available patient services, such as support groups, patient education classes, or spiritual care services.
- **Emergency Situations:**
  - **Emergency Protocols:** Understand what steps will be taken in case of an emergency or unexpected turn in your condition and who will be the point of contact.
- **Insurance and Financial Questions:**
  - **Coverage and Costs:** If applicable, ask about how your insurance coverage will be coordinated and about any out-of-pocket costs you may expect.
- **Documenting Answers:**
  - **Taking Notes:** Consider taking notes during discussions with your healthcare providers or asking a

family member to do so. This can be helpful in keeping track of important information and instructions.

Having a prepared list of questions for healthcare providers can greatly enhance the effectiveness of communication during your hospital stay and empower you to make informed decisions about your care. It can also alleviate anxiety by providing clarity on what to expect and how best to manage your health. This section of the chapter equips patients with the tools to actively engage in discussions with their healthcare team, ensuring a more informed and comfortable hospital experience.

Post-Hospitalization Care:

Navigating the Discharge Process and Aftercare

The period following a hospital stay is critical for recovery and long-term health. Understanding the discharge process and having a clear plan for post-hospitalization care are essential to ensure a smooth transition from the hospital to home and to prevent complications or readmission.

- **Discharge Planning:**
    - **Understanding the Process:** Familiarize yourself with the hospital's discharge process. This typically involves discussions with your healthcare team about your progress and readiness to leave the hospital.
    - **Coordination of Care:** Ensure that there is a coordinated plan involving your primary care physician or specialists for ongoing care after discharge.
    -

Fast-Track A&E

- **Follow-Up Care:**
  - **Scheduling Appointments:** Before leaving the hospital, make sure you have scheduled any necessary follow-up appointments with your primary care provider or specialists.
  - **Continuity of Care:** Communicate with your healthcare providers about any changes in medication or care plans to ensure continuity of care.
- **Medication Management:**
  - **Understanding New Medications:** Obtain clear instructions about any new medications prescribed, including dosage, frequency, and potential side effects.
  - **Reconciling Medications:** Review your pre-hospitalization medications with your healthcare provider to determine which should be continued, adjusted, or discontinued.
- **Home Care Instructions:**
  - **Recovery Guidelines:** Get detailed instructions on activities, dietary restrictions, wound care, signs of complications, and other specific guidelines pertinent to your recovery.
  - **Support Systems:** Identify who in your personal network can assist with your care at home, including help with daily activities, transportation, and attending follow-up appointments.
- **Rehabilitation Needs:**
  - **Therapy and Rehabilitation:** If required, arrange for physical therapy, occupational therapy, or other rehabilitation services.
  - **Home Adaptations:** Prepare your home environment as needed, such as installing safety rails or arranging a comfortable and accessible recovery space.

- **Understanding and Managing Symptoms:**
  - **Recognizing Warning Signs:** Be clear about which symptoms or changes in condition should prompt immediate medical attention.
  - **Self-Care Strategies:** Learn self-care strategies to manage symptoms and promote healing.
- **Insurance and Financial Considerations:**
  - **Insurance Claims:** Understand the process for filing insurance claims for post-hospitalization care and keep track of all related documentation.
  - **Coverage for Aftercare Services:** Verify what aftercare services are covered by your insurance and any associated costs.

Effective post-hospitalization care is a vital component of the recovery process, requiring careful planning and coordination. By understanding and actively participating in the discharge process and aftercare planning, patients can ensure a smoother transition to home care, reduce the risk of complications, and enhance their overall recovery. This section of the chapter provides a comprehensive guide to the various aspects of post-hospitalization care, empowering patients to take charge of their recovery journey.

Support and Resources for Post-Hospitalization Care:

Recovery and rehabilitation after a hospital stay can be a challenging phase, and having the right support systems and resources in place is crucial for a successful and smooth recovery. Identifying and leveraging these supports can significantly impact the effectiveness and comfort of the post-hospital care period.

- **Identifying Personal Support Systems:**
  - **Family and Friends:** Engage a network of family and friends who can provide emotional and practical support, such as assistance with daily activities, transportation to appointments, or help with household chores.
  - **Community Resources:** Explore community resources such as local support groups, senior canters, or charitable organizations that offer services and support for people recovering from illness or surgery.
- **Professional Home Healthcare Services:**
  - **Nursing Care:** For those requiring medical attention at home, professional home healthcare services can provide nursing care, wound care, or assistance with medications.
  - **Therapeutic Services:** Access to professional physical therapy, occupational therapy, or speech therapy at home can be arranged if needed for rehabilitation.
- **Social and Emotional Support:**
  - **Counselling Services:** Consider seeking counselling or therapy if you're coping with emotional stress or mental health concerns following your hospitalization.
  - **Online Support Groups:** Online forums and support groups can offer a platform to connect with others who have undergone similar experiences, providing a sense of community and shared understanding.
- **Financial and Insurance Assistance:**
  - **Navigating Insurance Benefits:** Seek assistance from insurance advisors or hospital financial counsellors to understand benefits related to post-hospitalization care.
  - **Financial Aid and Assistance Programs:** Research available financial aid programs, particularly if you

face high medical bills or require services not covered by insurance.
- **Patient Advocacy Services:**
    - **Advocacy and Navigation:** Patient advocates can help navigate complex healthcare systems, assist in coordinating care, and provide support in decision-making processes.
    - **Healthcare System Navigation:** Utilize resources provided by the hospital, such as patient navigators or care coordinators, to assist with scheduling follow-up appointments and connecting with necessary healthcare services.
- **Recovery and Wellness Resources:**
    - **Wellness Programs:** Participate in wellness programs focused on nutrition, exercise, and lifestyle modifications to aid in your recovery.
    - **Educational Resources:** Utilize educational materials and resources provided by the hospital or healthcare providers to better understand and manage your condition.

Having a robust support system and access to various resources can significantly enhance the recovery process following a hospital stay. By identifying and utilizing these supports, from personal networks to professional services and community resources, patients can navigate the post-hospitalization period more effectively, ensuring a more comfortable and successful return to daily life. This section of the chapter is dedicated to outlining the various types of support and resources available, guiding patients in assembling a comprehensive support system for their post-hospital care needs.

Chapter 10:

Mindset and Emotional Resilience

Embracing Positivity and Strength in the Face of Health Challenges

In "Mindset and Emotional Resilience," the tenth chapter of this enlightening journey through healthcare and wellness, we turn our focus inward to the power of the human spirit. Health challenges often test not just our physical endurance but also our mental and emotional fortitude. This chapter is dedicated to exploring and strengthening that often-overlooked aspect of healthcare – the resilience of the mind and heart.

Navigating the complex world of healthcare, managing chronic conditions, or facing acute health crises can be daunting. It can stir a myriad of emotions, from fear and anxiety to a sense of isolation or loss of control. How we mentally and emotionally respond to these challenges can profoundly impact our overall well-being and recovery process. This chapter serves as a comprehensive guide to cultivating a resilient mindset, offering practical strategies for managing health-related stress and anxiety.

We understand that resilience is not a journey taken alone. Hence, we also delve into inspirational stories from around the globe – tales of courage, perseverance, and triumph that remind us of the strength that lies in the human spirit. These stories are not just narratives; they are beacons of hope, teaching us invaluable lessons about facing adversities with grace and determination.

Moreover, this chapter underscores the importance of community and support networks in our health journey. Building a circle of support – whether through family, friends, healthcare providers, or support groups – is instrumental in navigating health challenges. We provide tips and insights on creating and nurturing these support systems, emphasizing the role they play in bolstering our emotional and mental health.

In essence, "Mindset and Emotional Resilience" is more than just a chapter; it's a companion in your health journey, guiding you through the emotional landscapes of healthcare and encouraging you to foster inner strength and positivity. It's a testament to the power of a resilient mindset and the importance of a supportive community in overcoming health challenges.

Managing Health-Related Stress and Anxiety:

Harnessing Mindfulness and Relaxation Techniques

One of the most effective ways to manage the stress and anxiety that often accompany health challenges is through mindfulness and relaxation techniques. This section of the chapter introduces several such practices, each designed to help calm the mind, reduce stress, and foster a sense of well-being.

- **Mindfulness Meditation:**
    - **Cultivating Awareness:** Mindfulness meditation focuses on cultivating a non-judgmental awareness of the present moment. It involves observing thoughts, feelings, and sensations as they arise, without getting caught up in them.
    - **Technique and Practice:** The practice can be as simple as sitting quietly and focusing on your breath. When

your attention wanders, gently bring it back to your breath. Regular practice, even for a few minutes a day, can significantly reduce anxiety and improve emotional stability.
- **Deep Breathing Exercises:**
  - **Calming the Nervous System:** Deep breathing is a quick and effective way to trigger the body's relaxation response. It involves taking slow, deep breaths, which can help lower heart rate and blood pressure.
  - **Various Techniques:** There are several techniques, such as diaphragmatic breathing, 4-7-8 breathing, or box breathing. These exercises can be practiced almost anywhere and at any time to relieve stress.
- **Progressive Muscle Relaxation (PMR):**
  - **Releasing Muscle Tension:** PMR is a technique that involves tensing and then relaxing different muscle groups in the body. This helps in identifying and releasing physical tension that often accompanies stress.
  - **Step-by-Step Approach:** Starting from one end of the body (like the toes) and gradually moving to the other end (like the head), tense each muscle group for a few seconds, then relax. The contrast between tension and relaxation helps to highlight and relieve muscle tightness.

Each of these techniques offers a unique approach to managing stress and anxiety and can be particularly beneficial in the context of health challenges. They empower individuals to take an active role in managing their emotional well-being, complementing the medical aspects of their healthcare journey.

Cognitive Behavioural Strategies:

Reframing Thoughts for a Positive Outlook

Cognitive Behavioural Therapy (CBT) offers a practical approach to managing the psychological challenges that often accompany health issues. This section explores how cognitive-behavioural strategies can be used to reframe negative thoughts, leading to a more positive and proactive outlook during health challenges.

- **Understanding Cognitive Behavioural Techniques:**
    - **Principle of CBT:** CBT is based on the concept that our thoughts, feelings, and behaviours are interconnected, and that altering one can change the others. It focuses on identifying and challenging negative thought patterns to bring about positive changes in feelings and behaviour.
    - **Self-Awareness:** The first step in CBT is becoming aware of one's negative thoughts and understanding how they affect emotions and behaviour.
- **Reframing Negative Thoughts:**
    - **Identifying Distorted Thinking:** Common cognitive distortions in health-related stress include catastrophic thinking (expecting the worst), overgeneralization (viewing a single event as a constant pattern), and personalization (blaming oneself unfairly).
    - **Challenging and Replacing Thoughts:** Once identified, these distorted thoughts can be challenged and replaced with more balanced and realistic thoughts.

- **Maintaining a Positive Outlook:**
  - **Focus on What Can Be Controlled:** Instead of fixating on aspects of health that are out of one's control, CBT encourages focusing on actions and thoughts that can be controlled, such as adhering to treatment plans or maintaining a healthy lifestyle.
  - **Positive Affirmations:** Using positive affirmations can help in reinforcing a positive self-image and outlook.
- **Behavioural Activation:**
  - **Engaging in Positive Activities:** CBT promotes engaging in activities that bring joy and satisfaction, which can improve mood and overall well-being.
  - **Setting Achievable Goals:** Setting small, achievable goals can provide a sense of accomplishment and purpose.
- **Journaling and Thought Records:**
  - **Keeping a Thought Diary:** Recording thoughts, emotions, and the situations in which they occur can help in identifying patterns and triggers of negative thinking.
  - **Problem-Solving:** Developing problem-solving skills to deal with challenging situations more effectively.

Cognitive-behavioural strategies offer powerful tools for individuals facing health challenges, enabling them to manage their mental and emotional well-being actively. By learning to reframe negative thoughts and engage in positive behaviours, patients can cultivate resilience and maintain a positive outlook through their health journeys.

Inspirational Global Stories of Resilience:

Global Tapestry of Courage:

Celebrating Resilience Across Cultures and Challenges

In the "Global Tapestry of Courage" section, we weave together a rich mosaic of stories that highlight the universal nature of resilience. These narratives span across continents, cultures, and ages, showcasing how individuals from various backgrounds confront and overcome their health challenges.

- **Diversity in Resilience:**
    - **Cultural Richness:** From the bustling streets of major cities to the quiet corners of rural villages, these stories bring forth experiences from every corner of the globe, reflecting a wide array of cultural backgrounds.
    - **Age and Experience:** The accounts range from young children facing life-altering diagnoses to elderly individuals battling chronic conditions, proving that resilience knows no age limit.
- **Health Challenges of Varied Nature:**
    - **Chronic Illness Warriors:** Stories include individuals managing long-term conditions like diabetes, heart disease, or autoimmune disorders, showcasing their daily battles and victories.
    - **Overcoming Acute Illness:** Narratives also highlight those who have faced acute medical crises, such as battling cancer, recovering from a serious injury, or undergoing major surgery, and their journey to recovery.
- **Universal Themes:**

- **Strength in Adversity:** These stories are bound by common themes of courage, determination, and the relentless pursuit of well-being, despite the odds.
  - **Shared Human Experience:** They remind us that while our struggles may be unique, the courage we muster in facing them is a shared human experience.
- **Inspiration Across Borders:**
  - **Global Resilience:** These accounts transcend geographical and cultural boundaries, offering universal lessons of hope and strength.
  - **Connectivity and Empathy:** They foster a sense of connectivity, as readers may find echoes of their own experiences in these stories, building empathy and understanding across diverse populations.

The "Global Tapestry of Courage" is a testament to the indomitable human spirit that unites us in our quest for health and happiness. By sharing these diverse and powerful stories of resilience, this section aims to inspire readers, offering them not just a glimpse into the lives of others, but also a mirror reflecting their own potential for courage and resilience in the face of health challenges.

Personal Journeys:

Intimate Narratives of Overcoming Health Adversities

In the section on "Personal Journeys," the focus shifts to the intimate, individual experiences of those who have navigated their way through health crises. These stories delve deep into the personal lives of individuals, revealing not just the challenges they faced but also their journey of overcoming and thriving amidst adversity.

- **Facing the Health Crisis:**
    - **Initial Reactions and Challenges:** Each story begins with the onset of the health crisis, capturing the initial reactions – shock, denial, fear – and the early challenges faced. This part of the narrative sets the stage for understanding the magnitude of the struggle everyone has encountered.
    - **The Diagnosis:** Descriptions of how each person received their diagnosis and the immediate impact it had on their life, both practically and emotionally.
- **Obstacles Overcome:**
    - **Physical and Emotional Hurdles:** The narratives detail the various obstacles encountered, from navigating complex medical treatments to coping with physical limitations and emotional turmoil.
    - **Social and Financial Barriers:** Many stories also touch upon the social and financial barriers that come with health challenges, such as dealing with societal stigma or managing the cost of care.
- **Coping and Thriving Strategies:**
    - **Finding Strength:** The heart of each story lies in the strategies and sources of strength that individuals tapped into. This might include turning to family and community support, finding solace in faith or spirituality, or drawing upon inner resilience.
    - **Adaptive Tactics:** Details of adaptive tactics employed, such as lifestyle changes, therapeutic approaches, or embracing new hobbies and interests that aid in coping and recovery.
- **Turning Points and Insights:**
    - **Moments of Realization:** Many stories feature pivotal moments or realizations that played a crucial role in

the individual's journey – a turning point that marked a shift in perspective or approach.
    - **Lessons Learned:** Insights and lessons gleaned from the experience, offering valuable takeaways for the readers.
- **Journey to Thriving:**
    - **Overcoming Adversity:** The culmination of each narrative is about overcoming adversity – not just surviving the health crisis but finding ways to thrive in its aftermath.
    - **New Perspectives:** Many individuals emerge with new perspectives on life, often with a renewed sense of purpose or a desire to help others facing similar challenges.

"Personal Journeys" is a profound section that brings to life the human side of health adversities. Through these intimate stories, readers are invited to witness the resilience, courage, and transformation of individuals who have faced their darkest hours and emerged stronger. These narratives serve as powerful reminders of the human capacity for endurance and hope, providing inspiration and practical strategies for anyone navigating their health journey.

Lessons in Resilience:

Finding Fulfilment Beyond Chronic Illness

The "Lessons in Resilience" section shines a light on the lives of individuals who have not only faced chronic illness but have also carved paths to fulfilling lives despite their ongoing health challenges. These stories are a testament to the human spirit's ability to adapt, overcome, and find joy and purpose in the face of long-term health adversities.

- **Living with Chronic Disease:**
  - **Everyday Heroes:** The narratives feature individuals from various walks of life who live with chronic diseases such as diabetes, arthritis, multiple sclerosis, or mental health conditions.
  - **Journey of Acceptance:** These stories often start with the initial diagnosis and the process of coming to terms with the reality of living with a chronic condition.
- **Adaptive Lifestyles:**
  - **Lifestyle Modifications:** Insights into how individuals have adapted their lifestyles to manage their conditions effectively, including changes in diet, exercise, and daily routines.
  - **Holistic Approaches:** Many find strength in adopting holistic approaches, incorporating practices like mindfulness, yoga, or alternative therapies into their management plans.
- **Empowerment Through Knowledge:**
  - **Self-Education:** A common theme is the empowerment that comes from self-education about their conditions, leading to better self-management and advocacy in healthcare settings.
  - **Community Engagement:** Involvement in support groups or online communities where experiences and tips are shared is often highlighted as a key component of living well with chronic illness.
- **Embracing New Challenges:**
  - **Pursuing Passions:** Stories often reveal how individuals rediscover or find new passions and

hobbies that accommodate and even enrich their lives amidst their health challenges.
  - **Career and Personal Goals:** Despite limitations, many individuals find ways to continue or adapt their careers or pursue new personal goals that bring fulfilment.

- **Giving Back:**
  - **Mentorship and Advocacy:** Many individuals become mentors or advocates for others living with similar conditions, finding purpose in helping others navigate their health journeys.
  - **Raising Awareness:** Actively participating in awareness campaigns and community events to educate and inspire others.

"Lessons in Resilience" in the context of chronic illness is not just about survival; it's about thriving. These stories offer valuable lessons on adapting to and managing life with a chronic condition, demonstrating that a fulfilling life is possible and attainable. They serve as powerful examples of resilience, hope, and the endless potential of the human spirit to rise above challenges.

Battling Acute Conditions:

Resilience Through the Storm of Sudden Illness

In this segment, we explore the compelling accounts of individuals who have faced acute health conditions. These narratives provide a window into their struggles and victories, offering insights into their journey through diagnosis, treatment, recovery, and the often transformative experiences that reshape their perspectives on life.

- **Facing Sudden Health Crises:**
    - **Initial Shock and Response:** Each story typically begins with the sudden onset of an acute health condition, such as a heart attack, stroke, or a severe injury, and captures the initial shock and urgent response that follows.
    - **Navigating the Healthcare System:** Accounts often detail the challenges of navigating emergency care, the complexities of receiving a diagnosis under pressure, and the whirlwind of starting immediate treatment.
- **Journey Through Treatment:**
    - **Medical Interventions:** Descriptions of the treatments undertaken, from surgeries to intensive therapies, and the physical and emotional toll of these interventions.
    - **Role of Healthcare Professionals:** Many stories highlight the crucial role played by doctors, nurses, and other healthcare professionals in managing the crisis and providing care.
- **Recovery and Rehabilitation:**
    - **Challenges of Rehabilitation:** The road to recovery is often fraught with challenges. Narratives typically share the hurdles faced during rehabilitation, whether relearning basic skills or coping with lasting impacts of the condition.
    - **Personal Determination:** A common thread is the determination and grit displayed in the face of daunting rehabilitation processes.
- **Newfound Perspectives:**

- **Life After the Crisis:** Many individuals emerge from their acute health crisis with a changed outlook on life. Stories often reflect on the lessons learned and how the experience has led to a newfound appreciation for life.
- **Shifts in Priorities:** Accounts frequently include shifts in personal priorities, whether it's fostering deeper relationships, pursuing new interests, or making significant lifestyle changes.
- **Inspiration and Motivation:**
  - **Resilience in Action:** These stories serve as profound examples of resilience in the face of unexpected health crises, inspiring others who might find themselves in similar situations.
  - **Sharing Hope:** Beyond their personal journey, these narratives often extend hope and motivation to others, showing that recovery and a fulfilling life post-crisis are possible.

The "Battling Acute Conditions" section is a tribute to the resilience and strength of individuals who have faced sudden and severe health challenges. Their stories are not just personal triumphs; they are beacons of hope and inspiration, offering valuable insights into the human capacity to overcome, adapt, and find new meaning in life after an acute health crisis.

Sources of Inspiration:

Embracing Role Models in Health Journeys

In the "Sources of Inspiration" section, we highlight the profound impact of role models – individuals who have turned their health adversities into opportunities for remarkable personal growth and transformation. These stories are not just about enduring hardships; they are about emerging stronger and becoming beacons of hope and guidance for others.

- **Role Models in Health Challenges:**
  - **Embodying Resilience:** The individuals featured in these narratives embody resilience and determination. Their journeys illustrate how facing health challenges head-on can lead to profound personal development.
  - **Diverse Backgrounds:** These role models come from various backgrounds, each bringing unique insights into how they navigated their health crises and turned them into opportunities for growth.
- **Lessons in Transformation:**
  - **Growth Beyond Recovery:** The stories show that recovery from a health issue can be more than just a return to normalcy; it can be a transformative experience that reshapes one's perspective on life, relationships, and personal goals.
  - **Finding Purpose:** Many individuals find new purpose after their health challenges, whether it's through advocacy, volunteerism, or simply by sharing their stories to inspire and help others.
- **Inspiring Resilience in Others:**
  - **Motivating Change:** By sharing their experiences, these role models motivate others to embrace change and find strength in their struggles.
  - **Encouraging Proactive Health Management:** They often become advocates for proactive health

management, encouraging others to take charge of their health and well-being.
- **Shared Experiences, Universal Lessons:**
  - **Common Threads:** Despite the diversity of their stories, common threads emerge – resilience, the power of a positive mindset, and the importance of support networks.
  - **Universal Lessons:** These narratives offer universal lessons on the human capacity to adapt and grow, regardless of the nature of the health challenge.

The "Sources of Inspiration" section celebrates the role models who demonstrate that health adversities can indeed be the starting points for remarkable journeys of personal growth and transformation. Their stories serve as powerful reminders of the resilience inherent in each of us and the potential for positive change even in the most challenging circumstances. Through their experiences, we find inspiration, motivation, and the courage to face our health challenges with hope and determination.

Shared Wisdom:

Applying Lessons of Resilience to Personal Challenges

The "Shared Wisdom" portion of the chapter is a vital culmination of the collective experiences and insights garnered from the stories of resilience. It distils the essence of what these individuals have learned through their health journeys and offers it as a guide for readers. This wisdom is not limited to those facing health challenges but extends to anyone navigating life's obstacles.

- **Practical Strategies for Life's Challenges:**
  - **Adapting to Adversity:** The section highlights practical strategies these role models used to adapt to their adversities, offering readers applicable methods for handling their own difficulties.
  - **Problem-Solving Techniques:** It includes insights into effective problem-solving techniques that were pivotal in managing health crises and can be equally effective in other life challenges.
- **Universal Insights:**
  - **Maintaining Hope and Positivity:** A key aspect of shared wisdom is maintaining hope and a positive outlook, even in the face of daunting challenges. The stories provide real-life examples of how this perspective can alter outcomes.
  - **Importance of Self-Care:** Emphasizing the importance of self-care, the narratives illustrate how taking care of one's physical, mental, and emotional health is integral to overcoming life's hurdles.
- **Building and Leveraging Support Systems:**
  - **Seeking and Accepting Help:** A common theme is the importance of building a support system – recognizing when to seek help and how to leverage this support effectively.
  - **Community and Connection:** The stories underscore the power of community and connection, highlighting how shared experiences can foster resilience.
- **Personal Growth and Development:**
  - **Learning from Experience:** The section focuses on how personal growth often stems from challenges, with insights on learning from experience and using adversity as a catalyst for personal development.

- **Embracing Change:** Tips on embracing change and the transformative power it holds are derived from the experiences shared by these role models.

"Shared Wisdom" in this chapter serves as a repository of collective insights, offering readers a wealth of practical strategies and universal truths. These are more than just stories; they are lessons in resilience, hope, and the human capacity for growth and transformation. Whether facing health issues or other life challenges, readers can draw upon this shared wisdom to navigate their paths with greater strength and clarity.

Global Connectivity:

Uniting Through Shared Experiences of Resilience

In "Global Connectivity," the focus shifts to the universal nature of the human experience, particularly in overcoming adversity. This section underscores that, regardless of geographic location or cultural background, the challenges we face and our resilience in overcoming them are threads that bind us together globally.

- **The Universal Language of Resilience:**
    - **Shared Human Experiences:** The stories presented in this section transcend cultural and geographical boundaries, highlighting that the experience of overcoming adversity is a shared human trait.
    - **Common Emotional Ground:** Despite diverse backgrounds, there is a common emotional ground found in the experiences of struggle, perseverance, and triumph, which resonates universally.

- **Learning from Global Narratives:**
  - **Diverse Perspectives on Resilience:** By exploring stories from various parts of the world, readers gain a broader perspective on resilience, learning from the diverse ways people cope with and overcome challenges.
  - **Inspiration Across Borders:** These narratives provide inspiration and wisdom that can be applied universally, offering comfort and guidance to people, no matter where they are in the world.
- **Connecting Through Stories:**
  - **Empathy and Understanding:** The power of these stories lies in their ability to foster empathy and understanding, creating a sense of connection among people who might otherwise feel isolated in their struggles.
  - **Shared Strength:** Recognizing the shared nature of overcoming challenges helps to reinforce the idea that we are not alone in our journeys, and there is strength to be found in our collective experiences.
- **A Tapestry of Human Endurance:**
  - **Cultural Richness and Commonality:** These stories weave a rich tapestry that not only celebrates cultural richness but also highlights our commonalities in facing and surmounting life's adversities.
  - **Global Community of Resilience:** They contribute to a sense of a global community united by resilience, fostering a feeling of belonging and solidarity among those facing health challenges.

"Global Connectivity" in this chapter is a profound reminder that the challenges we face in health and life, and our capacity to overcome them, are experiences that connect us all, regardless of where we are in the world. This section is a celebration of the human spirit's ability to endure and triumph, serving as a bridge that connects individuals across the globe through shared narratives of resilience and strength.

Building a Supportive Community or Network:

Strengthening Connections for Resilience and Recovery

In the journey of health and healing, the role of a supportive community or network cannot be overstated. "Building a Supportive Community or Network" is a section dedicated to guiding individuals on how to establish and leverage a network of support, encompassing family, friends, support groups, and online communities.

- **Leveraging Social Support:**
    - **Identifying Your Support Circle:** Start by identifying who in your circle – family, friends, colleagues – can provide emotional, informational, or practical support. Remember, support can come in different forms and from various sources.
    - **Engaging with Family and Friends:** Open communication with family and friends is key. Share your needs and challenges with them and let them know how they can support you. Sometimes, just having someone to talk to can make a significant difference.
    -

- **Finding and Joining Support Groups:**
  - **Seeking Shared Experiences:** Support groups provide a platform for connecting with others who are going through similar health challenges. These groups offer a sense of community, shared understanding, and valuable insights from peers.
  - **Local and Online Groups:** Explore both local support groups and online forums. While local groups offer face-to-face interaction, online groups can provide accessibility and a wider range of perspectives.
- **Utilizing Online Communities:**
  - **Digital Platforms for Support:** Social media platforms and online health forums can be excellent resources for finding support, advice, and encouragement. They can also offer anonymity and convenience, which might be preferable for some.
  - **Staying Informed and Connected:** Online communities can keep you informed about the latest in health care and provide a space to share experiences and coping strategies.
- **Maintaining and Nurturing Relationships:**
  - **Regular Check-ins:** Keep in touch regularly with your support network. Whether it's through phone calls, messages, or in-person meetings, regular interaction helps maintain and strengthen these relationships.
  - **Reciprocating Support:** Remember that support is a two-way street. Be there for your support network as they are there for you, fostering a nurturing and mutually beneficial environment.

Building and leveraging a support network is fundamental to navigating health challenges. This section provides practical tips on how to cultivate and maintain a strong network of support, highlighting the immense value of shared experiences, empathy, and mutual aid. A well-established support system not only offers practical assistance and emotional comfort but also plays a crucial role in enhancing resilience and promoting recovery.

Engaging with Healthcare Providers:

Fostering Communication and Partnership for Better Care

Effective engagement with healthcare providers is an essential aspect of building a support system within the medical community. This section focuses on encouraging patients to establish a collaborative and communicative relationship with their healthcare team, which is crucial for receiving optimal care and support.

- **Open and Honest Communication:**
    - **Expressing Concerns and Needs:** Encourage patients to be open and honest in communicating their concerns, symptoms, and needs to their healthcare providers. Clear communication can lead to more accurate diagnoses and effective treatment plans.
    - **Asking Questions:** Urge patients to ask questions about their conditions, treatments, and any other medical concerns. Understanding their health situation empowers them to make informed decisions.
- **Active Participation in Care:**
    - **Informed Decision Making:** Patients should be active participants in their care. This includes being informed about treatment options and participating in decision-making processes.

- o **Feedback and Follow-Ups:** Encourage patients to provide feedback about their treatment and to adhere to follow-up schedules, ensuring continuity and effectiveness of care.
- **Building Trust and Rapport:**
  - o **Consistent Communication:** Building a rapport with healthcare providers is facilitated by consistent communication. Encourage patients to see the same doctors and nurses when possible to foster familiarity and trust.
  - o **Respect and Understanding:** Mutual respect and understanding between patients and healthcare providers are key to building a strong relationship.
- **Leveraging the Healthcare Team:**
  - o **Multi-Disciplinary Approach:** Remind patients that their healthcare team might consist of various specialists, nurses, therapists, and pharmacists. Engaging with the entire team can provide comprehensive support.
  - o **Utilizing Resources:** Healthcare providers can offer or recommend additional resources such as patient education materials, support groups, or referral to specialists.
- **Advocacy and Self-Representation:**
  - o **Self-Advocacy:** Encourage patients to advocate for themselves, expressing their preferences and concerns. If necessary, they can bring a family member or friend to appointments for support.
  - o **Understanding Patient Rights:** Patients should be aware of their rights in the healthcare system, including the right to second opinions and to access their medical records.

Fast-Track A&E

Engaging effectively with healthcare providers is not just about receiving medical care; it's about building a partnership that supports the patient's overall health journey. This section provides strategies for patients to enhance communication and engagement with their healthcare team, emphasizing the importance of active participation, mutual respect, and informed decision-making in the pursuit of optimal health outcomes.

PART 2

PRACTICAL TIPS FOR BEATING A&E QUEUES

Chapter 1

When Health Challenges Arise

Fast-Track A&E

Introduction:

Welcome to Part Two, where theory transforms into action, and knowledge becomes your tool for navigating the often unpredictable waters of Accident and Emergency (A&E) services and hospitals. In this section, you're invited to dive into a compendium of practical tips and strategies, meticulously curated to empower you to potentially bypass A&E queues altogether.

Each chapter in this segment is a stepping stone towards a more informed, prepared, and proactive approach to your healthcare journey. From understanding when to call an ambulance, to recognizing symptoms that warrant immediate medical attention, these chapters are designed to offer clear, actionable advice.

The objective here is straightforward yet profound: to equip you with the wisdom to discern when A&E is essential and when alternative paths can be taken. By implementing these strategies, you not only alleviate the pressure on emergency services but also embrace a more efficient, less stressful healthcare experience for yourself.

In an ideal scenario, the knowledge from Part One combined with the practical tips in Part Two will enable you to effectively 'fast-track' your A&E experiences by avoiding unnecessary visits. This isn't just about skipping queues; it's about embracing a smarter, more efficient approach to managing health emergencies.

So, as you turn these pages, envision yourself as the captain of your health journey, armed with the insights and tactics to navigate swiftly and smoothly. Remember, the most efficient A&E visit could be the one you never had to make. Let's begin.

15 Strategies to Minimize Unnecessary A&E Visits

1. Basic First Aid Skills:

Learn how to manage minor injuries at home, such as treating minor cuts or nosebleeds, to avoid unnecessary A&E visits.

2. Timely GP Appointments:

Schedule regular appointments with your general practitioner (GP) for ongoing health issues. Avoid waiting until the weekend or when the situation worsens.

3. Proactive Health Monitoring:

Book an appointment with your GP as soon as you notice a change in your symptoms. Early intervention can prevent conditions from escalating.

4. Balanced Nutrition:

Adequate hydration and a diet rich in fiber can prevent common issues like constipation and dehydration, reducing the need for emergency care.

5. Establish Health Routines:

Create routines for critical health-related activities, like bowel movements. A change in routine can be an early sign to seek medical advice.

6. Regular Exercise:

Incorporate physical activity into your daily routine to prevent musculoskeletal pain. Even simple activities like stretching or walking can be beneficial.

7. Moderate Social Habits:

Limit smoking, alcohol, and recreational drug use. Excess in these areas is a frequent cause of A&E visits, especially among young adults.

8. Use Self-Referral Systems:

In many healthcare systems, you can directly refer yourself to specialists. Utilize these services early when health issues arise.

9. Assess the Urgency:

Before heading to A&E, evaluate the severity of your situation. Consider if alternative care, such as a local clinic or a future appointment, might be more appropriate.

10. Seek Expert Advice When Unsure:

In the UK, call 111 for guidance on whether your condition warrants an A&E visit. In other countries, consult a healthcare hotline or a primary care provider.

11. Stay Hydrated and Eat Healthily:

Regular intake of water and fruits is essential for maintaining bodily functions and preventing dehydration-related issues.

Fast-Track A&E

12. Maintain Regular Sleep Patterns:

Adequate and consistent sleep is crucial for overall health. Adjust your sleep based on your activity level and personal needs.

13. Understand Your Medical Conditions:

If you have a chronic illness, be well-informed about your symptoms and required actions, especially for potentially urgent situations.

14. Develop Physical and Mental Resilience:

A strong mindset can enhance your body's ability to resist and recover from illnesses. Cultivate positive thoughts and attitudes towards your health.

15. Use Health Services Responsibly:

Avoid using healthcare services as an escape from work or personal responsibilities. Seek counseling or support if you find yourself misusing medical resources.

Implementing these strategies can significantly reduce unnecessary A&E visits, allowing emergency services to focus on genuine emergencies and improving the efficiency of healthcare resources.

10 Habits for Avoiding The Emergency Room

1. Embrace an Active Lifestyle:

Engaging in regular physical activity, whether it's sports, walking, or even gardening, helps maintain cardiovascular health, manage weight, and reduce the risk of chronic diseases. An active lifestyle promotes better circulation and metabolic function compared to a sedentary life.

2. Establish a Healthy Routine:

Just as organizations thrive on routines, our bodies benefit from regular sleep, eating, and exercise patterns. Consistency in these areas can enhance bodily functions and prevent health issues.

3. Cultivate Happiness:

Positive emotions play a significant role in overall health. Happiness reduces stress levels and can improve heart health. Simple acts like smiling or engaging in enjoyable activities can have a profound impact on well-being.

4. Practice Forgiveness:

Holding onto grudges or past hurts can manifest as physical ailments. Forgiving and letting go of negative emotions frees the spirit and can lead to improved mental and physical health.

5. Live Honestly:

Honesty isn't just a moral virtue; it's healthy. Living a life of truth reduces stress and anxiety associated with deceit, leading to better mental and emotional well-being.

6. Choose Fulfilling Work:

Job satisfaction is crucial for mental health. Chronic stress from unfulfilling work can lead to depression, anxiety, and physical health problems. Finding joy in your work or transitioning to a more fulfilling job can have significant health benefits.

7. Maintain Balanced Nutrition:

A balanced diet, rich in fruits, vegetables, lean proteins, and whole grains, nourishes the body and reduces the risk of obesity and diet-related diseases. Moderation is key to a healthy diet.

8. Moderate Alcohol and Avoid Drugs:

Excessive alcohol consumption and drug use are common reasons for A&E visits. Moderation in alcohol and avoiding recreational drugs prevents many health issues and accidents.

9. Foster a Positive Mindset:

A positive outlook on life can enhance immune function and overall health. People with a positive mindset often experience faster recovery from illnesses and maintain better health overall. Practices like meditation can strengthen this positive outlook.

10. **Live a Balanced Lifestyle:**

A balanced life that includes hard work, adequate rest, hobbies, love, and social interaction can prevent burnout and health breakdowns. This balance is essential for long-term health and happiness.

Incorporating these habits into daily life can significantly reduce the likelihood of emergency health issues and visits to A&E. A holistic approach to health that addresses physical, mental, and emotional well-being is the key to a healthier, more fulfilled life.

10 Critical Conditions Warranting A&E Attendance

It's essential to recognize situations that require immediate medical attention in the Accident & Emergency (A&E) department. Here are ten scenarios where it's crucial to seek emergency care, even if symptoms seem to have subsided temporarily:

1. **Choking:** Even if the obstruction seems to have cleared, medical assessment is important to check for any residual damage or remaining blockage.
2. **Chest Pain:** Any chest pain, especially if it's sudden and severe, could be a sign of a serious heart condition and needs immediate attention.
3. **Severe Bleeding:** This includes heavy bleeding from any part of the body, such as wounds, the gastrointestinal tract, or after surgery.

4. **Collapse and Blackouts:** These can be symptoms of serious conditions like stroke, heart issues, or neurological problems.
5. **Falls and Fractures in Senior Citizens:** Falls in the elderly can lead to complications and often require immediate medical assessment, even if the person feels fine afterward.
6. **Swelling of the Neck, Mouth, or Throat:** Such swelling can indicate serious allergic reactions or infections that may obstruct breathing.
7. **Prolonged Diarrhea and Vomiting:** More than 48 hours of these symptoms can lead to dehydration and other complications, necessitating emergency care.
8. **Raised Temperature Post-Surgery:** A fever after surgery or along with signs of infection (like redness, swelling, or pain) can indicate a serious infection.
9. **Feeling Unwell During Chemotherapy:** Chemotherapy patients are at high risk for infections and other complications, making any feeling of illness a potential emergency.
10. **Persistent Cough:** Especially if accompanied by shortness of breath, chest pain, or if you're coughing up blood.

10 Common Illnesses or Issues That Don't Usually Require A&E Attendance

It's important to understand when to visit the Accident & Emergency (A&E) department and when it's more appropriate to seek other forms of healthcare. Here are ten common issues that typically do not require a trip to A&E, along with suggestions for alternative care:

Fast-Track A&E

1. **Alcohol Intoxication and Hangovers:** It's usually best to stay home, hydrate well, and rest. A&E should only be visited in cases of severe alcohol poisoning.
2. **Coughs in Adults:** Most coughs are not emergencies. Stay hydrated and consult your GP if the cough persists or worsens.
3. **Mild Sore Throats:** Rest and home remedies are often sufficient. See your GP if symptoms are severe or persistent.
4. **Minor Grazes and Scrapes:** For small grazes without swelling, home care is usually adequate. Seek medical care if there's significant pain, swelling, or signs of infection.
5. **Early Stages of Diarrhea:** Stay hydrated and monitor symptoms. If there's blood in your stool, severe pain, or prolonged symptoms, then consider medical attention.
6. **Mild Headaches:** Over-the-counter pain relief like paracetamol and rest often help. If headaches are severe, frequent, or accompanied by other symptoms, consult a doctor.
7. **Isolated Vomiting:** If it's not accompanied by other severe symptoms, rest and hydration are key. Seek immediate medical attention if there's blood in the vomit or signs of dehydration.
8. **Fever Without a Clear Infection Source:** Monitor the fever with a thermometer. If it's high, persistent, or accompanied by other severe symptoms, consult a healthcare provider.
9. **Runny Nose:** This is often due to a common cold and resolves on its own. Keep warm and stay hydrated.
10. **Fatigue and Dizziness:** Ensure adequate hydration, nutrition, and rest. If symptoms are severe, persistent,

or accompanied by other concerning signs, seek medical advice.

10 Essential Actions to Take After Calling an Ambulance

1. **Appropriate Clothing:**
   - Wear clothing that allows easy access for medical examination and treatment, particularly around the arms, chest, and abdomen. Choose garments that you wouldn't mind being cut off if necessary for emergency medical procedures.
2. **Secure Valuables:**
   - Remove jewellery and other valuables before the ambulance arrives. Store them safely at home to avoid misplacing them in the busy A&E environment, where items are easily lost.
3. **Keys and Personal Items:**
   - Keep your house and car keys in your pocket, ensuring you can secure your home before leaving. Consider taking a book or tablet for the wait, but only if it's convenient.
4. **Notify Your Contacts:**
   - Inform a family member, friend, or next-of-kin about your situation. If that's not possible, let a neighbour know so they can assist with any necessary communication.
5. **Pet Arrangements:**
   - Make provisions for your pet's care, either by arranging for someone to look after them or by contacting a local animal care service. Inform the ambulance staff about any pets left alone at home.
   -

Fast-Track A&E

6. **Home Safety Check:**
   - Ensure gas and electricity are turned off or adjusted appropriately, depending on the season, as you might be away for a few days.
7. **Arranging Care for Dependents:**
   - If you're responsible for children or other vulnerable individuals, quickly arrange alternate care for them. Inform the ambulance crew about any dependent left unattended at home.
8. **Medical History Recap:**
   - Write down or bring a list of your medical history, especially conditions relevant to your current situation. This information can expedite your treatment in the A&E.
9. **Current Medications:**
   - Pack all current medications, including over-the-counter drugs and supplements. This aids in continuity of care and provides healthcare providers with essential information about your treatment regimen.
10. **Resuscitation Status Documentation:**

    - If you're accompanying a patient, ensure their resuscitation status and any advance directives are known and documents are brought along. This information is crucial in an emergency and should return home with the patient post-discharge.

These actions, taken promptly after calling an ambulance, can streamline the subsequent medical care process, ensure personal and home safety, and help healthcare providers deliver the most effective treatment upon arrival at the hospital.

Chapter 2:

A&E Etiquettes

Mindset Thoughts for Healthcare Workers

Healthcare workers face unique challenges and situations daily. Developing the right mindset and strategies is key to navigating these effectively and compassionately. Here are some thoughtful approaches for healthcare professionals:

1. **Value Your Colleagues:** Your team is your biggest resource. A supportive, united team can significantly enhance your work experience.
2. **Embrace Each Day as New:** Treat every workday as a unique opportunity, even if the setting and routines seem familiar.
3. **Be Open to Challenges:** Healthcare brings diverse experiences and interactions. Embrace the learning and growth that come from this diversity.
4. **Prepare for the Worst, Hope for the Best:** Balancing optimism with realism helps in managing expectations and dealing with various outcomes positively.
5. **The Privilege of Patient Interaction:** Remember, your interaction may be a significant moment for a patient. Strive to make every encounter compassionate and positive.
6. **Acknowledge and Learn from Mistakes:** Everyone makes mistakes. The key is to acknowledge, learn, and grow from them.
7. **Don't Expect Praise:** Focus on doing your best. Recognition is gratifying, but self-satisfaction in your work's quality is more important.
8. **Explore Beyond 9-5:** If your job is taking a toll on you, remember there are many career paths within healthcare. Explore them for personal and professional growth.

9. **Speak Up or Move On:** If you witness wrongdoing, find a way to address it constructively. Staying silent might only perpetuate the issue.
10. **Develop Your Response Toolkit:** Have a set of responses ready for challenging situations. This preparation can help in managing difficult conversations effectively.

Handling Difficult Situations:

- Anticipate and prepare for complex interactions. Whether it's dealing with loss, confronting unethical behaviours, or managing personal emotions, being mentally prepared is crucial.

Continuous Learning and Development:

- Stay informed and educated. Continuous learning not only keeps you updated with medical knowledge but also helps in developing emotional intelligence and communication skills.

Balancing Empathy and Professionalism:

- Finding the balance between being empathetic and maintaining professionalism is key, especially in emotionally charged situations.

Maintaining Well-being:

- Prioritize your mental and physical health. Healthcare work can be demanding, and self-care is essential to sustain your ability to care for others.

How To Get Your Health Practitioner Help You Faster

Maximizing the benefit of a doctor's visit is crucial, especially given the time constraints in most healthcare settings. Here are some strategies to help ensure your doctor understands your health concerns more clearly and can provide the most effective support:

1. **Clearly Describe Symptoms:**
    - Start by telling your doctor the symptoms you are experiencing. Be specific about when they started, what seems to trigger them, and what, if anything, alleviates them.
    - Avoid medical jargon or self-diagnosis; instead, focus on describing how you feel in your own words.
2. **Avoid Leading Diagnoses:**
    - Resist the urge to suggest a diagnosis unless asked. Suggesting what you think might be wrong can inadvertently lead the doctor down a specific path, potentially overlooking other causes.
3. **Mention All Relevant Symptoms:**
    - Discuss any other symptoms you've been experiencing, even if they seem unrelated. Sometimes, seemingly disconnected symptoms can help doctors identify underlying causes or related health issues.
4. **Direct and Honest Answers:**
    - Respond to the doctor's questions as directly and honestly as possible. Remember that healthcare professionals are there to help, not to judge. Accurate information is key to effective diagnosis and treatment.

5. **Prepare Questions in Advance:**
   - Before your appointment, write down any questions or concerns you have. This ensures that you won't forget to mention important points during the consultation.
   - Examples of questions might include "What are the potential side effects of this treatment?" or "Are there lifestyle changes I can make to improve my condition?"
6. **Summarize Your Understanding:**
   - At the end of your appointment, summarize what you've understood from the conversation. This could be about your diagnosis, treatment plan, or next steps. It gives the doctor a chance to clarify if there's any misunderstanding.
7. **Discuss Treatment Options:**
   - Ask about different treatment options available, including their benefits and risks. Understanding all your options can help you make informed decisions about your care.
8. **Inquire About Follow-Up:**
   - Clarify what the next steps are. Ask if and when you should schedule a follow-up appointment, and what symptoms or changes you should watch for.
9. **Medication Clarity:**
   - If you're prescribed medication, ensure you understand how to take it, what it's for, and any potential side effects.
10. **Express Any Financial Concerns:**

    - If cost is a concern, discuss this openly with your healthcare provider. They may suggest cost-effective alternatives or generic medications.

25 Essential Questions to Ask Your Healthcare Practitioner

It's common for patients to have questions after their medical appointments or during their hospital stay. To ensure you have all the information you need, here's a modified and comprehensive list of questions you can ask your doctor, nurse, or healthcare professional. These questions are designed to provide clarity on your condition, treatment, and the impact on your daily life.

No.	Question	Notes
1	What exactly is my diagnosis?	
2	How will this illness affect my day-to-day activities?	
3	What is the expected progression of my illness?	
4	Can I continue my hobbies and activities, such as...?	Specify hobbies
5	What should I expect after discharge?	
6	Is it safe for me to plan a holiday in the near future?	
7	Will I manage my condition independently, or will I need ongoing medical support?	
8	Are there specific activities I should avoid or modify with my condition?	
9	Who can I turn to for support after leaving the hospital?	
10	Is this condition life-threatening?	
11	Is my illness contagious?	

Fast-Track A&E

No.	Question	Notes
12	Once cured or in remission, is there a chance of recurrence?	
13	What complications or secondary issues should I be aware of?	
14	What tests or examinations have been conducted during my stay?	
15	What are the treatment options available?	
16	If the initial treatment doesn't work, what are the next steps?	
17	What are the common side effects of the proposed treatment?	
18	Are there alternative or complementary therapies for my condition?	
19	What are the chances of fully recovering from my illness?	
20	What is my long-term prognosis?	
21	Am I eligible for any specific benefits or assistance due to my condition?	
22	What support services are available for me now and in the future?	
23	In case of an emergency, whom should I contact, and how?	
24	Do I need follow-up appointments, and who will organize them?	
25	Are there any lifestyle changes or precautions I should take?	

Using the Table: Before your appointment or during your hospital stay, review these questions.

- Check off or note down the ones most relevant to your situation.
- Feel free to add any specific questions or concerns you have.
- During your consultation, use this list as a guide to ensure all your important questions are addressed.

Remember, clear communication with your healthcare provider is key to understanding your health condition and the steps you can take to manage it effectively.

10 Things to Do While in A&E

A visit to the A&E department can often be unpredictable, with waiting times varying from an hour to several hours. While the wait can be filled with anxiety and uncertainty, there are ways to make this time bearable and productive. These tips can help you effectively navigate your time in A&E

1. **Stay Hydrated and Nourished:** Request a cup of tea, a biscuit, or water to stay hydrated. However, always check with a nurse or doctor before consuming anything, as it may affect your treatment.
2. **Reading:** Bring a favorite book or magazine. Reading can be a great distraction and help pass the time enjoyably.
3. **Engage in Conversation:** If you're feeling up to it, initiate a conversation with fellow patients or staff with a simple greeting or comment about the environment. Remember, not everyone may be in a mood to talk, so be mindful of their responses.
4. **Respect Privacy and Space:** Be considerate of others who may prefer quiet or are unable to engage in conversation. Keep discussions low-key and dispose of any litter properly to maintain a clean space.

5. **Research Your Condition:** Use this time to read up on your condition online. This can help you formulate questions to ask your doctor and better understand your situation.
6. **Prepare for Consultation:** Think about what you want to communicate to the healthcare professionals. Note down your symptoms, concerns, and questions. If you're worried about forgetting, record these on your phone.
7. **Be Patient and Informed:** Understand that assessments and reviews can take time. If you've been waiting for over two hours, it's reasonable to politely inquire about the status of your wait.
8. **Avoid Self-Discharge:** Leaving the hospital before being officially discharged can complicate your care. If you leave and need to return, you'll likely have to start the process from the beginning.
9. **Share Your Talents Discreetly:** If you have a subtle talent, like magic tricks, that can gently entertain or distract others, consider sharing it. However, be mindful of the environment and ensure it's appropriate and non-disruptive.
10. **Inform Your Contacts:** Use this time to inform a friend or relative of your situation. They can provide company or arrange transportation when you're discharged. This is especially important for those who might require additional assistance post-visit.

10 Things Not to Do in A&E

When visiting the Accident & Emergency (A&E) department, it's crucial to follow certain guidelines to ensure your safety and that of others. Here are ten things you should avoid doing while in A&E:

Fast-Track A&E

1. **Do Not Smoke:** Smoking can exacerbate health conditions and create additional risks. Respect hospital policies and the health of others, and refrain from smoking.
2. **Do Not Shout:** Keep your voice down. Loud noises can be disturbing to other patients, especially those in critical condition.
3. **Respect Privacy:** Do not open other people's curtains. Privacy is crucial, especially in a vulnerable state.
4. **Avoid Recording Conversations:** Recording others without consent is a breach of confidentiality and can have legal repercussions.
5. **Stay in Your Assigned Area:** Wandering around can delay your treatment and cause unnecessary confusion. Stay where the healthcare staff can find you.
6. **Refrain from Threats and Violence:** Aggression towards staff or other patients is illegal and counterproductive. It can affect the quality of care you receive and lead to legal consequences.
7. **Inform Staff If Leaving Your Area:** If you need to stretch your legs or use the restroom, let a nurse know so they can keep track of your whereabouts for safety and treatment coordination.
8. **Avoid Leaving for a Cigarette:** Smoking not only harms your health but also disrupts the flow of care in the A&E. If you leave for a cigarette, you may end up waiting longer.
9. **Dispose of Your Rubbish Properly:** Keep your area clean by using the bins provided. Leaving rubbish behind is disrespectful to staff and other patients.
10. **Be Honest About Your Symptoms:** Accurately describe your symptoms to healthcare providers. Exaggerating or downplaying symptoms can lead to incorrect diagnosis or treatment.

Addressing Aggression in Hospitals

Aggression in the Accident & Emergency (A&E) department can significantly impact both the healthcare environment and the level of care provided. Understanding the nature of aggression and its effects is crucial for maintaining a safe and effective clinical setting.

Types of Aggression:

- Aggression can manifest in various forms, including physical, verbal, emotional, psychological, and financial.
- It may stem from illness, emotional distress, vulnerability, or an inability to cope with life's challenges.

Impact of Aggression in A&E:

1. **Effect on Patients and Staff:**
   - Aggressive behaviour can create a hostile environment, affecting vulnerable and unwell patients who require a calm atmosphere.
   - Staff, while trained to handle aggression, are human and can be affected emotionally and psychologically by aggressive encounters.
2. **Legal Implications:**
   - Aggression towards healthcare staff, especially in the NHS, is a criminal offense. It can lead to police involvement and legal consequences for the aggressor.
3. **Resource Allocation:**
   - Dealing with aggression consumes time and resources that could otherwise be used to provide care to patients in need.

Dealing with Aggression:

- Healthcare providers employ various strategies to manage aggressive behaviour, prioritizing safety and attempting to de-escalate situations.
- Communication skills, empathy, and understanding the underlying causes of aggression can help in managing such incidents effectively.

Patient and Bystander Responses:

- Other patients often view aggression negatively, recognizing the dedication and effort of healthcare staff.
- There have been instances where patients have intervened to support staff, although this can also present safety risks.

Professional Training and Support:

- Regular training in conflict resolution and de-escalation techniques is essential for staff in high-risk areas like A&E.
- Psychological support and counselling services for staff affected by aggression can be crucial in maintaining staff well-being and effectiveness.

Preventative Measures:

- Clear communication regarding wait times and treatment processes can help in reducing patient frustration, a common trigger for aggression.

- Creating a supportive and understanding environment can also play a significant role in minimizing aggressive incidents.

10 Tips to Avoid Abuse in Hospitals

Having been physically assaulted by patients twice at separate A&E departments (like many of my colleagues too), leaving me with physical injuries, creating a respectful and safe environment in hospitals is essential for both patients and healthcare providers. Here are some strategies to prevent and address aggressive or abusive behaviours in these settings:

For Patients and Visitors:

1. **Develop Emotional Intelligence:** Recognize and manage your emotions, especially in stressful situations like a hospital visit.
2. **Practice Patience:** When feeling frustrated or angry, pause and count to five before responding. This simple act can prevent rash reactions.
3. **Adopt a 'My Turn Will Come' Attitude:** Understand that everyone in the hospital is being attended to based on their medical needs. Patience can reduce feelings of urgency and competition.
4. **Avoid Substance Influence:** Being under the influence of drugs or alcohol can impair judgment and increase the likelihood of aggressive behaviour.
5. **Practice Altruism:** Sometimes, allowing others to go ahead of you can make a significant difference in their life without impacting yours negatively.

6. **Self-Respect Leads to Respect for Others:** Remember that respecting yourself includes treating others with kindness and understanding.

For Healthcare Staff:

7. **Prepare for Possible Admission:** Remind patients and their families to be ready for potential admission. This can help manage expectations and reduce frustration.
8. **De-escalation Strategies:** If confronted with aggression, staff should be trained to safely disengage and seek security assistance.
9. **Reinforce Zero-Tolerance Policy:** Remind patients and visitors that abuse is not acceptable and that there are consequences for such behaviours.
10. **Flag Recurrent Aggressive Behaviour:** Document and report any patterns of aggression. This information can be crucial in developing policies to improve care and safety.

Additional Considerations:

- **Communication is Key:** Clear, compassionate communication from healthcare providers can help ease patient anxiety and pre-empt aggression.
- **Training in Conflict Resolution:** Regular training for staff in conflict resolution and de-escalation techniques can be invaluable in managing difficult situations.

Creating a Culture of Respect:

- Hospitals should foster a culture of respect and understanding, emphasizing that everyone deserves to be treated with dignity.

Fast-Track A&E

Chapter 3:

Navigating The Diagnosis

Navigating a Diagnosis of a Serious or Terminal Illness

Receiving a diagnosis of a serious or terminal illness in an A&E department can be a profound, life-altering moment. It often evokes a range of emotions from shock and sadness to, for some, an opportunity for profound self-realization or a shift in perspective. Here are some constructive steps to consider following such a diagnosis:

1. **Process Your Emotions:** Allow yourself time to process the range of emotions you might experience. It's normal to feel a gamut of emotions, including denial, anger, and grief.
2. **Seek Information:** Gather as much information as possible about your condition. Understanding the nature of your illness can help in making informed decisions about treatment and care.
3. **Discuss Treatment Options:** Have detailed discussions with your healthcare providers about available treatment options, including potential benefits and side effects.
4. **Consider Second Opinions:** Seeking a second opinion can provide additional perspectives on your diagnosis and treatment options.
5. **Explore Palliative Care:** For terminal illnesses, palliative care can significantly improve quality of life by managing pain and other symptoms.
6. **Plan Ahead:** Consider making plans regarding your care preferences, including advanced directives and end-of-life care.

7. **Build a Support Network:** Lean on family, friends, support groups, or counseling services for emotional support.
8. **Find Joy in Everyday Life:** Focus on activities that bring you happiness and fulfillment.
9. **Reflect on Life Goals:** A serious diagnosis can prompt reflections on personal goals, relationships, and experiences. Consider what is most important to you.
10. **Live in the Moment:** Try to live each day fully, appreciating the present moments.

Ethical Considerations in Terminology:

The use of the term "terminally ill" can indeed be a subject of ethical debate. Les Brown's concept of "Terminal Knowledge" suggests a shift in perspective – focusing on the limits of medical knowledge rather than the patient's potential lifespan. This approach could potentially offer a more hopeful outlook, acknowledging the possibilities beyond current medical understanding. Your thoughts and perspectives on this are valuable and can be shared via the email contacts provided at the end of this book.

Navigating Life After a Devastating Diagnosis

Receiving a diagnosis of a serious or terminal illness can be a transformative experience. While it's undoubtedly challenging, it can also be an opportunity to reflect, make significant decisions, and find meaning. Here are ten steps you might consider taking after receiving such a diagnosis:

Fast-Track A&E

A) **Contact Support Organizations:** Seek out organizations or charities related to your condition. These groups can provide support, guidance, and resources.

B) **Educate Yourself and Others:** Knowledge is empowering. Educate yourself about your condition and share this knowledge with family and friends to help them understand your situation.

C) **Say Goodbyes and Make Amends:** Use this time to strengthen relationships, forgive, and express love and gratitude. These actions can bring peace to both you and your loved ones.

D) **Reflective Retreat:** Take some time for introspection. Reflect on your diagnosis, its implications, and consider what adjustments you might need to make in your life.

E) **Make a Difference:** Consider how you can impact positively. This could involve raising awareness for your condition, participating in research, or engaging in charitable work.

F) **Reflect on the Past:** Look back at your life and achievements. Consider completing unfinished goals or using your experiences to benefit others.

G) **Organ Donation Consideration:** Think about the possibility of organ donation. This can be a powerful way to leave a lasting legacy.

H) **Organize Finances:** It's practical to get your finances in order. Planning for the future, including any inheritance matters, can bring clarity and peace of mind.

I) **Write a Will:** Ensure your wishes regarding your assets and care are documented legally. Consider setting up a Power of Attorney for when you're unable to make decisions.

J) **Plan Your Funeral:** If you have specific wishes for your funeral, document them. This can alleviate the burden on your loved ones and ensure your preferences are honored.

Ethical Consideration:

The discussion about terminal illness, end-of-life care, and preparation for death brings up significant ethical and personal considerations. It's a deeply individual journey, and each person's approach will vary based on their beliefs, values, and circumstances.

Dealing with Trauma in A&E

Trauma, whether emotional, physical, or psychological, is a common occurrence in the Accident & Emergency (A&E) environment. Understanding how to cope with trauma effectively is crucial for both healthcare professionals and patients. Here are some strategies and insights for dealing with trauma in A&E:

1. **Acceptance of the Event:** Recognize that the traumatic event has occurred. Acceptance is a crucial step in coping and moving forward.
2. **Focus on 'What Next':** Instead of dwelling on "what ifs," concentrate on the next steps and how to recover or help others.

3. **Seek and Accept Help:** A&E departments are supportive environments. Don't hesitate to seek help, and remember that staff members are trained and willing to assist.
4. **Express Emotions Authentically:** It's okay to show vulnerability. Expressing emotions can be a part of the healing process.
5. **Mental Preparation for Trauma:** While it's difficult to prepare for specific events, building mental resilience can help in managing trauma's impact.
6. **You Are Not Alone:** Trauma can be isolating, but it's important to remember that support systems exist, both personally and professionally.
7. **The Power of Prayer or Positive Thinking:** Regardless of religious beliefs, prayer or maintaining positive thoughts can be comforting and healing.
8. **Create a Letting-Go Ritual:** Develop ways to decompress and leave work-related stress at work, especially important in high-trauma environments like A&E.
9. **Engage in Hobbies and Activities:** Pursuing hobbies or activities outside of work can provide a mental break and help maintain a healthy work-life balance.
10. **Seek Professional Help for PTSD:** Be vigilant for signs of post-traumatic stress disorder, such as persistent anxiety, stress, or nightmares related to traumatic events. Early intervention with a therapist or psychiatrist is crucial.

Understanding Trauma's Impact

- Trauma can profoundly affect thinking, feeling, judgment, and decision-making.
- It can trigger various responses like fight, flight, or freeze and potentially lead to psychological or physical illness.

Coping Mechanisms for Healthcare Professionals

- Healthcare professionals in A&E are particularly susceptible to trauma exposure. Regular mental health check-ins, peer support groups, and professional counselling can be beneficial.
- Developing self-care routines, mindfulness practices, and ensuring adequate rest are essential for long-term resilience in such high-stress environments.

10 A&E Life-Saving Tips

In emergency situations, knowing how to react before professional help arrives can be crucial. Here are ten tips that could potentially save a life or prevent a situation from worsening:

1. **Stroke Response:** If you suspect a stroke, coughing vigorously might help dislodge a potential clot. However, immediate medical attention is crucial.
2. **Treating Burns:** Cool the burn under cold running water for about 20 minutes. This can help reduce tissue damage and pain.
3. **Managing Nosebleeds:** Lean forward and pinch your nose. Breathing through your mouth, keep the head above the heart to reduce bleeding.
4. **Bee or Wasp Stings, Snake Bites:** Gently squeezing out the area may help, but it's crucial to seek immediate medical attention, as some bites and stings can be life-threatening.
5. **Swallowed Objects in Children:** Attempting to induce vomiting can be risky. It's safer to seek immediate medical help, especially if the object is sharp or large.

6. **Dealing with Headaches:** Ensure you're well-hydrated as dehydration can cause headaches. Rest and over-the-counter pain relief like paracetamol can be effective.
7. **Diarrhea Management:** Eating dry, bland foods can help. Stay hydrated, especially if vomiting is also present.
8. **Fever Check:** If you have a fever, look for signs of infection. If no infection is apparent, monitor the fever closely. Seek medical advice if it's high, persistent, or accompanied by other symptoms.
9. **Cough and Flu Symptoms:** Stay hydrated and rest. Most minor respiratory infections clear up in about two weeks. Seek medical advice if symptoms worsen or persist beyond this period.
10. **Assessing Falls:** If you can't recall the cause of a fall or lost consciousness, seek medical help. Unexplained falls might indicate a more serious underlying condition.

Important Note:

- These tips are general guidelines and not a substitute for professional medical advice. Always prioritize seeking professional medical help in emergencies.

Fast-Track A&E

Chapter 4:
Pain Management in A&E and Beyond

Pain Management

Managing pain effectively in an Accident & Emergency (A&E) setting is crucial, as pain is a common and complex issue that brings many individuals to seek emergency care. Understanding the nature of pain and how to describe it can significantly aid healthcare professionals in providing appropriate treatment.

What Is Pain? Pain is a multifaceted experience encompassing physical, emotional, and psychological aspects. It's a signal from the body indicating that something is amiss. The perception of pain can vary greatly from person to person, influenced by a myriad of factors including individual pain tolerance, the nature of the injury, and psychological state.

Description of Pain Effectively communicating your pain to healthcare professionals is key to receiving appropriate care. Here's how you can describe your pain for better understanding and treatment:

- **Agony:** Indicates severe, overwhelming pain that is debilitating.
- **Discomfort:** A less intense form of pain, more of an annoyance or irritation than severe pain.
- **Affliction:** Suggests a pain that is persistent and troubling.
- **Suffering:** Implies a more profound experience of pain, often with emotional and psychological dimensions.
- **Torment:** Conveys an intense, possibly sharp or piercing quality of pain.
- **Soreness:** Typically describes a dull, aching type of pain.
- **Hurt and Aching:** General terms that can describe a range of pain sensations, from mild to severe.

Approach to Pain Management in A&E In A&E, healthcare providers take a proactive approach to pain management, which may include:

- **Assessment:** A thorough assessment of the pain, including its location, intensity, duration, and nature.
- **Medication:** Depending on the assessment, appropriate pain relief medication may be administered, ranging from over-the-counter analgesics to stronger prescription drugs.
- **Non-Medical Interventions:** In some cases, methods such as ice application, elevation, or immobilization may be used to alleviate pain.
- **Monitoring:** Continuous monitoring of the patient's response to treatment to adjust pain management strategies as needed.

Pain Management Education Educating patients about pain and its management is also a critical component of care in A&E. This includes informing patients about:

- **Pain Relief Options:** Understanding the various pain relief options available, including their benefits and potential side effects.
- **Self-Management Techniques:** Guidance on how to manage pain after discharge, such as rest, ice, compression, elevation (RICE), and when to take prescribed medications.

Chronic vs. Acute Pain: Understanding and Describing Pain in A&E

Differentiating between chronic and acute pain is essential in A&E settings, as it guides the approach to treatment and management. Here's a closer look at how pain can be described and its potential sources, which can aid in diagnosis and treatment.

Descriptions and Possible Sources of Pain

1. **Piercing Pain:**
   - Often associated with chest pain, possibly indicative of cardiovascular issues.
2. **Throbbing Pain:**
   - Common in chest pain, could signal conditions like angina or myocardial infarction.
3. **Shooting Pain:**
   - Also typical in chest pain, possibly suggesting nerve involvement or musculoskeletal issues.
4. **Stabbing Pain:**
   - Chest pain described as stabbing can be serious, warranting immediate investigation for causes like pulmonary embolism.
5. **Cramping:**
   - Often related to stomach pain, suggesting gastrointestinal issues such as indigestion or gas.
6. **Spasms:**
   - Also linked to stomach pain, possibly indicating muscle strain or gastrointestinal distress.
7. **Twinge:**
   - Common in muscle pain, suggesting a minor muscle pull or strain.

8. **Stinging:**
   - Associated with wound pain, often indicating an acute injury or infection.
9. **Bricking:**
   - Descriptive of vaginal pain, potentially indicating conditions like infections or pelvic inflammatory disease.
10. **Aching:**
    - A versatile description, relevant to head, tooth, stomach, or ear pain, and can indicate a range of issues from dental problems to headaches.
11. **Stiffening:**
    - Often experienced with neck, back, or leg pain, suggesting muscular or skeletal issues.

Broader Considerations in Pain Assessment

- **Irritation, Discomfort, Soreness, Stiffness:** These terms can describe less intense pain, often chronic, and linked to long-term conditions or musculoskeletal issues.
- **Pain from Disability or Long-term Illness:** Chronic pain management is crucial in these cases, requiring a comprehensive approach.
- **Hidden Pain Sources:** Pain can sometimes mask underlying issues such as stress, mental health problems, social difficulties, or medication-related problems.

Importance of Identifying Pain Source in A&E

- **Initial Step in Treatment:** Identifying the source of pain is a crucial step in treating or alleviating it.

- **Patient Communication:** Encourage patients to accurately describe their pain and its characteristics to help healthcare providers diagnose and treat effectively.

Your Pain Pathway in A&E

Understanding the pain management pathway in the Accident & Emergency (A&E) department can be crucial for patients. This knowledge can help set expectations and facilitate better communication with healthcare professionals.

Initial Pain Assessment and Management

- **Quick Pain Assessment:** Upon presenting with pain in A&E, a swift assessment is typically conducted to gauge the severity and nature of the pain.
- **Gradual Pain Management Approach:** The standard approach in pain management is to start with a lower dose of pain relief and then escalate if necessary. This ensures the patient receives adequate pain relief while minimizing potential side effects.

Typical Pain Relief Medications in Order of Administration

1. **Paracetamol:** Often the first line of pain relief due to its effectiveness and fewer side effects.
2. **Ibuprofen:** A non-steroidal anti-inflammatory drug, useful for mild to moderate pain.
3. **Codeine Phosphate:** A stronger painkiller, used for more intense pain.
4. **Co-codamol or Codydramol:** Combination drugs that include paracetamol and codeine.

5. **Naproxen:** Another anti-inflammatory medication, used for its longer-lasting effect.
6. **Diclofenac:** Often used for inflammation and pain.
7. **Tramadol:** A stronger opioid, used for moderate to severe pain.
8. **Oxycodone or Tapentadol:** Stronger opioids, typically used for severe pain.
9. **Morphine:** Often used in severe pain cases, particularly in emergency settings.
10. **Diamorphine:** Used in severe pain, particularly in palliative care settings.
11. **Gabapentin or Equivalents:** Often used for nerve pain.

Additional Pain Relief Options

Depending on the source and nature of the pain, as well as the required medical procedures, other forms of pain relief might be used:

- **Entonox (Gas and Air):** Often used for quick, short-term pain relief.
- **Fentanyl:** A very potent opioid, used in controlled settings.
- **Various Forms of Anaesthetics:** Used depending on the type of procedure, ranging from local to general anaesthesia.

Patient Advocacy and Follow-Up

- **Asking Questions:** Patients should feel empowered to ask healthcare professionals if the pain might return and what steps should be taken if it does.
- **Understanding Your Treatment:** Knowing the typical pathway of pain management can help patients

understand their treatment and advocate for themselves effectively.

Further Questions To Ask Your Practitioner about your Pain.

1. **How Long Should I Take the Pain Relief?** Ask about the duration of the treatment and whether there is a risk of dependency or tolerance with prolonged use.
2. **Are There Non-Medication Alternatives?** Inquire if there are other pain management strategies, such as physical therapy, that could be effective for your condition.
3. **How Should I Monitor My Pain?** Seek advice on how to track the effectiveness of the pain relief and what signs indicate that you should contact healthcare services.
4. **What Should I Do if the Pain Worsens or Doesn't Improve?** Understand the steps to take if your pain management plan is not effective.
5. **Can I Combine This Medication With Other Prescriptions or Supplements I'm Taking?** This is crucial to avoid potential drug interactions.
6. **What Lifestyle Changes Can Aid My Pain Management?** Ask about diet, exercise, or other lifestyle modifications that can complement your pain treatment.
7. **Is There a Follow-Up Plan for My Pain Management?** Discuss whether you need regular check-ins with your healthcare provider to assess and adjust your pain management plan.
8. **Are There Any Activities I Should Avoid While on This Pain Medication?** Certain medications might affect

your ability to perform specific tasks like driving or operating machinery.
9. **What Warning Signs Should Prompt Me to Seek Immediate Medical Attention?** Recognize serious symptoms related to your pain or its treatment that require urgent care.
10. **How Can I Effectively Communicate My Pain Levels to Family or Caregivers?** Discuss strategies for expressing your pain experience to those who support you.
11. **What Resources or Support Groups Are Available for Individuals With My Condition?** Access to support networks can be beneficial for ongoing pain management and emotional support.

Asking these questions can lead to a more comprehensive understanding of your pain management plan and enable you to participate actively in your care.

Additional Tips on Your Pain Management

1. **Communicate Effectively About Your Pain:** Be as specific as possible about the location, nature, and severity of your pain. Clear communication can help healthcare providers choose the most appropriate pain management strategy.
2. **Understand Potential Side Effects:** Familiarize yourself with the common side effects of the pain medications you are given. This knowledge can help you recognize and report any adverse reactions promptly.
3. **Follow Dosage Instructions Carefully:** Adhere to the prescribed dosage and timing of your pain medication. Taking more than directed can increase the risk of side effects or complications.

4. **Consider Non-Pharmacological Methods:** Alongside medication, techniques such as deep breathing, relaxation exercises, or guided imagery can be effective in managing pain and anxiety.
5. **Report Changes in Your Pain:** If your pain worsens or changes character, inform your healthcare provider immediately. Changes in pain can be indicative of evolving medical conditions that require attention.
6. **Stay Informed About Your Treatment Plan:** Ask about the planned approach for your pain management. Knowing what to expect can reduce anxiety and help you participate more actively in your care.
7. **Ask About Pain Management After Discharge:** If you're being discharged with pain, ensure you understand how to manage it at home, including when to seek further medical advice.
8. **Be Aware of Pain Medication Dependency:** Particularly with opioids, be conscious of the risk of dependency. Discuss with your healthcare provider about any concerns you may have.
9. **Explore Alternative Pain Relief Options:** In some cases, alternative therapies like acupuncture or physiotherapy may be appropriate. Discuss these options with your healthcare team.
10. **Stay Hydrated and Nourished:** Proper hydration and nutrition can aid in recovery and may also influence how your body responds to pain medication.

These tips are crucial for understanding and managing pain effectively, especially in a hospital setting. They hinge on patient participation, awareness, and communication.

Fast-Track A&E

Chapter 5:

Alternative Approaches to Pain Relief

Approaches to Pain Relief

Pain, an experience as universal as humanity itself, often brings people to seek both conventional and alternative methods for relief. Understanding pain and exploring various pain relief options can be instrumental in managing it effectively.

Understanding Pain

- Pain serves as a critical signal indicating injury, disease, or strain. It's the body's way of alerting you to potential harm.
- Chronic pain, different from acute pain, can linger and become a persistent part of life, often requiring ongoing management rather than a cure.

Alternative Pain Relief Methods

1. Acupuncture:

- Based on traditional Chinese medicine, acupuncture aims to release blocked energy (chi) within the body, believed to be the cause of pain.
- Thin needles are inserted at specific points, stimulating endorphins, the body's natural painkillers.

2. Herbal Medicine:

- Utilized for centuries, herbs offer natural pain relief options for various conditions.
- Examples include angelica for cramps, capsaicin for nerve pain, and ginger for joint pain.

3. Meditation:

- Aids in calming the mind, reducing stress, and managing pain.
- Techniques vary from concentrative meditation, focusing on a single point, to mindfulness and transcendental meditation.

4. Nutrition:

- A balanced diet rich in vitamins and minerals can enhance pain resistance.
- Certain supplements, like Vitamin E, calcium, and magnesium, are believed to alleviate specific types of pain.

5. Aromatherapy:

- Essential oils can alter brain chemistry to release endorphins, providing pain relief.
- Commonly used oils include lavender for relaxation and peppermint for headaches.

6. Guided Imagery:

- Involves visualizing mental images to control bodily functions like pain.
- Can be particularly effective for chronic pain management.

7. Biofeedback Techniques:

- Combines relaxation methods with instruments that monitor physiological responses.

- Teaches control over autonomic functions like heart rate, potentially reducing pain.

Pain Management: A Personal Journey

- Pain management is highly personal and may involve a combination of traditional and alternative therapies.
- It's crucial to educate oneself on different pain management methods to find the most effective approach for individual needs.

Consultation and Caution

- Always consult with healthcare practitioners before starting any new pain management regimen.
- These methods are not cures but strategies to better manage chronic pain.

The Role of Pain in Human Experience

Pain, an intrinsic part of the human condition, plays a multifaceted role in shaping our lives. While often perceived negatively due to the distress it causes, pain contributes significantly to the depth and richness of human experience.

Pain as an Influencer of Art and Personal Growth:

Pain, both physical and emotional, has historically been a profound influencer of art and music. It acts as a powerful muse, inspiring creativity and depth in artistic expression. Moreover, personal growth is often catalysed by pain, driving individuals to resilience and a deeper understanding of life.

Pain as a Catalyst for Empathy and Compassion:

The experience of pain can deepen one's empathy and compassion. Witnessing pain in others can evoke a sense of connectedness and humanity, fostering acts of kindness and support. It reminds us of our shared vulnerability and can inspire communal and individual acts of care.

Pain as a Teacher and Guide:

Pain acts as a crucial teacher, signalling the need for changes in lifestyle, environment, or behaviours. It encourages us to heed our bodies and minds for cues on self-care and wellness.

Pain as a Spiritual Force:

On a spiritual level, pain can be a powerful force that triggers introspection and spiritual growth. It often leads individuals to seek deeper meaning in life, understand their own resilience, and connect more profoundly with their faith or spiritual beliefs. This aspect of pain underscores its role not just as a physical sensation but as a catalyst for spiritual awakening and transformation.

Effective Pain Management as a Key to Enhanced Quality of Life:

Understanding and managing pain is crucial for enhancing life quality. A holistic approach to pain that includes medical, lifestyle, and psychological strategies can significantly reduce its negative impact, leading to a more satisfying and comfortable life. **Pain, though challenging, is an integral part of the human narrative**

Low Back Pain: Causes, Investigation, and Treatment.

Low back pain is a common ailment affecting a wide range of individuals. In my practice in A&E, this is one of the main reasons that people attend and A&E and never get a satisfactory diagnosis, treatment, or management plan. Understanding its causes, the necessary investigations, and available treatments is crucial for effective management and peace of mind.

Causes of Low Back Pain

1. Diseases in the Back

- **Injuries:**
    - Compression fracture of the vertebral column.
    - Rupture of intervertebral discs.
    - Injuries to ligaments and muscles of back.
    - Lumbosacral strain.
    - Intervertebral joint injuries.
    - Fracture of processes of vertebra.
- **Functional Imbalance:**
    - Pregnancy-related.
    - Pot belly.
    - Hip joint diseases.
    - Congenital spine curvature.
    - Leg length discrepancy.
- **Inflammatory Conditions:**
    - Bone infections (bacterial).
    - Tuberculosis of the spine.
    - Arthritis.
    - Brucellosis.

- Lumbago or fibrositis.
  - Muscle inflammation.
  - Anchylosing spondylitis.
- **Degenerative Diseases:**
  - Osteoarthritis.
  - Osteoporosis in elderly.
  - Intervertebral disc degeneration.
- **Tumours:**
  - Primary bone tumours in the spine.
  - Metastatic tumours (e.g., from prostate, lungs).

2. Gynaecological Problems

- Post childbirth.
- Post gynaecological surgeries.
- Uterine prolapse.
- Pelvic inflammatory diseases.
- Pelvic organ cancers.
- Endometriosis.

3. Problems in Other Body Parts

- Renal and ureteric stones.
- Prostate cancer.
- Pancreatitis.
- Biliary stones.
- Peptic ulcers.
- Pelvic organ inflammations.
- Aorta and iliac artery occlusions.

Investigation of Back Pain

1. Complete blood count (CBC).
2. Routine urine examination.

3. Ultrasonography (abdomen and pelvis).
4. X-ray (lumbar and sacral region).
5. MRI (spine).
6. CT scan (abdomen and pelvic region).
7. Examination (rectum, prostate, genitourinary organs).

Treatment of Back Pain

1. **Addressing the Root Cause:** Identification and treatment of the underlying cause.
2. **Symptomatic Relief:** Pain management, anti-inflammatory medications.
3. **Physical Therapies:**
    - Back exercises.
    - Traction.
    - Yoga.
4. **Surgical Interventions:** If necessary, based on the severity and underlying cause.
5. **Alternative Therapies:**
    - Homoeopathy.
    - Acupuncture.
    - Chiropractic care.

General Advice:

- Lifestyle modifications, such as improving posture and ergonomics at work, can help prevent and alleviate back pain.
- Regular physical activity and maintaining a healthy weight are also important preventive measures.

Back Pain Exercises: Strategies for Relief and Prevention

Back pain, a common issue among individuals under 45, can often be managed and prevented through targeted exercises. Understanding the spine's structure and the causes of back pain is crucial in selecting the right exercises.

Understanding the Spine and Causes of Back Pain

- The spinal column is crucial for stability and mobility, comprising 24 vertebrae from the skull to the pelvis.
- Muscles and ligaments tightly wrapping the spine can cause pain if injured.
- Causes of back pain may include muscle spasm, poor posture, sudden movements, osteoporosis, arthritis, infections, gynaecological issues, tumours, trauma, obesity, improper footwear, and heavy lifting.

Safe and Effective Exercises for Back Pain

1. **Posture Correction:**
    - Stand straight or sit in a chair that supports your back.
    - Avoid bending at the waist; instead, bend your knees to lower your body.
2. **General Guidelines:**
    - Avoid sitting or standing in the same posture for extended periods.
    - Use a supportive mattress for sleeping.
    - Avoid slouching or leaning forward.
    - Incorporate yoga and meditation for overall back health.

3. **Workplace Ergonomics:**
   - Ensure that your workspace is set up to support good posture and reduce strain on your back.
4. **Preventive Exercises:**
   - **Wall Slides:** Stand with your back against a wall and slide down into a crouch, then slide back up.
   - **Leg Raises:** Lie on your back and lift one leg at a time, holding it in the air for a few seconds.
   - **Leg Swings:** Gently swing each leg forward and backward while holding onto a stable object.
   - **Abdominal Strengthening:** Exercises like crunches or pelvic tilts to strengthen core muscles, providing better support for your back.

When to Consult a Physician

- If back pain is caused by factors beyond posture or if accompanied by bowel or bladder control issues, it's essential to consult a healthcare professional.

Tips for Ongoing Back Care

- Regularly engage in back-strengthening and flexibility exercises.
- Maintain a healthy weight to reduce stress on the back.
- Choose footwear that provides proper support.
- Practice lifting objects correctly, using your legs rather than your back.

It is very important not to take these suggestions and reflections to replace your healthcare practitioner's advice. I am not a specialist in this matter but only sharing my practical and researched knowledge. Always do what your physician or healthcare practitioner tells you above these.

Understanding Alzheimer's Disease and Managing Pain

Alzheimer's disease is a progressive neurological disorder that significantly impacts not only the individual but also their families and caregivers. As the disease progresses, understanding how to manage the symptoms, including pain, becomes essential.

The Progression of Alzheimer's Disease:

- **Early Stages:** In the initial stages, symptoms include memory loss and difficulty with daily tasks. Patients may struggle with short-term memory while retaining long-term memories.

Pain Management in Alzheimer's:

- As Alzheimer's progresses, it can affect the brain's ability to perceive pain. Patients might not respond to pain in typical ways.
- Caregivers and healthcare professionals need to be vigilant in observing signs of discomfort or pain, as the patient might not be able to communicate it effectively.

Caregiver Support and Strategies:

- **Educating Caregivers:** Caregivers should be equipped with skills to manage the changing needs of Alzheimer's patients, focusing on comfort and safety.
- **Legal Preparations:** Establishing a power of attorney and will early in the diagnosis is crucial, as the patient's ability to make decisions will decline over time.

Handling Behavioural Changes:

- In the moderate stage, patients may experience hallucinations, depression, and agitation. It's essential to maintain a calm and respectful approach.
- Never leave patients in the moderate stage alone, as they may wander and become lost.

Communication Techniques:

- Speak in a soft, calm voice and maintain eye contact.
- Avoid treating the patient like an infant and show respect for their dignity.
- Listen attentively and avoid pressing for clarifications if they seem to increase confusion or agitation.

Understanding the Severe Stage:

- In the severe stage, patients may have difficulty with basic motor skills and communication.
- Non-verbal cues become vital in understanding their needs and comfort levels.

How to Help:

- Be patient and understanding. The confusion and behavioural changes are symptoms of the disease.
- Create a safe, comfortable environment that minimizes the patient's stress and confusion.
- Families and caregivers should seek support groups or counselling to manage the emotional burden of caring for someone with Alzheimer's.
- Planning for respite care and exploring long-term care options early can be crucial.

Chapter 6:

Navigating Family Dynamics

Family Dynamics in Hospital Settings

The presence of family members in hospitals, especially in intensive care units, can be both beneficial and challenging. It's important to balance the needs of the patient, the functioning of healthcare staff, and the emotional needs of family members. Reflecting on personal experiences and observations can offer valuable insights into how these dynamics can be better managed.

1. Prioritizing Patient Rest and Recovery:

- Recognize that patients need ample rest for recovery. Continuous presence and interaction, even with the best intentions, can sometimes hinder the patient's rest and recuperation.

2. Respecting Healthcare Professionals' Workspace:

- Healthcare staff need space and access to the patient for regular check-ups and interventions. Family members should be mindful of this and cooperate to avoid impeding medical care.

3. Valuing Quality Time with Family:

- Hospitalization often brings into focus the importance of spending quality time with loved ones. This realization can encourage families to appreciate and prioritize relationships outside the hospital setting.

4. Managing Visitation and Emotional Support:

- Hospitals might consider implementing structured visitation policies to ensure patients get enough rest while allowing family members time to provide emotional support.
- Providing designated waiting areas or family rooms can help manage the number of visitors in patient areas.

5. Addressing Anxiety and Fear of Family Members:

- Clear communication from healthcare staff regarding the patient's condition can help alleviate anxiety.
- Offering counselling or support services to family members can also be beneficial.

6. The Role of Hospitalization in Family Dynamics:

- Hospitalization can sometimes serve as a catalyst for reuniting families or strengthening bonds.
- It's essential to acknowledge and facilitate these positive aspects while ensuring the patient's well-being remains the priority.

7. Educating Families on Patient Care:

- Providing families with information on how they can aid in the patient's recovery process can be empowering and helpful.

8. Encouraging Self-Care Among Family Members:

- Reminding family members to take care of their own health and well-being is crucial, as stress and worry can take a toll.

9. Understanding and Respecting Boundaries:

- Families should be encouraged to understand and respect the patient's need for privacy and quiet at times.

10. Promoting a Collaborative Environment:

- Encouraging a cooperative atmosphere where the medical staff and families work together can improve the overall care experience.

10 Considerate Actions While Visiting the Hospital

Visiting a hospital requires mindfulness and respect for the patients, staff, and the healthcare environment. Here are ten thoughtful actions to keep in mind:

1. **Practice Hand Hygiene:** Regularly wash and sanitize your hands to prevent the spread of infections.
2. **Maintain a Quiet and Respectful Demeanor:** Be aware of the hospital's atmosphere. Speak softly and move quietly to respect those who are healing and the staff who are focused on providing care.
3. **Be Mindful of Vulnerabilities:** If you're feeling unwell or have been exposed to communicable diseases, consider postponing your visit or take precautions like wearing a mask.

4. **Politeness Goes a Long Way:** Always interact with healthcare staff courteously. Polite requests are more likely to be met positively.
5. **Assist with Meals:** With permission from the nursing staff, help your relative with eating and drinking. It's a comforting gesture that can also be enjoyable for the patient.
6. **Facilitate Religious or Spiritual Needs:** If the patient practices a religion, consider arranging for a spiritual leader to visit or help them participate in religious activities, if their health permits.
7. **Encourage Mobility:** With the approval of healthcare staff, taking your relative for a short walk can be beneficial for their physical and mental health.
8. **Reconsider Bringing Flowers:** While a kind gesture, flowers can trigger allergies in some patients. Consider alternative gifts that are hospital-friendly.
9. **Check Visiting Hours:** Familiarize yourself with the hospital's visiting hours and policies to avoid inconvenience and ensure your visit is at a suitable time.
10. **Offer Transportation Assistance:** If you know elderly individuals who wish to visit their hospitalized relatives but have transportation challenges, offering them a ride can be a great help.

Ethical Dilemmas: Understanding and Resolving Challenges In Hospitals

In the dynamic and often high-pressure environment of Accident & Emergency (A&E) departments and hospitals, patients and healthcare professionals frequently encounter ethical dilemmas. Understanding and resolving these challenges requires a balance of empathy, practical wisdom, and adherence to ethical principles. Here, we explore some common ethical dilemmas and propose ways to address them.

Prioritization and Resource Allocation:

Dilemma: Healthcare professionals often face the challenge of prioritizing treatment, especially in A&E, where resources can be limited and patient influx is unpredictable. Decisions about who receives immediate care and who waits can be ethically complex.

Resolution: Utilizing triage systems effectively ensures that patients with the most critical needs receive immediate care. Continuous training and ethical guidelines can assist healthcare professionals in making fair and clinically justified decisions.

Informed Consent under Pressure:

Dilemma: Obtaining informed consent in emergency situations can be challenging, especially when patients are incapacitated or unable to comprehend their situation fully.

Resolution: When possible, healthcare professionals should communicate clearly and compassionately, ensuring that patients or their proxies understand the treatment options. In cases where patients cannot give consent, decisions should be based on the best interest principle, guided by ethical and legal frameworks.

Confidentiality vs. the Need to Inform:

Dilemma: Respecting patient confidentiality while recognizing situations where family members or authorities need to be informed (e.g., in cases of infectious diseases or abuse).

Resolution: Clear policies on patient confidentiality, balanced with legal and ethical obligations to report certain cases, should guide healthcare professionals. Communication skills training can help navigate these sensitive situations.

End-of-Life Decisions:

Dilemma: Decisions regarding life-sustaining treatments, especially for patients who have not articulated their end-of-life wishes, can be particularly challenging.

Resolution: Multidisciplinary discussions involving healthcare providers, patients, and family members (where appropriate) can aid in making decisions that align with the patient's values and best interests. Advance care planning should be encouraged.

Cultural Sensitivity and Care: Dilemma: Providing care that respects diverse cultural, religious, or personal beliefs can sometimes conflict with medical advice or standard practices.

Resolution: Cultivating cultural competence among healthcare professionals and advocating for patient-centered care can help navigate these dilemmas. Open, respectful dialogue is key to finding mutually acceptable solutions.

Mental Health Concerns:

Dilemma: Balancing respect for autonomy with the need to intervene in cases where patients may pose a risk to themselves or others due to mental health issues.

Resolution: Training in mental health, clear legal guidelines, and a compassionate approach to care are essential. Collaboration with mental health professionals can offer additional support and guidance.

Patient Autonomy vs. Healthcare Guidance:

Dilemma: Patients may refuse certain treatments or procedures, challenging medical recommendations.

Resolution: Respect for patient autonomy is fundamental, but it must be balanced with ensuring patients are well-informed about their choices. Effective communication and understanding the reasons behind a patient's refusal are crucial.

In resolving these dilemmas, continuous dialogue, ethical training, and a commitment to patient-centered care are vital. It requires a compassionate approach that respects individual rights while ensuring the highest standards of medical care.

Chapter 7:

Hospital From The Sky: An A-Z Journey

Resurfaced: A Journey from the Depths to Purpose.

On a fateful day, the 25th of August 2010, as the sun began its descent, painting the sky with hues of orange and pink, I encountered the brink of the beyond. It was around 6 pm, a family gathering humming with life beside a swimming pool that soon became the stage of my life's most dramatic turn.

In an inexplicable twist of fate, I found myself submerged, lost in the depths of the pool. Time warped around me as I lay motionless, embraced by the water's chilling hold. For what seemed an eternity, spanning 3 to 4 minutes, I was ensnared in a silent world, waiting for salvation. Tom, whom I now endearingly call 'Tom Saviour', emerged as my guardian angel. With a diver's grace and bravery, he plunged into the depths, pulling my lifeless form from the water's clutches, face down, back to the realm of the living.

Then came the paramedics, those unsung heroes, who worked tirelessly, expelling the invading waters from my body's every nook. Between that moment and 6 am the next day, I journeyed through an ethereal realm. It was an otherworldly experience, a serene voyage through a beautiful void. I was adrift in an endless expanse, surrounded by a sea of jubilant children, their faces glowing with innocence. They tossed flowers towards me, and I, in a state of blissful euphoria, reached out to grasp them, floating towards a bright, beckoning horizon, escorted by little angelic beings.

In that timeless space, I screamed out, a declaration of my plight: "I am drowning!" But it was 6 am the next day, and the world I returned to was different. A kind nurse, standing by

Fast-Track A&E

my bedside, gently reassured me, "It's ok love, that was yesterday." As I opened my eyes, a familiar and comforting presence greeted me – my beloved brother, Cyril, his friends Roland, and Ferdinand, seated nearby, with his eyes mirroring the ocean of emotions we both felt. Our eyes met, and a surge of tears flowed, blending our relief, love, and unspoken fears in silent understanding. His embrace was my anchor to life.

In that profound moment of vulnerability and gratitude, I made a silent vow to the nurse whose compassionate gaze met mine. I promised, in the depths of my being, to dedicate my life to saving others, just as I had been saved. This epiphany, born from the brink of death, was the genesis of my journey into nursing. Lying in the hospital bed on the 27th, inspirations flooded my mind, and I began to draft the verses of 'Hospital from the Sky', a poem that encapsulated the depth of my experience and the newfound purpose born from it. Miraculously appearing on page 333 – The Holy Trinity.

As I share this transformative narrative, for the first time, it is my heartfelt wish that it resonates deeply. As you peruse these verses, reflect upon the myriad of healthcare practitioners, the patients whose lives they touch, and those colleagues with whom they've crafted miracles - be they doctors, nurses, paramedics, healthcare assistants, or other vital members of the healthcare fraternity. Who do you envision in these lines? Take a moment to appreciate their presence in your life. This story is more than a personal journey; it's an invitation for introspection. What drives you in your professional path? What ignited that initial spark and continues to fuel your dedication? May the essence of this story reinvigorate your sense of purpose and strengthen your commitment to the noble calling of healthcare."

Fast-Track A&E

"Hospital From The Sky: An A-Z Journey"

Advocacy,
Voices for the voiceless, might for the meek.
Guardians of the fragile, champions of the weak.
Speaking for those silent, our words do seek,
To echo their needs, in every phrase we speak.

Blood,
Scalpels, gloves, the dance of healing arts.
From lifesaving surgeries to mending broken hearts.
Crimson tales in labs, where healing starts,
Each drop a story, of life's various charts.

Creation and Departure,
Beneath one roof, life's extremes do meet.
Births that bring joy, farewells bittersweet.
First cries to final sighs, in cycles replete,
Life's precious bookends, in one heartbeat.

Death,
A silent visitor, both feared and revered.
In shrouds and tags, life's finality mirrored.
A solemn journey, as the end is neared,
In death's quietude, life's fragility is cleared.

Empathy,
We share their pain, their hopes, their fears,
Mend their wounds through the years.
In every tear shed, empathy appears,
A shared connection that endears.

Fast-Track A&E

Forgiveness,
A release from past, a path to mend,
Forgiving self and others, let wounds tend.
In letting go, we allow our spirits to ascend,
In forgiveness, find the peace that will transcend.

Godliness,
In every soul and body, a divine spark resides,
In every fall and rise, His presence abides.
With faith diminished, yet in us, He confides,
In halls of healing, His spirit guides.

Healing,
In whispered words, in tender care bestowed,
In each act of healing, hope is sowed.
A journey from ailment to the health road,
In every cure, life's resilience glowed.

Infection,
Unseen foes in dances macabre,
Bringing forth fever, wound, and scar.
In sanitizing rituals, our defenses we bar,
Against microscopic battles that mar.

Joy,
Elusive in corridors of pain and heal,
Yet within reach, in every ordeal.
In choosing joy, life's colors we reveal,
Through struggles, life's joys we steal.

Kilograms,
Numbers that tell tales of health or strain,
In loss or gain, insights we obtain.

Fast-Track A&E

A measure of well-being, not disdain,
In every kilogram, a story plain.

Loneliness,
In silent wards, solitude's heavy cloak,
In every lonely heart, hope we evoke.
In companionship, life's connections we stoke,
Dispelling the shadows with words softly spoke.

Mystery,
Life's enigmatic dance of fate and chance,
In every survival, a mysterious glance.
Unanswered queries in medicine's advance,
In each healing, life's cryptic dance.

Newness,
In recovery's embrace, a rebirth sought,
From old ways to new, a transformation wrought.
In every healing, a battle bravely fought,
For newness of being, tirelessly we've sought.

Optimism,
In hopeful eyes, future bright foreseen,
In every recovery, where despair has been.
In optimism's light, life's true sheen,
A beacon through the dark, ever keen.

Pain,
A shared burden, in silence or scream,
In every grimace, a struggling dream.
Embracing pain as a healing stream,
In discomfort, life's enduring theme.

Fast-Track A&E

Questions,
Inquisitive minds seeking truth's clarity,
In every query, a quest for certainty.
In answers sought, life's perplexity,
Questions and answers, in perpetual parity.

Reassurance,
"It will be alright," a soothing balm,
In reassurance, finding peace and calm.
In every word, a healing psalm,
A harbor safe in life's stormy realm.

Service,
In selfless acts, humanity's best,
In every service, a noble quest.
Round the clock, without rest,
In serving others, we are blessed.

Tears,
From joy and sorrow, life's rivers flow,
In every tear, emotions that show.
Behind each drop, stories grow,
In tears, life's deeper truths we know.

Unique,
Each case a world, distinct and rare,
In every patient, unique care.
In diversity, medicine's flair,
Every individual, beyond compare.

Vulnerability,
Exposed hearts, souls laid bare,
In every frailty, a shared care.

Fast-Track A&E

In vulnerability, life's truths we declare,
A universal bond, all too rare.

Wisdom,
In every gesture, knowledge's grace,
In wisdom's light, life's challenges we face.
In corridors of care, a sacred place,
Wisdom's gift, humanity's embrace.

X-ray,
Through lenses that pierce life's veneer,
Revealing truths, both far and near.
In every image, clarity's frontier,
In X-rays, life's mysteries appear.

Y - **Youth** and Age in Harmony
Youthful energy and aged wisdom meet,
In corridors where life's extremes greet.
Babies cry their very first hello,
While elders whisper a soft, slow goodbye.
In every face, a story to show,
Of time's embrace under the same sky.

Z - **Zimmer Frames** and Steps of Time
Zimmer frames, steady companions in stride,
Echoing steps of a life's long ride.
They carry tales of years well-spent,
Supporting journeys, with age's bent.
In their silent glide, a dance of grace,
Each step a story in life's embrace.

References

Alzheimer's Association. (2023). 'Alzheimer's Disease: Symptoms and Stages'. [Online] Available at: Alzheimer's Association website

American Psychological Association. (2023). 'Coping with Trauma'. [Online] Available at: APA website

American Red Cross. (2023). 'First Aid/CPR/AED Participant's Manual'. [Online] Available at: Red Cross Website

Anderson, C. (2021). Managing Aggression in Healthcare. London: Medical Practice Publishing.

Anderson, G., and Hall, L. (2022). 'Balancing Family Involvement and Patient Care in Hospitals', Journal of Family Medicine and Health Care, 15(3), pp. 210-219.

Brown, J. (2022). Alzheimer's Disease: A Guide for Families and Caregivers. New York: Healthwise Publications.

Brown, L. (2022). Redefining Medical Prognoses: A New Perspective. New York: Health Insights Publishing.

Brown, L. and Davis, T. (2021). 'Utilizing Waiting Time Productively in Hospital Settings', Journal of Patient Experience, 18(3), pp. 200-205.

Brown, S. (2022). 'Opioids and Non-Opioids in Pain Management', Journal of Pain and Relief, 19(1), pp. 45-55.

Chen, L., and Wang, Y. (2021). Traditional and Modern Approaches to Acupuncture and Pain. Beijing: Traditional Medicine Press.

Davis, A., and Thompson, L. (2020). 'Recognizing Emergency Symptoms', Journal of Emergency Medicine, 45(3), pp. 234-242.

Davis, M. J., & Robinson, K. (2022). Alternative Treatments for Arthritis: An A to Z Guide. New York: Wellness Press.

Davis, R. (2022). 'Understanding and Communicating Pain: A Patient's Guide', Journal of Pain Management, 13(4), pp. 200-210.

Fisher, A., and Davis, M. (2021). The Healthcare Professional's Guide to Emotional Resilience. Boston: Medical Mindset Publishing.

Green, M. (2021). 'Comprehensive Management of Back Pain', Journal of Pain Management, 18(3), 77-85.

Green, M. (2022). 'Herbs and Natural Supplements for Pain Management', Journal of Natural Remedies, 18(4), pp. 200-215.

Green, M., and Harris, J. (2021). 'Ethical Considerations in Terminal Illness Diagnosis', Journal of Medical Ethics, 47(5), pp. 311-317.

Health and Safety Executive (HSE). (2023). 'Managing Violence and Aggression in Healthcare'. [Online] Available at: HSE website

Hospice Foundation. (2022). 'Coping with Terminal Illness'. [Online] Available at: Hospice Foundation Website

Hospital Visitor Guidelines. (2023). 'Best Practices for Hospital Visitors'. [Online] Available at: Hospital Visitor Information

Johnson, A. (2020). Emergency Medicine: Tips and Techniques. New York: Health Response Publishing.

Johnson, A. (2020). Mindfulness Techniques for Stress Reduction. New York: Wellness Books.

Johnson, L. R., & Greene, A. (2021). "The Role of Glucosamine in Arthritis Management," Journal of Alternative Therapies, 27(4), pp. 45-52.

Johnson, M. (2020). Life Beyond Diagnosis: A Guide to Living Fully. Boston: New Life Publishing.

Johnson, M. (2021). Preventing Aggression in Healthcare Settings. New York: CareSafe Publishing.

Johnson, M. (2021). 'The Psychological Impact of A&E Work', Journal of Emergency Medicine, 29(3), pp. 305-313.

Johnson, P. (2021). Patient Etiquette in Hospital Settings. New York: Healthcare Press.

Johnson, P. (2021). Understanding Pain: A Guide for Patients and Healthcare Providers. Oxford: Oxford Medical Publications.

Jones, M. and Patel, S. (2022). 'Symptom Management in Primary Care', Journal of General Practice, 80(2), pp. 120-130.

Martin, E., and Taylor, J. (2021). Principles of Pain Management in Emergency Medicine. London: Medical Care Press.

Martin, S. (2021). 'Pain Management in Alzheimer's Patients', Journal of Neurological Disorders, 19(4), pp. 112-119.

Miller, C.A., & Smith, Z.M. (2022). Low Back Pain: Causes, Diagnosis, and Treatment. New York: Health Publications.

Miller, J., and Taylor, A. (2021). Pain Relief in Emergency Medicine. London: Emergency Care Press.

Miller, S. (2021). 'Hospital Visitation Etiquette', Journal of Patient Care, 17(2), pp. 45-50.

National Center for Complementary and Integrative Health. (2023). 'Pain: Alternative Treatments'. [Online] Available at: NCCIH website

National Health Service (NHS). (2023). 'Accident and Emergency (A&E) Services'. [Online] Available at: NHS website

National Health Service (NHS). (2023). 'Coping with a Terminal Illness'. [Online] Available at: NHS website

National Health Service (NHS). (2023). 'Dealing with Aggression in Healthcare Settings'. [Online] Available at: NHS website

Fast-Track A&E

National Health Service (NHS). (2023). 'Family Presence in Hospital Settings'. [Online] Available at: NHS website

National Health Service (NHS). (2023). 'Mindfulness and Mental Health in Healthcare Professionals'. [Online] Available at: NHS website

National Health Service (NHS). (2023). 'Pain Management in A&E'. [Online] Available at: NHS website

National Health Service (NHS). (2023). 'Symptoms and Conditions That Require A&E'. [Online] Available at: NHS website

National Health Service (NHS). (2023). 'Types of Pain and Their Management'. [Online] Available at: NHS website

National Health Service (NHS). (2023). 'When to use A&E'. [Online] Available at: NHS website

National Health Service (NHS). (2023). 'Your Guide to A&E Services'. [Online] Available at: NHS website

National Institute of Neurological Disorders and Stroke (NINDS). (2023). 'Low Back Pain Fact Sheet'. [Online] Available at: NINDS website

Robinson, T. (2021). Emergency Medicine: What to Know. Cambridge: Medical Press.

Smith, A. and Green, L. (2022). 'Pain Descriptions and Their Clinical Implications', Journal of Pain Research, 16(2), pp. 155-164.

Smith, J. (2022). Effective Patient Communication in Healthcare. Oxford: Oxford University Press.

Smith, J., and Brown, L. (2022). Trauma Management for Emergency Professionals. New York: Healthcare Insights.

Smith, J., and Taylor, B. (2022). 'Aggression in Emergency Departments: Strategies for Prevention and Management', Journal of Emergency Nursing, 48(2), pp. 123-130.

Fast-Track A&E

Smith, L. (2020). 'Respectful Patient Behaviour: Expectations in A&E', Journal of Emergency Nursing, 46(4), pp. 445-450.

Smith, L., and Davis, R. (2019). 'Ethical Considerations in End-of-Life Care', Journal of Medical Ethics, 45(6), pp. 376-380.

Smith, L., and Davis, R. (2019). 'Home Management of Minor Emergencies', Journal of Family Medicine and Primary Care, 28(2), pp. 305-312.

Thompson, J. (2022). Caring for the Hospitalized: A Visitor's Guide. New York: Patient Care Press.

Thompson, L. (2022). 'Effective Communication in Healthcare Settings', Journal of Medical Communication, 16(3), pp. 234-240.

Thompson, R. (2021). Family Dynamics in Healthcare. London: Medical Family Press.

Williams, H. (2019). Understanding Primary Care: When to Avoid the ER. London: Health Education Press.

Williams, S., and Taylor, L. (2022). 'Dealing with Patient Aggression: Strategies for Healthcare Workers', Journal of Healthcare Safety and Compliance, 10(4), pp. 154-162.

Glossary

Advocacy: Supporting and representing the interests or rights of another person, especially in a healthcare context.

Alzheimer's Disease: A progressive neurological disorder that causes memory loss and cognitive decline.

Arthritis: A medical condition characterized by inflammation of the joints, leading to pain and stiffness.

A&E (Accident and Emergency): A medical facility specializing in emergency medicine, the acute care of patients without prior appointment.

Biofeedback: A technique that trains people to improve their health by controlling certain bodily processes that normally happen involuntarily.

BMI (Body Mass Index): A measure of body fat based on height and weight.

Chronic Pain: Pain that lasts for a long period of time, often resistant to medical treatments.

Cognitive Behavioural Therapy: A form of psychotherapy that treats problems by modifying dysfunctional emotions, behaviours, and thoughts.

Empathy: The ability to understand and share the feelings of another.

Glucosamine: A supplement used to alleviate the symptoms of joint pain, particularly in osteoarthritis.

Mindfulness: A technique involving focused awareness on the present moment, often used as a therapeutic technique.

MRI (Magnetic Resonance Imaging): A medical imaging technique used in radiology to form pictures of the anatomy and physiological processes.

Osteoporosis: A medical condition in which the bones become brittle and fragile from loss of tissue.

Palliative Care: Specialized medical care for people with serious illnesses, focused on providing relief from the symptoms and stress.

Paramedic: Healthcare professionals who provide emergency medical services outside of the hospital.

Physiotherapy: A therapy that uses physical techniques to improve movement, reduce pain, and promote overall health.

Resilience: The capacity to recover quickly from difficulties; mental toughness.

Telemedicine: The practice of caring for patients remotely when the provider and patient are not physically present with each other.

X-Ray: A form of electromagnetic radiation used for imaging or treatment in medicine.

Yoga: A group of physical, mental, and spiritual practices or disciplines which originated in ancient India, often used in therapy.

Coming soon!

About The Author:

Louistas Nyuyse's life epitomizes resilience and triumph. His early years, marked by challenges like carrying heavy sacks of potatoes to fund his education, laid the foundation for a life of hard work and perseverance. This resilience was further tested when he arrived in the UK with only £150, setting the stage for a remarkable journey of success.

Now, Louistas is a symbol of achievement. He has excelled as a coach, speaker, lecturer, trainer, and parent, transforming his humble beginnings into a legacy of inspiration and knowledge. His transition from modest roots to a beacon of success is a testament to his belief in diligence and ambition.

His venture into writing, inspired by his life experiences, has produced works like "Think Like a Virus," "The GREAT LIFE," "Due Diligence," and "Unplugged: Reclaiming Our Minds in the Digital Age." These books are not just narratives of his journey; they are motivational guides for those seeking to find and ardently pursue their purpose.

Louistas' mission is to empower others to follow their paths to success. He advocates for a success-oriented mindset and the creation of passive income streams alongside one's career. His books are designed to show that with determination, the right mindset, and guidance, one can achieve their dreams.

His story and teachings resonate with a powerful message: to seek purpose, embrace life's journey, and pursue success with tenacity and optimism. Louistas' life is a compelling reminder that with the right mindset and support, extraordinary achievements are within reach.

Fast-Track A&E

www.ingramcontent.com/pod-product-compliance
Lightning Source LLC
Chambersburg PA
CBHW050122170426
43197CB00011B/1686